SEXUAL SCIENCE

S·E·X·U·A·L
S·C·I·E·N·C·E

*The Victorian Construction
of Womanhood*

CYNTHIA EAGLE
RUSSETT

*Harvard University Press
Cambridge, Massachusetts
London, England*

First Harvard University Press paperback edition, 1991

Library of Congress Cataloging in Publication Data

Russett, Cynthia Eagle.
  Sexual science.

  Includes index.
   1. Sex differences.   2. Sex role—History—19th
century.   3. Women's studies—History—19th century.
I. Title.
QP81.5.R87   1989   305.3′09′034   88-24521
ISBN 0-674-80290-X (alk. paper) (cloth)
ISBN 0-674-80291-8 (paper)

For Bruce, who never needed a looking-glass

Contents

Acknowledgments

This study originated in my interest in two areas of history—the intellectual impact of Darwinism and the history of women. As long ago as 1965 Andrew Sinclair, in *The Emancipation of the American Woman,* gave a nod to what Victorian science had to say about women. Darwin and Huxley, he noted, "were not on the side of the feminists." Thomas Higginson, who was, worried that their writings "make woman simply a lesser man, weaker in body and mind." Remarking that Huxley had flatly denied the equality of the sexes, Sinclair concluded: "In fact, the very popularity of Darwin and Huxley in conservative American circles was due to their emphasis on motherhood as woman's vital role."

Since Sinclair's pioneering work, much has been written about women's health and the treatment of women by the medical profession in the late nineteenth century. Less attention has been devoted to the more strictly scientific appraisal of woman's nature. This book builds on the studies of Elizabeth Fee, Stephen Jay Gould, John and Robin Haller, and Rosalind Rosenberg in particular.

A rewarding year spent at the National Humanities Center in Research Triangle Park, North Carolina, got the book under way, and a term at the Netherlands Institute for Advanced Study in the Humanities and Social Sciences helped move it toward completion. The chapter on recapitulation benefited from the comments of Rosalind Rosenberg and of the audience at a session of the Berkshire Conference of Women Historians in 1982. I am also indebted to members of the history and American studies departments at Rutgers University for their criticisms at a seminar last year.

Frank Turner shared with me his knowledge of Victorian England and directed me to specific references. Beth Auerbach and especially Florence Thomas helped with the typing. Betty Paine provided an acerbic perspective on history and historians. Above all, I want to acknowledge the concern and support of John Morton Blum, mentor and—what is rarer—friend.

SEXUAL SCIENCE

NOTE ON TERMINOLOGY

This book is based on an examination of the scientific literature of the nineteenth and early twentieth century on the differences between men and women. The reconstruction presented here of the scientific evidence concerning the "woman question" necessarily employs many of the terms used in that literature, but it must be noted that those terms may be defined differently, or may no longer be used, in today's literature. For example, modern usage generally makes a distinction between the physical differences of sex, known as *sex differences,* and the cultural elaborations of these physical differences in personality, ability, and so forth, known as *gender differences.* Nineteenth-century scientists conflated the two terms, or, to be more accurate, simply denied the latter. I have for the most part chosen to use the term *sex difference* to conform to their usage, but this is not meant to imply a denial of the modern distinction. Non-European peoples, furthermore, were commonly referred to as "the lesser races" or "savages" in the nineteenth century; although these terms have no place in present-day science writing, I have followed Victorian usage for the sake of accuracy and context.

Finally, not every idea put forth in scientific literature may be considered a "theory." There are certainly coherent sets of propositions discussed in the following chapters that deserve the status of true theories, such as Darwin's theory of sexual selection. But I have also given the term, at times, to the work of some scientists, like G. Stanley Hall, whose undertakings do not meet the requirements of a strict construction of theory. Rather than cast about for some alternative term—*hypothesis, model, metaphor*—that might be technically more appropriate, I have simply chosen to use the term *theory* in a nonformal way.

Introduction

Have you any notion how many books are written about
women in the course of one year? Have you any notion how
many are written by men? Are you aware that you are, perhaps, the most discussed animal in the universe?

—Virginia Woolf (1929)

The distinction between masculinity and femininity has
served as a basis for metaphysical thinking at so many times
and in so many cultures that it ranks with the stars as an
object of superstition.

—Michael T. Ghiselin (1974)

In a small white stone house in Avignon near the banks of the
Rhone, John Stuart Mill worked during the morning hours of
1860 and 1861 on a first draft of *The Subjection of Women*. The essay
was in every respect, he would later insist, a collaborative venture
with his wife, Harriet Taylor. But she could no longer work with
him; she lay in the cemetery of St. Véran nearby, dead now some
two years.

Mill opened with a blunt challenge to the patriarchal foundation
of Victorian society: the subordination of one sex to the other was
"wrong in itself, and now one of the chief hindrances to human
improvement"; accordingly, it "ought to be replaced by a principle
of perfect equality, admitting no power or privilege on the one side,
nor disability on the other." Dismissing the argument that the long
history of sexual inequality should weigh in its favor, Mill turned to
"that most difficult question, what are the natural differences between the two sexes." It was a question, he insisted, that could not
really be answered: "Standing on the ground of common sense and
the constitution of the human mind, I deny that any one knows, or
can know, the nature of the two sexes, as long as they have only
been seen in their present relation to one another . . . What is now
called the nature of women is an eminently artificial thing—the

result of forced repression in some directions, unnatural stimulation in others." But of this Mill was sure—that nurture shaped character more than nature ever could. History displayed "the extraordinary susceptibility of human nature to external influences, and the extreme variableness of those of its manifestations which are supposed to be most universal and uniform." Any differences that might be found between the sexes could only be adjudged natural if they could not possibly be artificial, the effects of education or external circumstances. Meanwhile, a frank confession of ignorance was the only intellectually respectable position.[1]

Charles Darwin disagreed. Standing on a hillside path in Wales sixty feet above his summer neighbor, the redoubtable writer and reformer Frances Power Cobbe, Darwin shouted down to her his reaction to Mill's recently published essay on women. He was, he said, intensely interested in Mill's book, but "Mill could learn some things from physical science; and . . . it is in the struggle for existence and (especially) for the possession of women that men acquire their vigor and courage." Women's nature, like men's, was rooted in their biology. It was nature, not nurture, that mattered. Even then, Darwin was at work on the volume that would enshrine this view of human beings, The Descent of Man. Recording this scene in her autobiography, Cobbe was aware of some incongruity in the spectacle of two eminently genteel people, separated by "impenetrable brambles" and hence "exchang[ing] remarks at the top of our voices, being too eager to think of the absurdity of the situation." But she did not comment on the oddity of Darwin's emphasizing the natural inequality of the sexes to a woman who was an ardent and active suffragist.[2]

The distance between Avignon and Wales, stone house and hillside, nurture and nature precisely delimits the controverted terrain of the "woman question" in Anglo-American science in the late nineteenth century. The moment was one in which social and scientific developments converged to create the possibility and urgency of a science of male and female nature and of the differences between them. Such a science would, it was believed, shed light on vexing social issues raised by changes in women's roles and status that were taking place during the middle and later nineteenth century. The rise of sexual science needs, accordingly, to be seen both as part of an ongoing inquiry into the varieties of human existence and as a response to the particular historical moment in which women were asserting new claims to a life beyond the domestic hearth.

Interest in the scientific study of humanity had never been so lively. Nineteenth-century scholars responded with a will to Alexander Pope's admonition that "the proper study of mankind is man," but unlike most of their predecessors they worked under the assumption that human nature was not unitary but separate and diverse. If the proper study of mankind was indeed man, it was discrete, not universal, man—humanity divided by class, nation, and race. And increasingly it seemed, as the century wore on, that the proper study of mankind was woman.

What is man? What is woman? What are the differences between them? Before the midnineteenth century such questions were largely the province of folklore, theology, and philosophy. Yet science too entered the discussion. Aristotle argued that the female sex was a deformity of nature. Women, being colder and weaker than men, had insufficient heat to transform the menstrual blood into the more perfect form of semen. In conception, the woman contributed no seed but only the material substance and the place of incubation; the man supplied the form and the efficient cause. Galen similarly justified woman's inferior social status on the basis of her weaker nature. These assumptions survived to animate the speculations of medieval thinkers. And even when William Harvey challenged Aristotle's view that women produced no seed or ovum, he nonetheless insisted that the male contribution to conception was superior: the male supplied "reason" and excellence. Descartes, in like manner, held that the male semen endowed the offspring with soul.[3]

Scientific interest in women's nature had, then, a lengthy history. Yet the sexual science that arose in the late nineteenth century was something more than simply another chapter in that history. It was distinctive in a number of ways. In the first place, it attempted to be far more precise and empirical than anything that had gone before. In addition it was able to draw on new developments in the life sciences as well as on the new social sciences of anthropology, psychology, and sociology. And, finally, it spoke with the imperious tone of a discipline newly claiming, and in large measure being granted, decisive authority in matters social as well as strictly scientific.

In the natural sciences the great event was the emergence of biology out of a union of descriptive natural history and physiology. Both these fields had flourished independently in the previous century, when physiology, largely confined to the human body, was still the preserve of the medical profession and natural history remained classificatory and descriptive. Those who coined the term *biology* around 1800 hoped to move beyond narrowness and taxonomy to create a comprehensive study of the living organism, whether vegetable, animal, or human.

Biology in the second half of the nineteenth century was steeped in an atmosphere of evolution. Though the concept had not awaited the *Origin of Species,* Charles Darwin's collection of facts and powerful reasoning made evolution central to biological inquiry. The effect was revolutionary. Evolution gave new meaning and an entire history to the particular facts of anatomy, morphology, and embryology. Biologists began to study organisms with an eye to their ancestral linkages and to their change and variation over time, as well as to their adaptive fitness in the present.

The new social sciences bathed in the same evolutionary stream. These new disciplines were actually modernized forms of much older fields of inquiry. Physical anthropology, for example, proposed to bring precise empirical data to bear on anthropological questions going back a century and more, above all the question of race. Psychology, too, shook off its speculative past and determined to employ clinical tests and measurements as well as new information about the physiology of the nervous system in place of introspection and anecdote. The phenomena of moral philosophy, seen to be too diffuse to satisfy the new demands for specificity, empiricism, and precision, were parceled out among the social sciences of economics, political science, and sociology. In all these areas models of change and development, usually though not invariably indebted to Darwin, became the backbone of theory and research. Physical anthropologists studied the physical and mental traits of human beings in the context of their evolutionary relationships to the great apes. Cultural anthropologists assessed civilizations and races on an evolutionary scale of perfection. In psychology interest centered on the neurophysiological development of brain levels in the individual, as well as the development of intelligence and morality in humanity as a whole. Sociologists were fond of imagining societies as biological organisms writ large, undergoing a similar course from birth through maturity to death.[4]

Science and scientists had never enjoyed greater prestige, a prestige accorded them partly on the basis of the perceived connection between scientific knowledge and the great achievements of nineteenth-century technology and even more because they held out the dazzling promise of certain knowledge. The natural sciences were to undergo a crisis of faith around the turn of the century, but before that time it was possible to believe that nature was an objective reality "out there" apart from humanity but reliably knowable and predictable. Science was a product of human discovery, not an artifact of the human mind. Physics was generally conceded to provide the model of definite, exact knowledge. Biology had not yet attained that status, but Thomas Henry Huxley looked forward to a time when it would be "as deductive and exact" as mathematics. All the sciences, whatever their level of development, were alike committed to discovering the ground rules of the universe, those underlying principles that governed reality. Science was, quite simply, "the pursuit of *Law*."[5]

Charmed by the conception of a hierarchical order in human knowledge, charmed too by the evident successes of the scientific method, social scientists modeled their fledgling disciplines upon the natural sciences and set out to discover the regular laws that surely underlay the flux of social facts. Human life, they were convinced, was part and parcel of an orderly, law-bound universe: "The world," enthused the American psychologist G. Stanley Hall, "is lawful to the core." In support of this conviction they had little by way of proof (though the early work of the Belgian astronomer L. A. J. Quetelet on population statistics appeared promising) but a great deal by way of faith. Interested as they no doubt were in the study of society for its own sake, they were far more interested in it for the sake of the ethical and political norms they hoped by its means to discover. This interest extended beyond the social sciences to all realms of society. Finding "manifestations of a universal law" had become "the intellectual pastime of the nineteenth century." Reformers and conservatives alike searched for a new foundation for social and political action in the face of the weakening of religious belief and the growth of social unrest. By midcentury the bloom was off the optimistic social reform movements of the earlier part of the century both in Europe and in America.[6]

One measure of the European turn away from the Enlightenment faith in natural rights was the increasing emphasis laid by the social sciences on individual and group differences. It had been characteristic of social theory in the late eighteenth century to stress the commonalities shared by all human beings. Humanity was one in essence, however varied its particular manifestations might be. Eighteenth-century theorists did not deny the existence of differences among races and national groups; they did not even deny that some groups were better, or more advanced, than others. But in the main they did reject the notion that such differences were inborn or hereditary, and hence permanent, and accepted "the great surmise of the Enlightenment environmentalists concerning the power of enculturation."[7] Scottish Common Sense philosophy contributed to the notion of the psychic unity of humanity an analysis of mind into only a few relatively undifferentiated faculties like memory and judgment. It was thus content to suppose the division of labor in economic life a result not of specific constitutional abilities, but of environment and social conditions.

This congeries of ideas gradually gave way in the nineteenth century to a stress on differentiation and hierarchy. Environmentalism lost favor; categories hardened and were made permanent. Physical attributes were construed to be the determinants of character. Anatomists, physiologists, and psychologists grew increasingly concerned to classify individuals according to types with sharply differing constitutions and aptitudes. In the early years the new approach was sometimes put to the service of liberal reform, as with phrenology; later it served to buttress conservative, even racist, social and political philosophies. In either case the shift was, as Frank Manuel notes, "a momentous departure." It was so because it fractured the assumption of human unity, thereby encouraging invidious comparisons among groups; because it fostered typology at the expense of individual particularity; and because the new stress on measurable dimensions gave priority to just those physical attributes least amenable to change. According to the new doctrines a glance might suffice to read an individual's character and destiny.[8]

Of all the permutations of physical differentiation sex is, together with color, the most evident. Race and gender, not infrequently linked, are two of the great themes of nineteenth-century science. There are many reasons why this was so. The natural sciences, particularly after Darwin, were obsessed with the great issue of "man's place in nature" (the title of a book by Thomas Henry Huxley). New knowledge of comparative anatomy and physiology seemed to be laying the groundwork for a rigorously precise physical anthropology. Anthropological interest had been enormously stimulated by the accounts of late-eighteenth- and early-nineteenth-century missionaries, traders, and explorers. An "explosion of exploration" had sent Cook on three voyages to the southern Pacific and the coasts of Asia and America, Mungo Park to west Africa, Alexander von Humboldt to Spanish America, William Kirkpatrick to Nepal, and Alexander McKenzie to the Canadian Northwest, all by 1800. Contact with native peoples aroused interest not merely in race but in sex, since it revealed sexual customs, cultural beliefs, and labor patterns quite at variance with European expectations. Darwin himself raised the question of sex differences in *The Descent of Man, and Selection in Relation to Sex* (1871).[9]

Yet more was involved in this efflorescence of nineteenth-century anthropology than austere scientific inquiry. Race was a burning social issue in England and America. Abolitionist movements agitated the issue of black emancipation with increasing stridency. In this atmosphere science became a weapon, its findings useful as they legitimated or discountenanced the claims of black people to political and social equity. So too with sex. By the third quarter of the century women were laying claim to rights and opportunities previously reserved for men.

The lead in the agitation for women's rights gathering momentum in the last third of the nineteenth century was taken in America, where the movement could be dated from the Seneca Falls Convention of 1848. Though the movement later focused mainly on suffrage, the Declaration of Sentiments of 1848 represented a full-scale assault on the status of women, including the legal death of women in marriage, their exclusion from higher education and the professions, and the double standard of morality, as well as the franchise. Before the Civil War, women's rights in America were largely the concern of a numerically small but vigorous circle of reform-minded men and women, most of them abolitionists. After the war, the old alliance between abolitionists and women dissolved, and the women's rights movement emerged on its own. During these years organized feminism concentrated on winning the vote, with some modest successes in the West, but some voices continued to raise the grievances of 1848 and even (though more timidly) suggested reforms in marriage and divorce that would make the marital bond less restrictive.

Some changes were beginning to take place. Most of the private men's colleges continued to shut their doors against women, but coeducational state colleges and a few private ones were being founded, and, more important in the short run, a number of women's colleges sprang up to fill the void in the years after 1865. Postgraduate and professional training was still difficult to come by, but quite a few women had managed to obtain M.D.'s by 1900, and there were also some—though fewer—female lawyers and ministers. Perhaps of greater significance, the post–Civil War years saw an astonishing growth of women's organizations of all kinds, from those designed for self-culture to those with specific public policy concerns. This development, of which the suffrage organizations were only a small part, marked the real emergence of American women into public life, and resulted in awakening many to their disadvantaged and secondary status.[10]

These nascent changes in women's status came about partly through feminist agitation and partly for reasons unrelated to feminism, such as (in the case of the married women's property laws) the efforts to protect family property from improvident or unscrupulous sons-in-law. So too with the movement of women into the workforce, perhaps the greatest change in women's lives before the advent of reliable contraception: feminists applauded it and worked for it, but the trend resulted from the vast industrial expansion of the period with its insatiate need for human labor. Most women worked in factories through no desire of their own but simply to survive, yet they too, like the female doctors and the suffragists and the New Women of all persuasions, contributed to the perceived threat to the established social order.

British feminism followed a related but not identical course. It might be said that England led America in theory, while America led England in organization. The great fountainhead of Anglo-American feminist thought was Mary Wollstonecraft's *A Vindication of the Rights of Women* (1792), and in England a radical current continued to ripple through the early years of the nineteenth century. Influenced by the French Saint-Simonians and Fourierists, the utopian socialists under Robert Owen spoke and wrote on behalf of the social and intellectual emancipation of women. So too did the Unitarian radicals who wrote for the *Monthly Repository* and the Benthamite radicals whose organ was the *Westminster Review*. These latter circles initiated the youthful John Stuart Mill into the views that would find mature expression in *The Subjection of Women*.[11]

The material situation of women in England lagged behind that of American women. Married women there remained in coverture until passage of the Married Women's Property Acts of 1870 and 1883, whereas the American states began to pass property acts before midcentury. Divorce was more difficult to obtain in England. Higher education opened more slowly to women. Though the new civic universities welcomed men and women alike, Oxford and Cambridge, while accepting the presence of women by the 1880s, refused them degrees until well into the twentieth century.

Yet in England as in America feminism made itself felt. *The Englishwoman's Journal,* founded in 1858, became the focal point of feminists working for improved educational and professional opportunities for women, as well as for married women's property rights and, somewhat later, the vote. In 1866 Lydia Becker founded the first lasting suffragist organization. The next year John Stuart Mill introduced a woman suffrage amendment into the Reform Bill of 1867; its failure provided the real impetus for the creation of a nationwide suffrage movement, marked by the founding of the National Society for Woman Suffrage (1868). Shortly thereafter

Josephine Baker embarked on her crusade against the Contagious Diseases Acts, which provided for the registration and medical inspection (by force if necessary) of prostitutes in garrison towns. This "revolt of women" challenged not only the curtailment of women's civil liberties but also the Victorian code of propriety that mandated female innocence in such matters. Feminists succeeded in establishing women's colleges at Cambridge (Girton and Newnham) and Oxford (Somerville and Lady Margaret Hall). They also contributed to a change in the climate of opinion regarding the rights of married women that made possible passage of the two Married Women's Property Acts. And in England, with an even longer history of female wage labor than America, women continued to pour into the marketplace, each a living contradiction of the cult of true womanhood.[12]

The feminist challenge was sweeping: it embraced education and occupation, together with legal, political, and social status. It even dared broach the subject of equality in personal, and especially matrimonial, relationships. Such assertiveness was more unsettling than the racial threat because it was more intimate and immediate: few white men lived with blacks, but most lived with women. Scientists responded to this unrest with a detailed and sustained examination of the differences between men and women that justified their differing social roles. Anatomy and physiology, evolutionary biology, physical anthropology, psychology, and sociology evolved comprehensive theories of sexual difference. Scientists in all these fields were guided, with few exceptions, by the beacon of evolution, but they turned more specifically to several theories common in the scientific literature of the time. From physics they took the principles of the conservation of energy and the correlation of forces: from biology, sexual selection, the biogenetic law ("ontogeny recapitulates phylogeny"), and the physiological division of labor. These theories were utilized and adapted to explain how and why men and women differed from each other and, often enough, what these differences signified for social policy, and conclusions drawn from them display such a remarkable degree of uniformity that it is fair to say that a genuine scientific consensus emerged by the turn of the century.

It is my aim in this book to examine these theories in the context of their time. I have focused on the Anglo-American scientific community because my primary interest is in American history. Science, however, does not observe national boundaries, and many of the materials are Continental. There are, I think, some differences in tone between the prescriptive proposals of European and American scientists, but the materials on which they drew were common to both. We need to understand first of all what the theories had to say and what kinds of evidence were adduced in their support. The nature of the evidence is an interesting issue in itself because of the absence at the time of most—indeed, virtually all—of the data we would today deem relevant to a discussion of sex differences: data from genetics and endocrinology, from neuroanatomy and neurophysiology, from Freudian psychology and measurements of intelligence and personality. Today we would want in addition to examine the role of culture and society in differentiating the sexes, but this vast topic, now so critical to the discussion, was dismissed by the great majority of Victorian scientists as of little consequence.

The situation was one in which a truly modest quantity of reliable data was made to support a formidable body of theory. This lack of empirical data did not inhibit theorizing, but it made the validation of theories much more difficult. It forced scientists to rely for the most part not on clinical results or laboratory evidence but on common knowledge and the obiter dicta of their predecessors. Again and again the same names were cited, gaining authority with each citation. Alternatively, some scientists became masters of extrapolation, the classic instance being that of Patrick Geddes and J. Arthur Thomson's interpretation of sex differences based on the distinction between sperm and ovum.

The overwhelming consensus of this work was that women were inherently different from men in their anatomy, physiology, temperament, and intellect. In the evolutionary development of the race women had lagged behind men, much as "primitive people" lagged behind Europeans. Even as adults, they remained childlike in body and mind, never developing traits, such as beards, that distinguished the men from the boys. The reason for woman's arrested development was the need to preserve her energies for reproduction; she suffered a foreshortened maturation, but the race gained. And her weaknesses were actually strengths: Darwinian sexual selection explained physical and behavioral differences between the sexes as advantageous in finding mates. Thus women became fragilely attractive, while men grew muscular and courageous, each sex loving in the other what it did not find in itself. It followed, therefore, that women could never expect to match the intellectual and artistic achievements of men, nor could they expect an equal share of power and authority. Nature had decreed a secondary role for women. The great principle of division of labor was here brought to bear: men produced, women reproduced. This was called complementarity.

Women, and those men like Mill who sympathized with them, naturally found this message unpalatable. Particularly in America, feminists rejected their scientific relegation to a separate and lesser status. They did so, essentially, in two ways. Writers like Antoinette Brown Blackwell and Eliza Burt Gamble denied that Charles Darwin and Herbert Spencer had correctly interpreted the significance of sex differences, but they did not deny the existence of innate differences themselves; indeed, they emphasized them. Other women, particularly students of the newly developing social sciences, attacked the issue of difference directly. The alleged sex differences lacked proof, they argued, and even those that might be shown to exist were unlikely to be innate, but were probably the result of social factors.

In the long run the environmental argument proved a far more reliable tool to combat scientific antifeminism, since the acceptance of innate sex differences—and thus, in effect, of biological determinism—reinforced traditional stereotypes and lent credence to the validity of separate spheres. For this reason modern scholars have criticized the work of innatists like Blackwell as "entrapped within the same framework of biological determinism as Darwin." Certainly the example of John Stuart Mill and the power of his skeptical environmentalism appear immensely preferable in retrospect, yet in the 1870s and 1880s such was not the case. Contemporary scientists and scientific popularizers dismissed Mill as one who ignored science. Darwin, who respected Mill, nonetheless lamented his scientific ignorance. The London Anthropological Society, devoted to racial and sexual inequality, excoriated the "school of Mill." The editor of the *Popular Science Monthly* scolded the "philanthropists, sentimentalists, and politicians" promoting women's rights as people who, like Mill, refused to be guided by science: "And yet the fundamental questions of this important movement belong solely to scientific investigators." Only at the very end of the century did cultural interpretations begin to achieve respectability; prior to that time they were simply dismissed as unscientific. So it is understandable why, given the enormous prestige of science and the universal acceptance of its authoritative status in matters of sex difference, some women tried to confront scientific antifeminism on its own terms.[13]

The liveliest and arguably the most effective challenge to scientific orthodoxy around the turn of the century was that of Charlotte Perkins Gilman. A devoted Darwinian, Gilman gave her whole allegiance neither to the environmentalists nor to the innatists. She believed in the shaping power of the environment; her books are searching critiques of the social forces that distort and stunt the lives of women. At the same time she accepted the innatist notion that men had a greater share of genius than women, whose innate gifts were for constructive labor and altruism. Her suspicion that there existed a bedrock residuum of sex distinction played second fiddle, nonetheless, to her exasperation with the social overemphasis on sexual distinction. Both men and women shared a common human nature; this, not the accident of sex, was the most important fact about them.

Witty and penetrating, Gilman had a talent for accepting the premises of men like Darwin and Spencer and exploding their perspectives to arrive at wickedly revolutionary conclusions. Thus she drew on sexual selection while exploiting to the full the awkward break in Darwin's account between human beings, among whom the females were kept, and other mammals, among whom the females were free and independent. She extolled the division of labor with an enthusiasm equal to Spencer's but insisted on pursuing it to its logical conclusion in the one enterprise as yet untouched by modern methods of work—household industry. In the end Gilman's social evolutionism wore no better than theirs, but such was the force of her logic that her argument remained intact, as fresh today as when it first appeared.

A great deal of the late-nineteenth-century writing on gender difference is overtly emotion-laden. Though some scientists, like Darwin, were content to speculate fairly judiciously about the social significance of their conclusions, others—and they seem to have been more numerous—pontificated. Many writers expressed anxiety at women's restiveness, while others expressed outrage. The subject of women and their status in society clearly touched a deep nerve. I believe that this issue became interwoven in complex ways with other concerns of this period, religious, philosophical, social, and economic, to form a tapestry of uncertainty: about changes in the economy and social structure deriving from industrialism, and more profoundly about evolution and humanity's kinship with the brutes, and about the eclipse of divinity in the universe and the relation of matter and spirit. Educated Victorians of all kinds felt the impact of change, but scientists were particularly aware of the cosmic instabilities that evolution disclosed. In denying to women a coequal role in society, scientists sought to stabilize at least one set of relationships and by inserting lesser orders (women, savages) between themselves and the apes, to distance themselves from the animality and erosion of status that Darwinism seemed to imply. If human beings could no longer lay claim to being a separate creation just a little less exalted than the angels, then a human hierarchy of excellence was needed more than ever. Women and the lesser races served to buffer Victorian gentlemen from a too-threatening intimacy with the brutes.

The terms of this controversy are by now obsolete, yet the fundamental issues have not been laid to rest. In the twentieth century sex and scientific inquiry continue their uneasy relationship in new areas with new vocabularies—hormonal research, brain lateralization, and sociobiology among them. The level of discourse is in every way more sophisticated, and the content less overtly tendentious. Moreover, science no longer speaks with a single voice, and in recent years a vigorous critique of science has emerged. Still, the historical emphasis on difference continues to be put to the use of an ideology of incapacity, though the two concepts are not logically linked. Difference does not have to imply inequality. And even if it did, no particular social policy would necessarily follow. As Richard Lewontin has pointed out, "there is no reason that differences in ability, whether intrinsic or not, need imply differences in status, wealth, or power. We might build a society in which picture painters and house painters, barbers and surgeons would be given equal material and psychic rewards."[14] Such a society would have chosen to sever the causal connection between science and social policy. It would, that is to say, have denied the assertion, so strenuously made by Victorian scientists, that scientific knowledge ought to govern social and political decision-making. We have not created that society, any more than the Victorians did. Meanwhile, women and other marginal groups will continue to view the scientific pursuit of group and individual differences with suspicion. The dismal history of sexual science suggests that they will be right to do so.

CHAPTER 1

How to Tell the
Girls from the Boys

If there be any truth in science, the intellect of woman not
only has but must have, a certain relation to her structure;
and if it could be shown that there exists no difference between the male and female minds, there would be an end of
Anthropology.

—Luke Owen Pike (1869)

Just, therefore, as higher civilization is heralded, or at least
evidenced, by increasing bulk of brain; just as the most intelligent and the dominant races surpass their rivals in cranial
capacity; and just as in those races the leaders, whether in the
sphere of thought or of action, are eminently large-brained—
so we must naturally expect that man, surpassing woman in
volume of brain, must surpass her in at least a proportionate
degree in intellectual power.

—*Popular Science Monthly* (1878–1879)

Physical anthropology inaugurated the sustained effort to measure and record the differences among human beings in the
middle and late nineteenth century. The story of the search for
empirical indices of temperament and intelligence has roots in
earlier theorizing, however—in eighteenth-century physiognomy
and more immediately in the doctrines of phrenology, popular
from about the 1820s onward. The story of phrenology, in turn,
begins with Franz Joseph Gall.

In the late eighteenth century Gall, as a young Austrian medical
student, observed that those of his fellow students who were gifted
with good memories and did well on examinations frequently also
had bulbous eyes. Later, as a neuroanatomist disturbed by the
metaphysical cast of psychology, Gall had occasion to recall his
youthful observation and to wonder whether intellectual traits
might not affect external appearance. Physiognomists supposed

that character could be read in the face, but Gall went further: might it not be revealed in the entire physique, and most particularly in the conformation of the head? The prospect of a material basis for what had hitherto been shrouded in metaphysics was exhilarating, and Gall began to work out an analysis of the mind in terms of observable characteristics. His work, and its popularization and extension by his disciple Johann Gaspar Spurzheim, inaugurated the new science of phrenology, pledged to "an extensive induction of facts." Henceforward introspection and the deliverances of an epistemology unsupported by anatomical observation would not suffice to penetrate the mysteries of mind.[1]

The fundamental doctrine of phrenology was the material foundation of intellect: "the brain is the organ of mind." Phrenologists were careful to add that the dependence of thought on the brain did not mean that mind and brain were one, but rather that the faculties of mind manifested themselves by means of the brain. A favorite analogy pictured the brain as the instrument of mind in much the same way as a violin created the music that issued from it. No one could confound the music with the instrument that gave it life; in like manner no one need construe the identity of mind and brain. This care did not, however, prevent critics from charging phrenology with rank materialism and irreligion. Though some ministers, like the American Henry Ward Beecher, were phrenological enthusiasts, probably the majority of clergymen in America and England were hostile to the new science. They had reason to be, since phrenology opposed the belief that mind was independent of the body and emphasized instead their integration. However pious their protestations of neutrality, phrenologists did challenge the orthodox religious explanation of the nature of the human constitution. In its successive elaborations—and above all that of George Combe, Scottish popularizer of phrenology—phrenology provided an alternative, not a correlative, to religion.[2]

Phrenology supposed the existence in the brain of numerous distinct faculties, each located in a particular area of the cerebral cortex. From the correlation of certain striking behavioral traits with specific cranial prominences, Gall inferred the location within the brain of organs giving rise to these faculties. The faculties themselves were not observable, nor were the cortical organs—

not, at least, in living organisms. Phrenologists did conduct post-mortem dissections on the brains of individuals whose personalities were known (and who could be induced to contribute in this way to scientific progress). By and large, however, phrenology's claim to an empirical base rested on the accumulation of correlations between behavior and skull configuration, and phrenologists accordingly built up large collections of skulls and of casts of the heads of prominent persons. Though the enterprise was flawed, it could indeed boast of its empiricism in comparison to the psychology it hoped to unseat. Gall, writes Robert M. Young, sought "to replace the speculatively derived, normative, intellectual categories of the sensationalists with observationally determined faculties which reflected the activities, talents, and adaptations of individual organisms."[3]

The precise enumeration and specification of the faculties required a great deal of research. It was decidedly not a matter to be settled dogmatically. Gall and Spurzheim themselves differed over details. Still, over time a general consensus did develop about the number (roughly thirty-seven) and definition of the faculties. Part of that consensus concerned sex distinctions. Phrenology in no way disturbed the conventional nineteenth-century wisdom about differences between the sexes; rather, it confirmed it. "There is a natural difference in the mental dispositions of men and women," wrote Spurzheim, "not in essence but in quantity, and quality, which no education can remove. Certain mental powers are stronger, and others weaker in men than in women, and *vice versa.*" There was "less vigor in the female intellect" and smaller reflective power: "women do not extend their reasoning beyond the range of the visible world. Nor do they make any great or daring excursions into the regions of fancy." In men, intellect predominated over feeling; in women, the reverse: "It is almost an axiom that women are guided by feelings, whilst men are superior in intellectual concentration." Phrenologists methodically tabulated the particular areas of affective difference. Women had more of the organ of cautiousness, being "more timid and careful" than men; men possessed more combativeness. Approbativeness (vanity) showed itself stronger in women; self-esteem, in men. Because they remained at home, women had a greater share of inhabitiveness, or love of place. Similarly, women had more of adhesiveness, the "instinctive tendency to attach one's self to surrounding objects, animate and inanimate." This faculty, which "disposes to friendship and society," expressed itself differentially in young children—in boys, by attachment to dogs, rabbits, horses, birds, and other animals; in girls, by "affectionate embraces of the doll."[4]

Far outweighing any of these emotional differences was the marked distinction between the kinds of love peculiar to each sex. Men had a decided edge in amativeness, or sexual love, as manifested in the larger male cerebellum, seat of the amative organ. Women, by contrast, felt philoprogenitiveness (love of young) much more intensely, so intensely, indeed, that as children they selected dolls and cradles for their play in preference to the drums, horses, and whips beloved of little boys. George Combe testified to the magnitude of the sexual division of love: "by the *difference in these organs alone* [amativeness and love of offspring], Gall could tell, when a brain was presented to him in water, whether it were that of a male or female . . . The skulls of women are, by this difference of development, readily known from those of men." Combe added that Gall and Spurzheim had examined the heads of twenty-nine women guilty of child murder, and in twenty-five "this organ [love of young] was *very feebly* developed." (Whether and how these infanticidal women's brains, so conspicuously wanting in parental love, could have been identified as feminine if "presented in water" to the distinguished founders of phrenology, Combe did not say.)[5]

Phrenology and Reform

Preaching the physical basis of mental powers, phrenologists perforce accepted a kind of physiological determinism. An individual's particular faculties were "determinate and ordained," fixed in the body's constitution. "Men will never feel like women," pronounced Spurzheim, "nor women like men." Logically, such pronouncements led straight to fatalism: one's destiny was written in one's skull. The connection did not escape hostile observers like the Scottish philosopher Sir William Hamilton, who bluntly asserted that "Phrenology is implicit atheism; . . . Phrenology—Physical Necessity—Materialism—Atheism—are . . . the precipitous steps of a logical transition." Logical such a transition might have been; the fact is that, logic notwithstanding, phrenologists shared the zeal for reform that swept over England and America in the first half of the nineteenth century. Phrenologists were reformers, and they were optimistic about what human beings, properly educated in self-knowledge, might achieve. Though mental endowments were assuredly diverse and unequal, it was incumbent upon individuals to make the most of the talents they possessed and, conversely, to minimize their liabilities. Mental deficiencies could never be completely eradicated, but organs could be redirected or retrained to better purpose. Weak faculties could be strengthened by exercise, overly powerful ones curbed.[6]

Reformist optimism was abundantly evident in the writings of the foremost Scottish phrenologist, George Combe, whose popular *Constitution of Man* spread the gospel of "gradual and progressive improvement" both in nature and in humanity. Optimism reached a crescendo in America under the benevolent dispensation of the brothers Orson and Lorenzo Fowler and their partner Samuel Wells. Their *Self-Instructor in Phrenology and Physiology,* while stressing the centrality of heredity as "infinitely more potential than education, and all associations and surrounding circumstances," was nonetheless a hymn to self-improvement through phrenology, "the great reformer." Another Fowler publication promised clients that

> A correct Phrenological examination will teach, with SCIENTIFIC CERTAINTY that most useful of all knowledge—YOURSELF; YOUR DEFECTS, and how to obviate them; your EXCELLENCES and how to make the most of them; your NATURAL TALENTS, and thereby in what spheres and pursuits you can best succeed; show wherein you are liable to imperfections, errors, and excesses; direct you SPECIFICALLY, what mental faculties and functions you require especially to cultivate and restrain; give all needed advice touching self-improvement, and the preservation and restoration of health; show, THROUGHOUT, how to DEVELOP, PERFECT, and make the VERY MOST POSSIBLE out of YOUR OWN SELF.

Human nature was in short fixed, but malleable, constitutionally determined, yet improvable.[7]

On both sides of the Atlantic phrenology seems to have been

cordial to the aspirations of women. British feminists in the 1820s and 1830s appealed to phrenological studies to prove the lack of demonstrable difference between men's and women's brains. (This despite Gall. There appears to have been more than a single school of brain interpretation.) One Scottish feminist told her audience that "phrenologists had proved, and she herself would prove, that women's brains were capable of being improved to a degree which would make them equal and even excel the men in all the better accomplishments of our common nature, and give them power to break the chains of the tyrant and the oppressor, and set them completely free."[8]

In America phrenologists supported women's entry into the medical profession at a time when most doctors were firmly opposed. The Fowlers chastised Harvard for refusing admission to Harriot Hunt, a medical practitioner who sought to enter the Harvard medical school in 1850. The issue was one that touched the Fowlers with some immediacy: Lydia Folger Fowler, wife of Lorenzo, entered Central Medical College in Syracuse in 1849. The first medical school to admit women on a regular basis, Central had only a short time to glory in its uniqueness; it dissolved in 1852, but not before appointing Lydia Fowler to its faculty. She thus became, though briefly, the first woman professor in an American medical school. Subsequently she maintained a private practice for many years. Folger did all this with the enthusiastic support of the male Fowlers, whose pro-woman views were based, according to their biographer, on "the phrenological concept of woman as a human being in her own right endowed with many, if not all, human potentials."[9]

Jessie Fowler, daughter of Lydia and Lorenzo, inherited the phrenological apostolate. Toward the end of the century she wrote a brief summa of sexual differences that amplified the phrenological view of human potential. Man was organized "to take the lead, to be the responsible partner." Woman was organized "to act the gentler part of man's life-work, so as to be the counterpart of him." Fowler did not contend for identity of mind in the sexes (no phrenologist could); rather, she seconded the position voiced by the English suffragist Millicent Fawcett: it was not needful or desirable to maintain that men and women were endowed with the same gifts, but social and political arrangements must permit women freedom to express the gifts they had. Almost entirely conventional in its attribution of specific sexual traits, Jessie Fowler's summation breathed nevertheless the same spirit of amplitude as her mother's life. Women could *do* as well as *be*. They might not be destined for the rude outdoor world of farming and surveying and mining that beckoned men, but they had talents meant to radiate beyond the home circle: Woman "makes a capital nurse, doctor, musician, milliner, dressmaker, artist, writer, and speaker."[10]

Insofar as it encouraged feminine potential, phrenology appears to have been that rarity, a scientific (or presumably scientific) doctrine that did not insist on the cultivation of separate spheres. Here was a theory that accepted conventional nineteenth-century wisdom about sexual distinctions and yet accommodated, even encouraged, distinctly unconventional aspirations for women. Committed to human betterment, phrenologists were convinced of the malleability of human nature. If an individual were deficient in memory, let him cultivate it; the faculty would grow. If another craved constant praise, let her curb her approbativeness; it would diminish.

Phrenology Eclipsed

Later in the nineteenth century a different understanding of human nature came to prevail. Scientists stressed not the body's possibilities but its limitations. Human beings lived out their destiny governed by "the tyranny of their organization." Inequality of gifts was a law of nature, as before, but an inequality underlined and hardened into permanence. The difference between earlier and later views is not absolute, of course; it is a difference of emphasis rather than kind. Both phrenologists and their successors agreed on the innateness of mental traits; both stressed the importance of heredity; both believed they had a mission to enlighten and educate their lay audience about nature's laws. But the change of atmosphere is palpable, and it had an effect on the messages these experts conveyed to women. "You are women, and hence by nature different," instructed the phrenologists of the first half of the century, "but you must express the gifts you have, even beyond the household." "You are women and hence different," repeated the scientists of the Victorian era, "and your differences disqualify you for the worldly roles you seem, most unwisely, to wish to assume."

By the middle of the century phrenology was losing momentum and credibility. Its pioneering attempt to localize cerebral functions had never been based on experimental work, despite the fact that Gall was a distinguished neuroanatomist. The phrenological method was anecdotal and, although allowing in theory for falsification (the Boston Phrenological Society offered a prize for the best essay critical of phrenology), was much more geared to confirmation. Nor did phrenologists have the benefit of control procedures or statistical methods. Phrenology was never accepted by the major authorities in psychology and physiology. Nor did it capture the universities; it remained at the fringe of scientific respectability. Alfred Russel Wallace, codiscoverer with Darwin of the principle of natural selection, was virtually alone among scientists of note to accept as scientific the claims of phrenology. Scientists were much more likely to agree with the psychologist Alexander Bain, whose sympathetic yet telling critique of phrenology assailed its inability to explain the nature of the character traits it professed to discover. These had still to be determined by observation and experience, to which the reading of "bumps" added nothing. Bain's criticisms joined those of continental physiologists whose work on animal brains seemed to refute the concept of cerebral localization and to point instead to the functional unity of the cerebrum. The experimentalists found no trace of local seats of amativeness, ideality, approbativeness, and the rest.[11]

Under an accumulated weight of hostility and ridicule, which its inability to prove its assertions did nothing to dispel, phrenology eventually collapsed. So ignominious was its rout by the forces of establishment science that it was denied all claim to the status of true science. Edward Boring in his standard *History of Experimental Psychology* writes, "it is almost correct to say that scientific psychology was born of phrenology out of wedlock with science." The judgment is too harsh. True, phrenology's scientific credentials did not in the end pass muster; its central contention that character and intellect could be read in the skull proved illusory. But its conception of psychology as an empirical science shaped the future of that discipline. "The central message of phrenology," writes the historian of its American phase, "was that man himself could be brought within the purview of science and that mental phenomena could be studied objectively and explained by natural causes." Phrenology achieved this shift, as Bain and subsequent chroniclers of the history of psychology acknowledged, by its insistence on the brain as the locus of mind. In so doing, it stimulated brain research and encouraged scientists and philosophers to view human beings as integrated mind–body organisms. Franz Joseph Gall inaugurated functional psychology.[12]

The legacy of phrenology was immediate as well as long-term. To the rising science of physical anthropology phrenology bequeathed its general concern with empiricism and its specific concern with the measurement of skulls. While Gall and Spurzheim relied on sight and touch, their followers invoked higher standards of scientific accuracy. Skull measurement became the hallmark of phrenology. George Combe in his *Elements of Phrenology* commended use of both the caliper and the craniometer. Physical anthropology, drawing on the tradition of physiognomy as well as phrenology, added to these a truly formidable battery of cranial instrumentation: the facial goniometer for measuring facial angle, the craniograph for making sketches of skulls, the stereograph, the micrometric compass, and the craniophore (an apparatus for holding skulls) and other devices for obtaining cranial capacity.[13]

Phrenology bequeathed to physical anthropology as well its faith in the biological basis of human capacity. Human beings were what they were because of the tilt of their faces and the shape of their skulls. To this contention physical anthropologists were able to add a great deal of anatomical and physiological data, but the message was the same: bodies determined minds. Hence the great human differences of color and sex and shape mattered; indeed, they were of paramount importance in establishing a new science of man. Nor was there any escape from the dictates of nature. The new anthropology preached permanence and scoffed at reform. Gladly accepting the tools of phrenology, it rejected the latter's belief in the possibility of change.

The Rise of Physical Anthropology

Anthropologists study human diversity. By the middle of the nineteenth century that diversity was strikingly apparent in reports about alien races and cultures emanating from missionaries, travelers, traders, colonialists, and, increasingly, ethnologists in far-off lands. Midcentury scientists expressed their perplexity with this mass of new knowledge in a bitter controversy over the origin of the human race: Had humanity been created as one species or many? Were all human beings kindred under the skin, or had different groups of people been created as so many separate and immutable species? The issue had many ramifications—theological, philosophical, and humanitarian. George Stocking points out that monogenism, the one-species theory, and polygenism, the many-species theory, reflected alternative attitudes to human diversity: "Confronted by antipodal man, one could marvel at his fundamental likeness to oneself, or one could gasp at his immediately striking differences. One could regard these differences as of degree or of kind, as products of changing environment or immutable heredity, as dynamic or static, as relative or absolute, as inconsequential or hierarchical."[14]

The anthropological tradition of the eighteenth century had tended to favor monogenism because its commitment to a universal history of cultural evolution required the assumption of human psychic unity. Even the minority of polygenists among the eighteenth-century progressivists did not put too much stress on human plurality lest it endanger their cherished belief in uniform and continuous human progress. Nineteenth-century ethnology, a kind of progenitor of anthropology more interested in cultural than in biological diversity, generally sounded this strain as well. Convinced of European racial superiority as they assuredly were, ethnologists did not question the lesser rank of dark-skinned, non-European peoples in the racial hierarchy, but they usually understood their inferiority to be the result of environment rather than biology. Races were, in this perspective, not the cause but the result of cultural and environmental diversity, and their inferior status could in principle be remedied. Benevolent concern for the darker brother was very much a motivating force behind the creation in 1843 of the Ethnological Society of London. This offspring of Quaker and Evangelical philanthropy maintained a firm allegiance to the brotherhood of man.[15]

Not so with physical anthropology. Emerging at midcentury out of anatomy, zoology, and medicine, it displayed from the start a *physical anthropology*

bias for medical analysis and an emphasis on the classification of races by physical structure. In 1859 Paul Broca, surgeon, neurologist, discoverer of Broca's area of the brain (responsible for speech), and giant among early anthropologists, founded the Anthropological Society of Paris. It became the European center of racial typology and the model for a number of similar societies, including the Anthropological Society of London. In America anthropological work proceeded under the aegis of the anatomist Samuel G. Morton at the University of Pennsylvania. Favorably impressed by the doctrines of phrenology, Morton had published a series of cranial studies culminating in his magnum opus, *Crania Americana,* in 1839. The existence of slavery in the United States lent the study of racial types particular immediacy. The eminent zoologist Louis Agassiz, encountering blacks for the first time in Philadelphia, found their appearance so strange and repellent that he classed them as a separate and lesser species, distinct from the Caucasian. This doctrine of the diversity of human species characterized the "American school" of anthropology. Other important loci of physical anthropology by the latter nineteenth century were Germany and Italy.[16]

Whether on the continent, in England, or in the United States, physical anthropologists focused not, like the ethnologists, on language and culture but on physical characteristics. The important things to know about people were their skeletal structure, the texture of their hair, the slope of their faces, the color of their skin and eyes, the size of their skulls, and the convolutions of their brains. Racial classification proceeded on the assumption that pure racial types existed, to which particular human beings more or less closely approached. Measuring individual variety, physical anthropologists confidently expected to distill from it the fundamental hereditary type. The enterprise was intensely Platonic, investing the ideal type with more reality than the individual. Timeless, changeless, the types of humankind might overlap at their boundaries but their essences remained pure.[17]

So construed, physical anthropology aggressively asserted the inequality of man. James Hunt, doctor and founder of the Anthropological Society of London, resigned from the Ethnological Society partly in protest at its views on racial unity. Nature presented to Hunt a cosmic hierarchy:

> Her suns rule their subordinate planets, surrounded again by their subject satellites. The vegetable and animal kingdoms are a succession of organic stages, separated, as Swedenborg would say, by "discrete degrees." While at the very apex of this pyramid of form and function, we find regal man, the virtual king of the earthly sphere. And are we to suppose that there are no innate and hereditary transmissible diversities among men? Reason as well as fact revolts at so absurd a conclusion.

In founding the Anthropological Society as a rival of the Ethnological, Hunt intended it "to show that human equality is one of the most unwarrantable assumptions ever invented by man."[18]

Among physical anthropologists Hunt's outspoken views were not particularly extreme. There is an "unequal degree of *perfectability*" among races, wrote Paul Broca. Some could, others could not, attain a high degree of civilization: "Never has a people with a black skin, wooly hair, and a prognathous face, spontaneously arrived at civilization." In America the "inferior character of the Negro" sanctioned the institution of slavery; in Africa, colonial subjugation. Yet not only blacks but also Polynesians, Chinese, Celts, and, in general, "such races as, since historical times, have taken little or no part in civilization" were consigned to the ash heap of history.[19]

To that same ash heap anthropologists relegated women. While it is true that the main thrust of physical anthropology was toward the classification of races, the problem of the sexes posed too many similarities to ignore. This was all the more true because midcentury women were exhibiting a disturbing propensity to challenge long-established social arrangements with respect to their rights and duties. A note of apprehension is surely detectable in a paper read by James McGrigor Allan to the London anthropologists, in which he denounced the "superficial, flat-chested, thin-voiced Amazons, who are pouring forth sickening prate about the tyranny of men and the slavery of women." The same note, more soberly expressed, is to be found in Paul Broca's warning that any change in the nineteenth-century sexual and social order "necessarily induces a perturbation in the evolution of races, and hence it follows that the condition of women in society must be most carefully studied by the anthropologist."[20]

In the brief publication annals of the *Anthropological Review* (1863–1869), the analogy between blacks and women was several times explicitly drawn. Thus Thomas Bendyshe, having heard James Hunt's paper, "On the Negro's Place in Nature," remarked that women were "in some respects as inferior to man as Negroes are to Europeans," because of their swifter maturation and decay and their imperfect development. In a scathing attack on his arch-enemy John Stuart Mill, Hunt mocked the reductio ad absurdum to which Mill had been driven by his "metaphysical assumptions . . . of political right and social justice": "John Stuart Mill cannot help claiming the suffrage for the Negro—and the woman. Such conclusions are the inevitable result of the premises whence he started." For physical anthropologists the issues of race and sex were intimately related—not two separate problems but two aspects of the same problem.[21]

Anthropologists focused their inquiry on three dimensions of the human soma: anatomical, physiological, and cranial, of which the last was certainly the most important. From the 1860s to the end of the century data on sex differences in these three areas accumulated; a convenient summary is to be found in Havelock Ellis's *Man and Woman,* published in 1894. Ellis, a doctor by training and a pioneer British sexologist, went to some trouble to gather the best-informed material he could find. His book, widely read in the many editions that followed, represents the consensus of medical and scientific opinion of the day.

Sex in Body

Ellis's experts found that, in general, women were anatomically more childlike than men. On average they were of course shorter and lighter, but even relative to total height women had longer heads, shorter necks, longer trunks, and shorter limbs than men. Ellis cited the German physiologist J. Ranke's assertion that a short trunk in a human being was a sign of superiority, but dismissed it on the ground that while it was true that yellow races were characteristically long-trunked, Negroes were the shortest-trunked of all. Hence shortness of trunk could not be a mark of superiority. Women's shorter limbs were certainly infantile, but again Ellis disputed the opinion of some continental anatomists that short limbs were simian or savage. His caution was warranted. As with data on the trunk, correct interpretation of limb length foundered on contradictions: women were at one extreme, but blacks, according to the extensive anthropometrical tests performed on soldiers in the American Civil War, were at the other. Anatomy proved frustratingly recalcitrant in the search for conclusive measurements.[22]

The final and most radical skeletal distinction between men and women was the structure of the pelvis, "a sexual distinction which immediately strikes the eye and can scarcely be effaced." The generous amplitude of the European female pelvis managed to be both sexually and racially significant, since "in some of the dark races [the pelvis] is ape-like in its narrowness and small capacity," whereas the European pelvis was "the proof of high evolution and the promise of capable maternity."[23]

Phrenologists, earlier in the century, had been sure that "the skulls of women are . . . readily known from those of men." So too Carl Vogt, a professor of natural history at the University of Geneva whose interests embraced anthropology, emphasized the sexual as well as the racial distinctiveness of skulls. Men's and women's skulls could be separated as if they belonged to two different species. The years did not confirm this confidence. Writing in the 1890s, Ellis stated, to the contrary, that skulls were difficult to distinguish by sex. Men tended to have a prominent glabella (the bony prominence over the nose), and women had larger parietal and frontal protuberances. A woman's face was small compared to her large head (an evolutionary superiority) and she was more prognathous than man, that is, her jaws and teeth protruded more (an evolutionary inferiority). In no detail, however, was the distinctiveness great enough to be definitive.[24] By the end of the century many anthropologists were seeking more sophisticated indicators of sexual difference.

Physiologically, the processes of life manifested themselves more deeply and vigorously in men than in women. Men ate more, and their blood was denser and redder than that of women, which appeared, by contrast, watery. Women's blood had fewer red corpuscles and a lower specific gravity. Men possessed a slower pulse rate and greater respiratory power. Women consumed less oxygen and produced less carbonic acid than men of equal weight, thus exhibiting lesser respiratory power (although Ellis sensibly believed that women's impaired respiration resulted in large part from their restrictive clothing). Men enjoyed an immense muscular superiority, their strength being "not less than twice as great as that of women." They were also able to discipline their strength: "The movements of men are more precise than those of women. Thus men make the best pianists."[25]

Totally eclipsing in significance these rather trivial sexual differences was the great physiological fact of woman's existence, her periodicity. The phenomenon of menstruation was alone fully sufficient to explain why women could never hope to stand on a level of social and professional equality with men. Whatever may have been the reality of the menstrual cycle in Victorian women's lives (and it would be reasonable to suppose that burdensome clothing, scant exercise, physiological ignorance, and a culture that encouraged female invalidism increased their discomfort), scientists and medical men wrote of it more as a primal curse than a natural process. James McGrigor Allan thought it explicable in terms of woman's greater approach to the animal type "if it be true that this [the menstrual discharge] is also a characteristic of female anthropoid apes, and of other mammalia." He agreed wholeheartedly with the French historian Jules Michelet's definition of woman as a nearly perpetual invalid: "Such she emphatically is, as compared with man." During menses women "suffer under a languour and depression which disqualify them for thought or action, and render it extremely doubtful how far they can be considered responsible beings while the crisis lasts." Not surprisingly, Allan believed menstruation an insuperable obstacle to feminine aspiration in the intellectual realm: "Even if woman possessed a brain equal to man's—if her intellectual powers were equal to his—the eternal distinction in the physical organisation of the sexes would make the average man in the long run, the mental superior of the average woman. In intellectual labour, man has surpassed, does now, and always will surpass woman, for the obvious reason that nature does not periodically interrupt his thought and application."[26]

Allan's tone in writing of women was decidedly vituperative, but neither the passage of time nor a more sympathetic perspective altered the negative appraisal of female physiology. Wrote Havelock Ellis, "women are thus, as it were, periodically wounded in the most sensitive spot in their organism . . . even in the healthiest woman a worm, however harmless and unperceived, gnaws periodically at the roots of life." Examples of this sort could readily be multiplied. Medical authority seems to have been all but unanimous that one-half the race was irremediably handicapped in the attempt to live a productive life. No wonder that an early dissenter from this creed, the American physician Mary Putnam Jacobi, marveled at the scientific double standard that viewed the male reproductive apparatus as a source of power, while "as soon as there is question of the other [sex], the fundamental conception of the subject seems to be changed. Not alone the accidents of sex or the abnormal exercise of its functions, but the sex itself seems to be a pathological fact, constantly detracting from the sum total of health, and of healthful activities."[27]

Sex in Skull

Though bodily anatomy and physiology were pressed into the service of racial and sexual differentiation, the characteristic and crowning achievement of nineteenth-century physical anthropology was craniology, the study of the skull and brain. A heritage of phrenology, craniology flourished as never before in the period after 1860, a period Elizabeth Fee aptly denominates "the Baroque period of craniology." New instrumentation proliferated, much of it attributable to the fertile mind of Paul Broca. No one did more to ensure that the hallmark of physical anthropology would be the calipers and measuring tape. At his death the indefatigable Frenchman had accumulated 500 skulls and 180,000 measurements. Nor was he unique in his concern for method and thoroughness: it was said of another investigator that he thought it necessary to take 5,000 measurements on a single skull.[28]

Underlying the zeal for cranial measurement was the core assumption inherited from phrenology that the body—more specifically, the head and brain—revealed the mind. At a time when intelligence testing and for that matter psychological testing of any kind did not exist, such a premise was not unreasonable. It appeared to offer the only feasible alternative to the speculations of metaphysics and introspective psychology. As Edward A. Spitzka, a leading American neuroanatomist, enthused:

> When we remember that in the human species the brain has attained the highest degree of perfection, and experience teaches that the manifestations of brain-action differ considerably in the races and social classes; when we remember that all that has ever been said or written, carved or painted, discovered or invented, has been the aggregate product of multifarious brain-activity, it seems but reasonable to seek for the somatic bases for these powers and their differences in different individuals.

Nor were the craniologists alone in their preoccupation with the somatic basis of thought; physiologists and psychologists were even then joining forces to explore the intimate but mysterious relationship between body and mind.[29]

Perhaps the crudest index of mental capacity was the facial angle, essentially a measure of the verticality of the face. Pieter Camper, who developed an instrument to measure facial angle around 1770, explained: "The idea of stupidity is associated, even by the vulgar, with the elongation of the snout, which necessarily lowers the facial line." Elongated snouts displayed, in the scientific jargon, prognathism; more vertical profiles were orthognathous, the ideal having been attained in the noble proportions of the ancient Greeks. Nobility did not shine forth from the female profile; quite the contrary, women shared the prognathous jaw with "the lowest races of man," according to Carl Vogt. Hermann Schaaffhausen, a contributor to the *Anthropological Review* in 1868, agreed that prognathism, "the most palpable mark of an inferior organisation," linked women with primitive peoples: "We so frequently find in ancient female skulls so decided a prognathism that they almost resemble the Ethiopian skulls, and have been mistaken for them." Duly recording the scientific consensus on the "savage" character of female prognathism, Havelock Ellis injected a lighter note by suggesting, "Perhaps the naive forward movement of slight prognathism in a woman suggests a face upturned to kiss . . ."[30]

Of greater import was the cephalic index, devised by Swedish anthropologist Anders Adolph Retzius, perfected by Broca, and touted by Broca's disciple Paul Topinard as "the first measurements on the skull which should be taken, when we have no time to take more." The cephalic index, the ratio of skull length to skull breadth, divided human beings into three all but unpronounceable groups: the dolichocephali (long-heads), the brachycephali (broad-heads), and the mesaticephali or orthocephali (middle-heads). As with skeletal structure, however, it proved easier to take the measurements than to interpret them. Retzius supposed that dolichocephaly indicated high mental capacity. Nordic and Teutonic peoples were decidedly dolichocephalic. Broca, on the other hand, French and brachycephalic, discovered that African blacks and Australian aborigines were also dolichocephalic. The scales shifted; anthropologists began to associate dolichocephaly with primitivism and brachycephali with civilization: "increase in width is commensurate with the increase of intelligence." But what about the Mongolians, who were by any measure broad of head? With women too the scientists ran into difficulty. Respected anatomists argued that women were certainly dolichocephalic; others, equally respected, that they were not. Topinard attempted to salvage the cephalic index by suggesting that woman was "less dolichocephalic in the dolichocephalic races but also less brachycephalic in the brachycephalic races." Understandably unable to convince even himself of the utility of this makeshift effort, Topinard by 1867 advocated abandoning the cephalic index to distinguish the sexes.[31]

Pride of place among craniological indices goes without question to the size and weight of the brain; by far the greatest amount of ink and the largest number of pages in the literature were devoted to measuring the brain in the firm belief that bigger was better. At least until the end of the century, probably a majority of scientists believed in a correlation between brain size and intelligence. "Other things being equal," wrote Paul Broca, "there is a remarkable relationship between the development of intelligence and the volume of the brain." William Hammond, a leading American neurologist, explained why: "it may be said that the largest brain will produce the greatest amount of mental energy. This deduction is based upon the fact that, as a rule, the larger the brain as a whole, the greater is the quantity of gray matter upon which its activity depends."[32]

But how to measure the brain, particularly since few brains presented themselves for measurement after death? In the vast majority of cases anthropologists had to satisfy themselves with calculating the volume of the skull. It was frustratingly difficult to obtain reliable results. Samuel Morton, one of the pioneers in the field, experimented with several substances, including white pepper seeds and lead shot, for filling the skull and then measuring the volume of the filler in a graduated metal cylinder. Other researchers used water, mercury, sand, millet, mustard seed, pearl barley, peas, haricot beans, rice, linseed, and inflated rubber bags. Shot, Topinard concluded, probably made the best filler. The problem was that results seemed to vary widely according to the substance used.[33]

One can understand, given these difficulties, the eagerness with which physical anthropologists sought out actual brains—fresh ones, if possible, from persons recently deceased, or, second best, brains already preserved in alcohol, formalin, or formaldehyde. Such brains were not easily come by. Hitherto, as one scientist lamented, few people of the better class had been aware of the great value of cerebral examination, and anatomists had had to content themselves with "the brains of pauper ne'er-do-wells and criminals." Hoping to remedy this lack, scientists in Europe and America banded together in groups dedicated to the postmortem preservation and analysis of their own brains together with those of such public-spirited individuals as could be persuaded to donate them. The Mutual Autopsy Society of Paris took the lead in 1881, followed by the American Anthropometric Society (1889) and, shortly thereafter, the Cornell Brain Association.[34]

To later generations there is a certain macabre humor in the desperate seriousness of the quest for great brains. Edward A. Spitzka, whose father was a founding member of the American Anthropometric Society, bemoaned the loss to science of the superior brains of the past—those of Newton, Shakespeare, Michelangelo, Beethoven, and Edgar Allan Poe: "how elevating, how inspiring would their lessons be." What was even worse, another brain of the same caliber had only recently been lost through sheer carelessness, that of Walt Whitman. Whitman had donated his brain to the AAS (in his younger years he had been intensely interested in phrenology and had his head read several times). The brain was carefully preserved after his death, but "some careless attendant in the laboratory let the jar fall to the ground; it is not stated whether the brain was totally destroyed by the fall, but it is a great pity that not even the fragments of the brain were rescued."[35]

Eventually Spitzka accumulated sufficient brain-weight data to construct a cranial hierarchy, beginning at the top with the massive organ of Turgenev (2,012 grams) and descending to the pitifully insufficient brain of a Bushwoman (794 grams). Spitzka drew from his work some conclusions about the population at large:

> Men of the kind who never remain steadily employed and who usually fail to learn even a trade stand lowest in the scale. Above them come the mechanics and trade-workers, the clerks, the ordinary business men and common-school teachers. Highest of all we find the men of decidedly mental abilities; the geniuses of the pencil, brush and sculptor's chisel, the mathematicians, scholars, and statesmen.[36]

Sex in Brain

With the possible exception of the common-school teachers, Spitzka peopled his scale exclusively with men. Yet women were not ignored in the great brain race. Far from it: masculine prodigiousness benefited by the contrast with feminine insignificance. And certainly the data were readily available. Paul Broca, dean of craniologists, actually collected more information about the contrasts between men's and women's brains than about any other kind of group difference. Scientists all over Europe and America joined Broca in a unanimous conclusion about the nature of the contrast: women's brains were smaller and lighter than those of men. Carl Vogt cited a British researcher who had weighed the brains of 2,086 males and 1,061 females of all ages. The male brains, he found, varied from 1,285 to 1,366 grams; the female brains, from 1,127 to 1,238 grams. The lightest male brains thus outweighed the heaviest female brains. A German scientist obtained somewhat different figures—an average brain weight of 1,390 grams for men and 1,250 grams for women. Broca's comparable figures were 1,323 grams and 1,210 grams. But the relationship between the sexes remained the same: men had an advantage of about 10 percent in the volume and weight of their brains. To the educated English-speaking public this difference became familiar as "the missing five ounces of female brain," from a phrase in the widely read and reprinted articles entitled "Mental Differences between Men and Women" by the Darwinian psychologist George John Romanes.[37]

Lest anyone doubt the significance of this disparity, the plain-spoken Frenchman Delauney spelled it out: "Diagrams of the feminine brains of different races show that even in the most intelligent populations . . . the skulls of a notable proportion of women more nearly approach the volume of the skulls of certain gorillas than that of better developed skulls of the male sex." Indeed, scientists offered little comfort to women of the highest races. Not only did a sexual disparity in intelligence exist; it had actually increased with civilization. On the basis of a decidedly small sample of prehistoric skulls from l'Homme Mort cave (thirteen in all), Broca found a cranial difference of only 99.5 cubic centimeters in volume, while his modern sample yielded a difference of from 129.5 to 220.7 cubic centimeters. Broca's European colleagues concurred: "the male European excels much more the female than the negro the negress." Evolution was not always, it appeared, a friend of women.[38]

As an index to mental capacity brain weight (or, failing that, brain volume) had the elegance of simplicity, and it claimed the hearts of some researchers until well after the turn of the century. But there were indications long before 1900 that their faith might be misplaced. Havelock Ellis noted that the German T. L. W. Bischoff had set out the facts in 1880 in his book *Das Hirngewicht,* as did Ellis himself in 1894. They and others pointed to what Elizabeth Fee has called "the elephant problem," the fact that in sheer size and weight the most massive human brain is completely outclassed by the brain of an elephant or whale. A feminist of the period caustically observed that "Almost any elephant is several Cuviers in disguise, or perhaps an entire medical faculty." Even excluding other species and restricting the discussion to the human race, there was room for skepticism. Havelock Ellis recorded the heaviest brain weights yet obtained; they belonged, in descending order, to "a totally undistinguished individual, an imbecile, the Russian novelist Turgenev, an ordinary workman, a bricklayer, and the French zoologist Cuvier."[39]

By no means every scientist was persuaded by this kind of counterevidence. Vogt, who had accepted the validity of the elephant argument thirty years before Ellis, nevertheless reaffirmed "an approximative relation" between brain weight and intelligence. Spitzka went further, refusing to concede the relevance of very heavy brains among "idiots, imbeciles, criminals, insane, and other defectives" as well as some blacksmiths and bricklayers; the phenomenon could readily be explained by "pathological hypertrophy" and grave structural defects. Spitzka spared no compassion for the owners of abnormal brains: "Those great water-logged pulpy masses in the balloon-like heads of hydrocephalic idiots did not discover and never could have discovered the laws of gravity, invent the ophthalmoscope, create 'Hamlet,' or found modern natural history." His faith in the correlation of size with excellence remained unshaken.[40]

Other anthropologists, acknowledging the force of the case against absolute brain weight, searched for a more sophisticated index that could take account of the fact that brains existed not in disembodied isolation but in intimate relationship with bodies. How to capture that relationship? Many ratios were tried—of brain weight to height, to body weight, to muscular mass, to the size of the heart, even (one begins to sense desperation) to some one bone, such as the femur. All proved, for one reason or another, inadequate, as indeed all were. Stephen Jay Gould points out that even today students of brain size cannot agree on the proper way to make allowance for the effect of body size. It is instructive, in this context, to consider the reasoning with which Paul Broca dismissed the need to take account of the body-size discrepancy between men and women:

> We might ask if the small size of the female brain depends exclusively upon the small size of her body. Tiedemann has proposed this explanation. But we must not forget that women are, on the average, a little less intelligent than men, a difference which we should not exaggerate but which is, none the less, real. We are therefore permitted to suppose that the relatively small size of the female brain

depends in part upon her physical inferiority and in part upon her
intellectual inferiority.

The circularity of Broca's argument is apparent, but that did not
hinder its popularity, and Broca became one of the acknowledged
leaders in the field of differential intelligence.[41]

Late in the nineteenth century anthropologists increasingly followed the lead of neuroanatomists into the fissures and recesses of
the brain. Edward Spitzka expected the best brains to possess not
only massiveness but also "the best material" and the "most elaborate and efficient plan of construction." Structural complexity, that
is, a greater number of fissures and convolutions, indicated superior
brain quality. Spitzka vividly illustrated the point with a trio of
plates showing how brains decreased regularly and dramatically in
both size and complexity from the heights of intellect inhabited by
the mathematical genius Karl Friedrich Gauss, the famed physicist
and physiologist Hermann von Helmholtz, and the physicist Per
Siljestrom, through the plain of savagery (represented by a Bushwoman, a Papuan, and "Sartzee," also known as the "Hottentot
Venus") to the depths of animality (the brains of a gorilla, a chimpanzee, and an orangutan). Obviously the more numerous the
convolutions, the greater the amount of gray matter, and therefore
the greater the capacity for thought.[42]

The overall shape of one's brain mattered too. Though phrenology had been discredited, a new modified form of cerebral localization emerged after 1860 from the research of Broca and others in
which particular areas of the brain were assigned the motor processes, other areas the higher processes of abstract thought. In brief,
as Gould puts it, front was better. People thought with the frontal
lobes, felt emotions with the occipital lobes, and moved about
through the good offices of the parietal lobes.[43]

To no one's surprise, sexual differences seemed to impress themselves on the appearance of the brain in all the aforementioned
respects. William Hammond noted that both the gray substance
and the white substance of the cerebellum were heavier in specific
gravity in the male brain. Others testified to the lesser development
of the frontal lobes and the greater development of the occipital
lobes in women. Hammond, agreeing that the masculine frontal

lobes were both larger and more convoluted, thought the parietal lobes dominant in women. Either way, of course, men monopolized thought.[44]

To our minds the details of neuroanatomy may appear wearisome and arcane, but they were the stuff of heated controversy in the scientific and popular press of a century ago. Nor was the controversy simply theoretical. Time and again scientists spelled out the social implications of their scientific conclusions, especially with reference to education. The magnitude of the stakes for women can be seen in the reaction of Helen H. Gardener, a freethinking journalist and feminist, to several articles by William Hammond in the *Popular Science Monthly*. Hammond, widely respected for his work on insanity and nervous diseases, had asserted on the basis of the structural differences in the brain reviewed above that girls ought to be educated differently from boys. Gardener challenged the assertion in a letter to the magazine, since, as she wrote, "the published opinions of such a man as Dr. Hammond, and in such a magazine as 'The Popular Science Monthly,' are likely to have a wide influence upon the welfare and prospects of a large number of women." His writings would, she feared, "inevitably influence school directors, voters, and legislators." The two antagonists attacked and counterattacked in the pages of the journal through August, September, and October of 1887, until the editor declared the controversy closed.[45]

So seriously did Gardener view the threat to women that she sought out Dr. Edward C. Spitzka, distinguished father of Edward A. and a man recommended to her by physicians as "the best brain anatomist in America and second to none in the world." Gardener learned from him that "any statement to the effect that an observer can tell by looking at a brain, or examining it microscopically, whether it belonged to a female or a male subject is not founded on carefully-observed fact." Gardener interpreted this as a refutation of Hammond and carried the good news, in a speech entitled "Sex in Brain," to the International Council of Women in 1888. The victory would have to be considered Pyrrhic, however, for Gardener found in her research not one scientist who believed in woman suffrage or sex equality.[46]

Darwinian Psychology Defines Woman

Some of the same threads of fact and fancy that informed the work of the physical anthropologists also went into the making of the new science of psychology. Already being reshaped by physiological research on the brain and nervous system, psychology felt the shock waves of the Darwinian revolution and began to adopt an evolutionary perspective. Darwin himself was intensely interested in the intellectual and moral as well as physical continuities between animals and human beings. In 1871 he coupled a tract exploring these interests with a lengthier one on sexual selection as a necessary corollary to natural selection and published what was in effect two books in one, *The Descent of Man, and Selection in Relation to Sex.* The work became the source book for a generation and more of research in evolutionary psychology. It became, in addition, the starting point for a psychology of sex difference. Though hardly more than a sketch, Darwin's treatment of mental distinctions between the sexes had behind it the immense prestige of his name. It set the terms for subsequent discussion.

"Some writers," Darwin began, "doubt whether there is any . . . inherent difference in the mental powers of the sexes." (He was surely thinking of Mill.) But such a difference "is at least probable from the analogy of the lower animals which present other secondary sexual characters." Analogy with the animal kingdom was the evolutionary argument par excellence, and one that Darwin used extensively throughout the *Descent.* Here his interest was in differences of temperament, and he appealed to the experience of breeders and wild-animal handlers to bear him out: "No one disputes that the bull differs in disposition from the cow, the wild-boar from the sow, the stallion from the mare, and, as is well known to the keepers of menageries, the males of the larger apes from the females." This artful selection included both domesticated and wild animals, as well as those most akin to human beings. Turning to men and women, Darwin recited a familiar Victorian litany. Men excelled in courage, pugnacity, energy, and preeminently in the higher intellectual faculties of abstraction, reason, and imagination. Women's powers of intuition, of rapid perception, and perhaps of imitation were more strongly marked than the comparable powers of men. Women's "greater tenderness and less selfishness" contrasted to men's "ambition which passes too easily into selfishness." Darwin summoned the testimony of Mungo Park's well-known African travelogue and that of "many other travellers" as to the greater altruism of women even among the savages.[47]

Darwin had no other evidence of a sexual disparity in temperament. In view of the paucity of the evidence, it is pleasing to observe the tentative tone of his discussion. The analogy with the lower animals made temperamental differences between the sexes "probable." Woman "seems to differ" from man principally in greater tenderness and unselfishness, which she manifests toward her young and which, therefore, "it is likely" that she would extend to all her fellow human beings. But Darwin abandoned this tentative tone when he moved on to "intellectual powers" proper. Here there could be no doubt: man attained "higher eminence, in whatever he takes up, than can woman—whether requiring deep thought, reason, or imagination, or merely the use of the senses and hands." The evidence on this point was conclusive (albeit hypothetical). Imagine two lists, one of men and one of women, of those most eminent in poetry, art, music, history, science, and philosophy: "the two would not bear comparison." To clinch the argument Darwin called on "the law of the deviation from averages," recently developed by his cousin Francis Galton, from which Darwin inferred "that if men are capable of a decided preeminence over women in many subjects, the average of mental power in man must be above that of woman." (Here Darwin appears to have made an illegitimate inference. Men's "preeminence over women in many subjects" could equally well have resulted from a curve in the distribution of male intellect such that more men than women were found at the extremes of intelligence *and* stupidity. A distribution of this sort would not require any difference in the average levels of male and female intelligence.)[48]

Darwin's foray into the uncharted terrain of sexual psychology was followed by that of his disciple, the comparative psychologist George John Romanes, who with William Hammond was named by Helen Gardener an "honored representative" of "the so-called scientific school of objectors to human equality." Romanes, probably more than any other man in England, established psychology firmly on a Darwinian basis. His work, together with that of Herbert Spencer, Francis Galton, the British psychiatrist Harry Campbell, the American psychologist G. Stanley Hall, and a few other authorities, provided the core of the scientific consideration of sex differences in psychology. These men constructed a feminine psyche very much in accord with prevailing cultural views of womanhood—gentle, emotional, nurturant, weak-willed, and dependent.[49]

Less cautious than Darwin, Romanes sweepingly asserted that "in the animal kingdom as a whole the males admit of being classified, as it were, in one psychological species and the females in another." This was a bold assertion. Darwin had demonstrated bodily differences between the sexes as far down the animate scale as the Articulata, but, said Romanes, "I think it is evident that secondary sexual characters of a mental kind are of no less general occurrence." The implications of this assertion are arresting: do male spiders think and feel differently from female spiders? (Fans of E. B. White will think at once of the spider Charlotte and her tender concern for Wilbur the pig.)[50]

Whatever the tenability of a differential psychology for crabs and spiders, Romanes was, needless to say, principally interested in his own species. Employing the old tripartite division of mind into intellect, emotions, and will, he discerned wide disparities of sex in all three. The marked intellectual inferiority of woman, most evident in her comparative lack of originality, revealed itself also in poorer judgment and acquisition, that is, "power of amassing knowledge." These deficiencies were, however, offset by certain strengths: "refinement of the senses, or higher evolution of sense-organs," and rapidity of perception and thought, expressed in "intuitive insight" and "nimbleness of mother-wit."[51]

Emotion was universally acclaimed as woman's element. If men characteristically thought, women characteristically felt. It was part of their charm, this propensity to feel deeply, but it was not without danger. Romanes cautioned that "we find that in women, as contrasted with men, [the emotions] are almost always less under control of the will—more apt to break away, as it were, from restraint of reason, and to overwhelm the mental chariot in disaster." In extremis, the result was hysteria, but even the normal emotional state of woman was one of "comparative childishness," that is, a generally unreasonable temper. As with her feebler intellect, however, so too with her erratic emotions: strength counterbalanced weakness. Woman excelled in affection, sympathy, devotion, self-denial, piety, and morality.[52]

Finally, Romanes found the will less tenacious in women, who as a consequence tended toward indecision and fickleness. Taken as a whole, the mental characteristics of women were "those which are born of weakness," just as those of men were "born of strength." Woman's mental weakness arose directly from her physical weakness and her consciousness of dependence. It therefore behooved men to be generous about female frailties, Romanes concluded chivalrously, since "it is the privilege of strength to be tolerant."[53]

Not for one moment were Victorian women permitted to forget that their essence was reproductive. Nature had created in woman "a being whose principal functions are evidently intended to be love, leading to generation, parturition, and nutrition." Few writers stated this truth with the bluntness of the English biologist and novelist Grant Allen, who, in a controversial article, described woman as "not even half the race at present, but rather a part of it told specially off for the continuance of the species . . . She is the sex sacrificed to reproductive necessities." The message, nonetheless, was clear: maternity defined womanhood, imparting "a fulness of emotional life, the whole quality of which is distinctively feminine." Herbert Spencer attributed the psychical as well as physical differences between the sexes to "their respective shares in the rearing and protection of offspring." Admitting that parental instinct was common to both men and women, Spencer hastened to add that it was not identical in both: "That the particular form of it which responds to infantine helplessness is more dominant in women than in men, cannot be questioned." Physiology helpfully specified a physical basis for woman's greater fund of emotion: the greater development of her viscera. Feeling originated, according to some naturalists, not in the brain but in the abdomen, and woman had more abdomen. Among the lower animals reproduction did not engender bonds between parent and offspring. Among mammals, however, intrauterine fetal development combined with a maternal instinct for postpartum nurturance to create close ties between mother and child. Biology decreed love, and woman loved: "The expansion of the abdominal zone in the female . . . is the physical basis of the altruistic sentiments."[54]

Woman's instinctive motherliness did not, it should be made clear, presuppose an instinctive sexuality. Scientists and medical men in the late nineteenth century were uncertain about the existence and strength of the sexual instinct in women, but it was generally agreed that it was weaker than in men. A rather interesting attempt to gather some empirical data on the subject is contained in Harry Campbell's *Differences in the Nervous Organisation of Man and Woman* (1891). Campbell, a specialist in nervous disorders who provided Havelock Ellis with much of the psychological information for *Man and Woman,* found formidable difficulties in the path of his inquiry. He could not, in propriety, direct questions of a sexual nature to any woman, nor apparently even to the middle-class gentlemen of his acquaintance. He settled on the working-class men whom he treated at a hospital out-patient clinic. These he questioned about the sexual instincts of their wives. Of fifty-two respondents, only twelve reported the presence of any sexual feeling at all in their wives prior to marriage; forty said it had been completely absent. After marriage desire was less strong in wives than in their husbands in almost all cases. Thirteen women, according to their husbands, had never experienced any sexual feeling at all.[55]

Campbell concluded from his primitive survey that the sexual instinct was "very much less intense" in women than in men. As a convinced Darwinian, this finding made sense to him: strong passion induced men to marry and fulfill their reproductive role, but women did not need that spur. They could conceive and bear children perfectly well with no arousal at all. Campbell even speculated that female sexuality was on the decrease. If one could assume that strongly sexed women were those most likely to be recruited into prostitution and that prostitutes had fewer children than other women—both reasonable assumptions, he believed— then it followed that prostitution (a flourishing Victorian institution) might actually be diminishing the level of female sexuality.[56]

The Nature of Admissible Evidence

Dubious as the physiology and anthropology of the period may have been, these disciplines were models of empiricism in comparison to psychology. They could at least lay claim to some figures and facts. Psychology was all but bereft of both. Heavily reliant on casual observation, anecdote, and folk wisdom, this infant discipline was only just beginning to acquire the experimental and clinical grounding that would justify its inclusion among the sciences. The state of the art is readily apparent in the frequency of comments such as "no one can question," "it is a matter of universal recognition," "everyone admits."

The first serious attempt to study the psychology of sex differences did not come until Helen Bradford Thompson's *Psychological Norms in Men and Women* (1903). Havelock Ellis, unlike most of his colleagues, candidly admitted the inconclusive nature of the evidence at his disposal, which consisted of a few experiments, a certain number of observations, and a great deal of speculation, giving as reason that "Psychology as a science was only born yesterday." At the turn of the century psychologists knew hardly more about the male and female psyches than had Charles Darwin when he was forced to rely on animal analogies and the travel narratives of Mungo Park.[57]

Conclusions reared on such insubstantial foundations proved vulnerable. Take, for example, the question of sense perception. Francis Galton, cousin of Darwin and father of eugenics, believed that acute sensibility was correlated with high intellectual powers, and was consequently greater in men. He appealed to the marketplace for evidence that men possessed greater powers of discrimination: they and not women filled the positions of tea and wine tasters, piano tuners, and the like. "If the sensitivity of women were superior to that of men, the self-interest of merchants would lead to their being always employed; but as the reverse is the case, the opposite supposition is likely to be the true one."[58]

Two aspects of this interesting inference are worth remarking on, or three if we note Galton's tacit acceptance of a sexual double standard in wages (for why else would "the self-interest of merchants" favor women over men but that they could be had more cheaply?). First, the argument completely discounts the intervention of sociological factors. Were these occupations considered suitable for women? Were women encouraged to fill them? Were merchants really as sex-blind in their hiring policies as Galton assumed? Second, it flatly contradicts Romanes's compensatory ascription to women of "refinement of the senses, or higher evolution of the sense-organs," to offset their intellectual inferiority. Romanes, however, unlike Galton, had not linked perceptivity to what he called "the deeper qualities of the mind." Discovering in a timed reading test that women both read more and retained more than men, he quickly deduced that this faculty could have no relation to intelligence, "some of my slowest readers" being "highly distinguished men." Such lack of agreement is perfectly understandable in the absence of solid information, but it does point up the subjective nature of early differential psychology.[59]

Havelock Ellis initially took his cue from Galton rather than Romanes. He argued that the common belief in women's greater delicacy of sense perception arose from a confusion between two distinct nervous qualities—sensibility (precision and intensity of perception) and irritability or affectability (readiness or quickness of response). Women excelled men in the latter, but not in the former. Taking note of the fragmentary nature of the evidence, Ellis nonetheless felt justified in concluding "that there is little reason to suppose that women have more delicate sense, and considerable reason to suppose that most of their senses are somewhat less keen."[60]

By the fourth edition of *Man and Woman* Ellis was compelled to make some revisions. Men, it appeared, did not after all have a better sense of smell than women, and women were clearly superior to men in tactile sensibility. And women were more, not less, sensitive to pain. Ellis provided a new, albeit somewhat grudging, conclusion: "it would not seem that men are clearly and decidedly superior to women in sense perception . . . In so far as the balance of advantage is on the side of women, it is less emphatically on their side than popular notions would have led us to suspect."[61]

Ellis's openness to new evidence does not appear to have been widely shared. Confronted with a doctoral thesis challenging the correlation between skull capacity and intelligence, Galton, for example, simply told its author that "he totally disagree[d]." Equally firm was his dismissal of social and environmental factors in the formation of mind. Nature, not nurture, was what counted. So convinced was Galton of the insignificance of environment in shaping lives that he made achievement and public renown the measure of intelligence: "If a man is gifted with vast intellectual ability, eagerness to work, and power of working, I cannot comprehend how such a man should be repressed." Nor could his scientific colleagues. Hardheaded Henry Maudsley sniffed, "Village Hampdens, mute inglorious Miltons, and bloodless Cromwells do *not* sleep in the graves of the rude forefathers of the hamlet." As for gifted women, that potential legion of "Shakespeare's sisters," their case was the same. They "suffered no other hindrance to the exercise and evolution of their brains and their intellect than those that are derived from their constitution and their faculties of development." No obstacles hindered, no customs entrapped them: "in poetry, music, and painting, if not also in history, philosophy, and science, the field has always been open to both." Indeed, "women by tens of thousands have enjoyed better educational as well as better social advantages than a Burns, a Keats, or a Faraday; and yet we have neither heard their voices nor seen their work."[62]

It was the old cry, where are the female geniuses? Show us your distaff Newtons and Bachs and Michelangelos and Shakespeares. And if they cannot be found, surely it is because female genius does not exist. With one voice scientists derogated the environmentalist views of John Stuart Mill and denied the force of his argument that the absence of female Homers to date was only "a negative fact," which "at most leaves the question uncertain, and open to psychological discussion." For his part, Mill was perfectly aware who the enemy was—all those in "the prevalent schools both of natural history and of mental philosophy" who viewed "with a kind of supercilious contempt" any effort to take account of external causes in the creation of human character. Whether or not it is true, as Galton wrote in 1892, that Mill's views prevailed in the public mind during the 1860s, scientists in succeeding years labored strenuously to promulgate their own conception of mental capacity as inborn and hereditary, and to a large extent they succeeded.[63]

When we ask, then, on what evidence natural and social scientists based their discussions of the nature of men and women, the issue is twofold. We need to know not only what kinds of information they accepted, but what kinds they ruled out. It can be seen that Victorian scientists harbored an intense somatic bias. Real knowledge about individuals could come only through their bodies—measuring them, probing their reactions to stimuli, testing their physiological functions, observing the convolutions of their brains. This ardor for the material was understandable, and much of it was justified. These were the very years during which physiological psychologists first began to scrutinize the physical basis of the mind, affording hope of some ultimate resolution to that mystery of mysteries, the relationship of mind and body. Yet preoccupation with bodies, with things tangible and measurable, narrowed the vision and cramped the understanding of many. They became blind to the play of forces that could not so readily be dissected. Somatic determinists, these men belittled the significance of social and cultural factors. Long before Freud they were apostles of the doctrine that anatomy is destiny.

When the fabric of scientific orthodoxy began to fray after the turn of the century, it was because of challenges on both fronts—to the facts as they were then supposed to be, and to the standard by which facts were judged to be significant. New facts emerged as the natural sciences continued to develop, but in addition the range of admissible evidence was greatly enlarged. The analysis of human nature took on new complexity as the social sciences, moving beyond biological explanations, staked out for themselves a separate dimension of culture. Even in the social sciences nurture did not completely efface nature; over their respective claims fierce battles were waged. But the Victorian scientific faith in the simple correspondence of mind and body, that innocent conviction that in probing the soma one tapped the soul, was not destined to survive.

CHAPTER 2

Up and Down
the Phyletic Ladder

We are influenced in our deeper, more temperamental dispositions by the life-habits and codes of conduct of we know
not what unnumbered hosts of ancestors, which like a cloud
of witnesses are present throughout our lives, and our souls
are echo-chambers in which their whispers reverberate.

At the gill-slit period of human life, man is at the stage of
his very ancient progenitors, who once lived a pelagic life
when there was nothing but water over the earth's surface.

As no carnivores were so well fitted to their wild environment as the cat family, so that its feral traits are still almost
intact, it appeals most to girls, relatively useless as it is, in
part because the old instinct which made her the domes-
ticator of wild animals survives best in her.

—G. Stanley Hall (1904)

For some empiricists the mere accumulation of facts about sex
differences sufficed. They were prepared to let the facts, as
outlined in Chapter 1, speak for themselves, with but a little interpre-
tive assistance. More often, however, Victorian men of science
tried to fit their data on divergence between the sexes into some
larger theoretical framework. This move was essential if they were
to provide causal explanations of their findings, and it was in
accordance with the period's eagerness to bring human beings
under the domain of universal law. Broadly speaking, scientists had
recourse to four of the great organizing principles of nineteenth-
century science: the biogenetic law; sexual selection with its corollary, the greater variability of the male; the conservation of energy
and the correlation of force; and, in social thought, the physiological division of labor. This and the next three chapters address these
principles in turn.

Ontogeny recapitulates phylogeny. The phrase reverberates down the corridors of biological thought to the present day. In the nineteenth century its influence extended beyond the borders of biology into anthropology, psychology, child study, and pedagogy. Not much was known about the life history of the individual, still less about the history of the species, but if there were parallels between them, comparison might illumine both.

In its simplest form the concept of recapitulation asserts that every individual organism repeats in its own life history the life history of its race, passing through the lower forms of its ancestors on its way to maturity. By the late nineteenth century recapitulation theory had become closely linked to the name of the great German Darwinian Ernst Haeckel. An enthusiastic morphologist, Haeckel hoped to make recapitulation an integral part of a comprehensive evolutionary synthesis. To him we owe the terms *ontogeny* and *phylogeny* as well as the terse formula in which they figured: "Ontogeny is the brief and rapid recapitulation of phylogeny." This was the biogenetic law that Haeckel formulated in 1866 and applied to human beings as well as the lower animals:

> As so high and complicated an organism as that of man . . . rises upwards from a simple cellular state, and as it progresses in its differentiating and perfecting, it passes through the same series of transformations which its animal progenitors have passed through, during immense spaces of time, inconceivable ages ago. . . . Certain very early and low states in the development of man, and other vertebrate animals in general, correspond completely in many points of structure with conditions which last for life in the lower fishes. The next phase which follows on this presents us with a change of the fish-like being into a kind of amphibious animal. At a later period the mammal, with its special characteristics, develops out of the amphibian . . .

The French anatomist Etienne Serres had earlier described the process more clearly: "Man only became man after traversing transitional organisatory states which assimilate him first to fish, then to reptiles, then to birds and mammals." The evidence was plain to see in the human embryo, which early in its career possessed gill-slits and a tail like those found in adult fish. Man thus came into possession of an ancient, if perhaps lowly, pedigree.[1]

Recapitulation gave tremendous impetus to the young science of embryology by investing each developmental stage with phylogenetic significance. The record of the individual was the record of the race: "Evolution tells us that each animal has had a pedigree in the past. Embryology reveals to us this ancestry, because every animal in its own development repeats its history, climbs up its own genealogical tree." By analogy three biological disciplines became parallel and mutually reinforcing: embryology, comparative anatomy, and paleontology. Embryology furnished the record of ontogeny, or individual development; comparative anatomy showed phylogeny, or race development, viewed as a range of contemporaneously existing forms; and paleontology illustrated phylogeny viewed as a temporal sequence.[2]

In this manner recapitulation unified a number of diverse biological disciplines, an outcome that was pleasing both aesthetically and pragmatically, since it satisfied the desire for parsimonious explanation and contributed to the establishment of the grand evolutionary paradigm that was the goal of much late-nineteenth-century morphology. It served a unifying function in relation to the study of humanity as well, strongly reinforcing the Darwinian lesson that human beings were part of nature with an ancestral pedigree that could be traced back through their nearest relatives, the great apes, to the lower mammals, the amphibians, the fishes, and ultimately, in Haeckel's schema, to the Gastrea, progenitor (albeit, as it turned out, imaginary) of all multicellular organisms.

Anthropology Recapitulates Biology

Recapitulation theory proved irresistible to the social sciences. It provided a program for greater anthropological understanding of all those groups outside the charmed circle of Caucasian male adulthood—children, women, and the lower races. In so doing it became the thematic core of anthropology, of psychology, and of child study. That women, children, and savages shared many traits in common was a finding that appeared to emerge from the evidence of physical anthropologists and psychologists. Recapitulation shed light on why this might be so.

Anthropologists taught that primitive societies represented cultural stages that fell short of the complete civilization exemplified by the societies of western Europe. In the phylogeny of the human race the nineteenth-century savage, together with his prehistoric forebear, was assigned the role of child. Speaking before the Anthropological Society of London in the 1860s, C. S. Wake sketched a racial hierarchy in which the Australian aborigine occupied the childish or selfish niche; the American Indian, the willful level of boyhood; the oriental, the empirical level of early manhood; and the European, rational maturity. Another theorist pushed the analogy back to fetal development:

> The leading characters of the various races of mankind are simply the representatives of particular stages in the development of the highest Caucasian type. The Negro exhibits permanently the imperfect brow, projecting lower jaw, and slender bent limbs of a Caucasian child some considerable time before the period of its birth. The aboriginal American represents the same child nearer birth. The Mongolian, the same child newly born.[3]

Underlying racial hierarchies of this kind lingered the pre-Darwinian conception of nature as a Great Chain of Being, a single, ladder-like scale of relative levels of perfection. On this ladder one, and only one, being occupied the highest rung, all others failing to achieve perfection in greater or lesser degree. Long before Darwin biologists within the tradition of the Chain of Being did not hesitate to ascribe degrees of perfection to different races. It would therefore be foolish as well as false to imagine that invidious scaling of races waited upon evolution. Stephen Jay Gould in his study *Ontogeny and Phylogeny* has included an example from the eighteenth-century preformationist Charles Bonnet: "We may oppose the impropriety of the Hottentot to the propriety of the Hollander. From the cruel cannibal, we pass rapidly to the humane Frenchman . . . We mount from the Scottish peasant to the great Newton." Most of these earlier views, however, rested their case on differences in culture rather than differences in biological endowment. Since cultural inferiority could conceivably be remedied, ethnocentrist hierarchies were less fixed and enduring than hierarchies based on color and stature and head shape. Somatic determinants gained prominence in recapitulatory physical anthropology after midcentury.[4]

Strictly construed, the biogenetic parallel barred savage races from further development. "Half-devil and half-child," they could not hope to attain the heights of civilization. It thus devolved upon the mature races to assume perpetual guardianship over those who could not govern themselves. This conviction of mission was widespread in England and America, even among those who might (unlike the majority of members of the London Anthropological Society) be considered racial moderates. Alfred Russel Wallace believed, for example, that "the relation of a civilized to an uncivilized race, over which it rules, is exactly that of parent to child, or generally adults to infants."[5]

Given the kinship of savage and child, each presumably had much to tell scientific inquirers about the other. What was known about the psychology of childhood could illuminate the darkness of the savage mind and, conversely, primitive behavior could provide clues to an understanding of the Caucasian child. But only rarely was this likeness heuristically employed to elicit new information, partly no doubt because of the lack of mental or behavioral measurements, partly because the analogy seemed self-evident. For the most part the claim was affirmed rather than explored. It functioned as a way of ordering old, not of gaining new, information. Carl Vogt, for example, remarking on the generally accepted fact that Negro children learned as readily as did white, spoke of the transformation that occurred in them at "the fatal period of puberty": their jaws began to project and their cranial sutures to close, thus depriving their brains of further space for growth. (The same process, significantly, took place among the anthropoid apes.) From puberty onward, their faculties remained stationary, incapable of further progress. Hence the childlike propensities of the Negro: love of pleasure and of music and dancing, inconstancy of feelings, and lack of soaring imagination. Similarly Harry Campbell itemized the psychological characteristics shared by children and savages: lack of will power, reflection, and persistence; feeble attention span; weak capacity for abstraction; imitativeness and lack of originality; impulsiveness and general emotionalism; fearfulness and a concomitant sense of dependence. These traits of children, "such as belong to an inferior grade of mental evolution," were all shared by primitive man, so that the savage had aptly been called " 'the baby of the race.' " Had research actually been undertaken during these years to test racial differences in development, it would have shown, contrary to the assertions of Vogt and Louis Agassiz and others, first, that there is no difference in the timing of closure of the cranial sutures in Negroes and whites and, second, that the closure takes place in any event long after brain growth has been completed.[6]

Woman as Child and Savage

In the dual sequences of ontogeny and phylogeny child and savage neatly counterpointed each other. Woman, however, played a role in both: in ontogeny she represented eternal adolescence, in phylogeny she recalled the ancestry of the race. Parallels could be drawn between women and children, on the one hand, and, making due allowance for their higher culture as Europeans and Americans, between women and primitives, on the other.

Evidence for the childishness of woman was particularly abundant. It could be read in her skeleton, which the French anthropologist Paul Topinard in an oft-cited passage located midway between the skeletal structure of the infant and that of the man. It could be read in her skull as well: "The outlines of the adult female cranium are intermediate between those of the child and the adult man; they are softer, more graceful and delicate, . . . the forehead is . . . more perpendicular . . . the superciliary ridges and the gabella are far less developed, often not at all; the crown is higher and more horizontal, the brain weight and cranial capacity are less." Rudolf Wagner believed that the brain of woman as a whole was always in a more or less infantile condition; Emil Huschke, that woman was only a child in growth, her brain, like her body, remaining true to the infantile type. A glance at the average woman sufficed: compared to the adult male body, the female form approached the infantile condition in relatively longer length of trunk and shorter extremities.[7]

Psychologically, too, woman remained a child, weak-willed, impulsive, perceptive, markedly imitative rather than original, timid, and dependent. (Perceptivity, be it noted, was often held to stand in inverse ratio to high intellectual development, since the latter induced reflection and this in turn retarded perception.) According to Harry Campbell, women craved sympathy as children did, although unlike children they were equally ready to bestow it.[8]

In identifying woman as a kind of immature man the logic of recapitulation suggested that the fully evolved human male himself passed through a female stage of development. So convinced were most students of psychology of a polar opposition between male and female that they rarely pursued this suggestion. One who did was Edward Drinker Cope, leader of the "American School" of neo-Lamarckians and a well-known paleontologist. In discussing the relationships between human physique and human nature, Cope remarked that men when young experienced a phase of feminine emotionality:

> The gentler sex is characterized by a greater impressibility . . . ; warmth of emotion, submission to its influence rather than that of logic; timidity and irregularity of action in the outer world. All these qualities belong to the male sex, as a general rule, at some period of life, though different individuals lose them at very various periods . . . Perhaps all men can recall a period of youth when they were hero-worshippers—when they felt the need of a stronger arm, and loved to look up to the powerful friend who could sympathize with and aid them. This is the "woman stage" of character.

G. Stanley Hall, the American evolutionary psychologist, similarly noted the "feminized stage of psychic development" through which adolescent boys normally passed. Men, of course, were expected to mature beyond the "woman stage," but for women the "powerful friend" was a lifelong necessity.[9]

The childlikeness of women was a mark of inferiority. "Physically, mentally, and morally," avowed James McGrigor Allan of the London Anthropological Society in his sometimes rather intemperate assessment of female capacities, "woman is a kind of adult child . . . [But] Man is the head of creation. The highest examples of physical, mental, and moral excellence are found in man." Even more telling of woman's inferiority, however, was her resemblance to the savage. Observing that "the female European skull resembles much more the Negro skull than that of the European man," Carl Vogt added, "We may be sure that, whenever we perceive an approach to the animal type, the female is nearer to it than the male." Paul Albrecht pointed out that as the black man, grinning, chattering, shambling, preserved primate characteristics, so too did woman:

> In woman the stature is less than that of man; both dolichocephaly and prognathism are more marked and of more frequent occurrence; the inner incisors are more powerfully developed; the *trochanter tertius* [bony prominence on the femur] occurs more frequently (more frequently indeed than in the apes); . . . hypertrichosis [excessive hair] is more frequent, baldness less frequent; resort to biting and scratching is more frequent.[10]

Though most of the scientific description of feminine peculiarities reads like a transcription of familiar Victorian wisdom, this was not always the case. To anyone acquainted with the nineteenth-century stereotype of exquisitely sensitive, vaporous womanhood, one of the more startling assertions in the literature was that of woman's physical insensibility relative to man. In this once again women resembled primitive peoples. Everyone knew about the insensibility of savages to pain. Havelock Ellis told the tale of the Maoris who cut off their toes to fit into European boots, and the Italian founder of criminal anthropology, Cesare Lombroso, wrote, "All travelers know the indifference of Negroes and American savages to pain: the former cut their hands and laugh in order to avoid work; the latter, tied to the torture post, gaily sing the praises of their tribe while they are slowly burnt." This tolerance of physical stress was a residue of the power of lower animals to restore a lost organ. Lost at higher stages of life, the power lingered in truncated guise as superior tolerance of trauma and surgery among "the lower human races, the lower classes of society, women and children."[11]

Querying medical men about the alleged stoicism of women in the face of pain, Lombroso reported a uniform response:

> Carle assured me women would let themselves be operated upon almost as though their flesh were an alien thing. Giordano told me that even the pains of childbirth caused relatively little suffering to women, in spite of their apprehensions. Dr. Martini, one of the most distinguished dentists of Turin, has informed me of the amazement he has felt at seeing women endure more easily and courageously than men every kind of dental operation. Mela, too, has found that men will, under such circumstances, faint oftener than women.

Courage being an attribute of men of higher race, it was unthinkable that it might be found in women or savages. Their courage must be indifference; their endurance, insensibility. They did not—could not—suffer. Savages, women, and children might no longer regenerate limbs as the newt does, but their tolerance of discomfort linked them securely with their amphibian ancestry.[12]

The Romantic Psychology of G. Stanley Hall

Arguably the most influential, and certainly the most colorful, exploration of recapitulation occurred in America under the aegis of a peculiar and compelling figure, one of the founding fathers of American psychology, G. Stanley Hall. As a young man in the 1870s Hall, like so many seekers of his generation, had fallen under the spell of Darwin, Huxley, Spencer, and Tyndall. Electing a lifework in psychology rather than in the ministry for which he had originally trained, he committed himself to fashioning an evolutionary science on the twin bases of recapitulation and the inheritance of acquired characteristics. These concerns Hall, a powerful personality, passed on to the numerous students who came under his influence at Johns Hopkins University and later at Clark, an entirely graduate university which he served as professor of psychology and first president from its inception in 1888 until 1920. Devoted to the study of childhood and adolescence, Hall and his disciples forged the recapitulatory linkages among savages, children, and women at greater length and with greater imagination than any other writers of their time.[13]

Hall's approach to psychology was strongly genetic. "We really only know things," he wrote, "when we trace their development from the farthest beginning through all their stages to maximal maturity and decay." The farthest beginning in the development of the human psyche Hall located in the minds of animals, and he advocated careful study of animal psychology. But closer to hand was the mind of the child, also immensely valuable in explaining human beings to themselves. Hall confessed to a romantic infatuation with childhood, and especially adolescence, a period "more worthy, perhaps, than anything else in the world of reverence . . . These years are the best decade of life."[14]

Children represented the precious heritage of the race in a particularly accessible way, since they were open, direct, and spontaneous. In children was revealed with clarity the emotional life all but smothered in adults. Exhibiting considerable emotion of his own, Hall inveighed against the extinction of primal passion among civilized adults:

> in our day and civilization, the hot life of feeling is remote and decadent. Culture represses, and intellect saps the root . . . What does the psychologist of the study know of hate that makes men mad or bestial, of love that is not only uncalculating but is stronger than life, of fear that shakes the pulses, and courage that faces death in its cruelest forms unflinchingly, of the wages of battle where men fight beasts or each other with teeth and knives and spitting revolvers, of torture, of joy that threatens sanity? Our sensibilities are refined, but our perspective is narrow . . . What we have felt is second-hand, bookish, shop-worn, and the heart is parched and bankrupt.

Across this arid landscape of the soul children frolicked with the freshness of living emotion,

> freighted, as they are, body and soul, with reminiscences of what we were so fast losing. They are abandoned to joy, grief, passion, fear, and rage. They are bashful, show off, weep, laugh, desire, are curious, eager, regret, and swell with passion, not knowing that these last two are especially outlawed by our guild. There is color in their souls, brilliant, livid, loud. Their hearts are yet young, fresh, and in the golden age.[15]

These same qualities, so near exhaustion among civilized adults, could also be found among primitive peoples. Hall's attitude toward primitive cultures was deeply paternalistic, as indeed it must be in anyone who equates primitivism with immaturity. At the same time, writing at the turn of the century, when social scientists were beginning to have second thoughts about the validity of racial typology, Hall did not utilize the child-savage analogy in the old way to brand the primitive with eternal inferiority. He urged the abandonment of terms like *upper* and *lower* when applied to race, in favor of *forward* and *belated*. "We must drop," he wrote, "the view that seeks in the lower races missing links between animals and men." Insofar as the savage, like the child, remained closer to his emotional roots, he represented a precious repository of feeling for the emotionally enfeebled:

> Most savages in most respects are children, or, because of sexual maturity, more properly, adolescents of adult size . . . Their faults and their virtues are those of childhood and youth . . . Primitive peoples have the same right to linger in the paradise of childhood. To war upon them is to war upon children . . . Without them our earthly home would be left indeed desolate. They have a life of feeling, emotion, and impulse, and scores of testimonials from those who know them intimately, and who have no predilection for Rousseau-like views, are to the effect that to know a typical savage is to love him.[16]

Hall was especially excited about the clues child psychology afforded to the mystery of ancestral man. Consciousness in the civilized mind floated atop the many layers of subconscious life. In these strata were recorded the hereditary bequests, the habits and codes of conduct, of countless prehistoric ancestors, so that "our souls are echo-chambers in which their whispers reverberate." Maturation hushed those whispers, and civilization drowned them out in the roar of city streets. Of the long prehistory of the race only the child and adolescent could tell. The child from about nine to twelve, healthy, active, vigorous, newly independent of his parents, relived "an old and relatively perfected stage of race maturity, still in some sense and degree feasible in warm climates, which . . . stands for a long continued one, a terminal stage of human development at some post-simian point." Puberty shattered the child's physical and psychic equilibrium; "driven from his paradise," the child endured the storms and stresses of adolescence. At this time began the acquisition of traits phyletically newer, superimposed on the "paleopsychic traits" of childhood. "The child comes from and harks back to a remoter past; the adolescent is neo-atavistic, and in him the later acquisitions of the race slowly become prepotent." Now morality awakened, and sentiment and religion. The adolescent felt the first stirrings of sexual love, and his social instincts, hitherto dormant, unfolded. Though still plastic, he began to develop character. In short, adolescence was "a marvelous new birth" to humanity.[17]

Hall composed imaginative variations on the theme of recapitulation. He pointed out that childish fear of strangers was perhaps a legacy of " 'the ancient war of all against all in the long and bitter struggle for existence.' " The child's habit of clutching the hair or beard of adults suggested a remoter origin, "the necessity for anthropoids of arboreal habits to cling to the shaggy sides of their parents." Reflection might even discern something of the "very ancient progenitors, who once lived a pelagic life when there was nothing but water over the earth's surface" in the enthusiasm of children for water: "To paddle, splash, swim and sun sometimes constitutes almost a hydroneurosis, and children pine all winter and live only for the next summer at the sea . . . Alas for the child who has not access to a beach! and nowhere in the world perhaps are children so happy or in their element as when there."[18]

Alexander Chamberlain, Hall's student and colleague at Clark, called attention to the way in which the periods of childhood and youth might be correlated with the stages of race development. This kind of information, while inherently important as part of the genetic history of humanity, had pedagogical implications as well. It suggested that the modern haste to incarcerate young children within the four walls of the elementary school was tragically misguided. Children needed to live out to the full the savage phase of human phylogeny. Hall deplored "transplant[ing] the human sapling" too soon to the schoolhouse, where it was forced to "sit on unhygienic benches and work the tiny muscles that wag the tongue and pen, and let all the others, which constitute nearly half its weight, decay." Far better to return to the more natural pedagogy of Rousseau:

> Rousseau would leave prepubescent years to nature and to these primary hereditary impulses and allow the fundamental traits of savagery their fling til twelve. Biological psychology finds many and cogent reasons to confirm this view if only a proper environment could be provided. The child revels in savagery, and if its tribal, predatory, hunting, fishing, fighting, roving, idle, playing proclivities could be indulged in the country and under conditions that now alas! seem hopelessly ideal, they could conceivably be so organized and directed as to be far more truly humanistic and liberal than all that the best modern school can provide. Rudimentary organs of the soul now suppressed, perverted, or delayed, to crop out in menacing

forms later, would be developed in their season so that we should be immune to them in maturer years.

The first education should be that of home and environment, teaching, through nature study and "tales of the heroic virtues," the lessons of the ancestral past.[19]

Hall's romanticism extended to women as well as children. In a lengthy chapter on "Adolescent Girls and Their Education" that owed much to Havelock Ellis, Hall depicted women as above all else repositories of both ontogenetic and phylogenetic human traits. As a kind of perpetual adolescent, woman "represent[ed] childhood and youth in the full meridian of its glory in all her dimensions and nature"; as a perpetual savage, she "fulfill[ed] the function of seeing to it that no acquired good be lost to mankind . . . Her whole soul, conscious and unconscious, is best conceived as a magnificent organ of heredity."[20]

Since women were designed to be racial conduits rather than racial catalysts, Hall had some very definite ideas about their intellectual capacities and the education suited to them. In woman, the "sympathetic and ganglionic system is relatively to cerebro-spinal more dominant." And this was well and beautiful: Hall himself had over the years become "penetrated with the growing sense of the predominance of the heart over the mere intellect." He feared that modern woman in the blind pursuit of intellectual training was endangering all that was characteristically womanly and losing sight of woman's true goal—motherhood: "The madonna conception expresses man's highest comprehension of woman's real nature." Might not Catholics, who worshipped a Virgin Mother serenely indifferent to mind, be on to a profound truth? "Who ever asked if the holy mother, whom the wise men adored, knew the astronomy of the Chaldees or had studied Egyptian or Babylonian, or even whether she knew how to read or write her own tongue, and who has ever thought of caring?" Girls must be educated "primarily and chiefly for motherhood."[21]

The proper course for educators, then, was to establish a regimen that would "broaden by retarding, . . . keep the purely mental back and by every method . . . bring the intuitions to the front." Women must at all costs resist the influences that encouraged psychological precocity and avoid premature intellectual specialization. Hall was a vociferous opponent of coeducation. Two sexes so different in nature, capacity, and destiny ought not to sit side by side in the classroom. Girls could not be held to "the same standards of conduct, regularity, severe moral accountability, and strenuous mental work that boys need." The physiological rhythms of the young girl mandated a different schedule of work and rest, leaving to man his week and "giving to her the same number of Sabbaths per year, but in groups of four successive days per month."[22]

Hall bathed his commentary on women in the mauve tints of nineteenth-century sentimentalism; the words *reverence* and *glorification* and *worship* recur. He did not share the hard-bitten misogyny of European writers like Henry Maudsley, Cesare Lombroso, and Carl Vogt, for whom recapitulation certified the inferior status of women. Yet his discussion was profoundly ambivalent. Women were, he wrote, less emancipated from nature than were men, their "processes" more unconscious; they often appeared "volatile and desultory." They tended to employ duplicity and deception. Their softness threatened the robustly virile traits like anger and militance: "To be angry aright is a good part of moral education, and non-resistance under all provocations is unmanly, craven, and cowardly . . . Real virtue requires enemies, and women and effeminate and old men want placid, comfortable peace, while a real man rejoices in noble strife which sanctifies all great causes, casts out fear, and is the chief school of courage." Fear of emasculation constituted an important element in Hall's dislike of coeducation: male teachers suffered from the progressive feminization of coeducational public schools, and male principals surrounded by female teaching staffs risked "deterioration in the moral tone of their virility" as well as decreased ability to cope successfully with other men.[23]

The evidence suggests that Hall was himself a man of divided mind. Civilization was progress, but savages enjoyed "the hot life of feeling." Adults had "full ethical maturity" but children had more fun. Men were the movers and shakers, but women possessed the secret of eternal youth. Hall's biographer suggests that in the achievement of a mature masculine identity Hall felt compelled for many years to suppress within himself elements he identified with femininity, such as altruism and an interest in aesthetics. By the time he was writing *Adolescence* he felt free to give these "feminine" elements their due, but he still could not integrate successfully the masculine and feminine ideals. The result is an account notable for its unresolved tensions, one which exonerates women from most of the charges lodged against them by European theorists while relying heavily on the antifeminist interpretations of those same theorists, and which reverently replaces women on their Victorian pedestals while ensuring that men remain very much in charge.[24]

The Underside of Evolution

Women and savages, together with idiots, criminals, and pathological monstrosities, were a constant source of anxiety to male intellectuals in the late nineteenth century. (Children, though less than fully human, would eventually become so.) Man's place in nature, so long established as a thing apart, separate and distinct from the rest of creation, had suffered a radical revaluation. The human species was now seen as sharing a common animality with the beasts that walked and flew and crept over the earth. Man differed in degree rather than in kind from his nearest relatives, the anthropoid apes, and this was as true of the mind as of the body. Psychologists postulated an evolutionary theory of mind, frighteningly vivid, that supposed gradual development from the lower to the higher functional centers. Rather than something distinctively human, "all our highest faculties and sentiments are differentiations and evolutions of instincts and desires which are represented in the lowliest organisms by the most simple and most general vegetative instincts." This process might go awry, stranding its victim at some lower level of evolution. Equally, it might reverse itself in a process of undevelopment, as happened in insanity when, the higher inhibitions stripped away, "the savage in man springs to the surface."[25]

Even for its ardent supporters, this view of human nature was not without cost; it seems to have occasioned among scientists and those aware of scientific trends a most extraordinary obsession with evolutionary failures, those who never quite made it to complete human perfection or who, having made it, regressed. These "outcasts from evolution," women, savages, and criminals among them, were a nagging reminder that nature sometimes miscarried without warning and without pity. If man was after all only an ape of higher development, the sickening possibility existed that some small developmental quirk, some ancestral lack of self-control, some injury or illness, might consign an individual to an existence that was less than fully human.

Nineteenth-century fiction is rich in evolutionary tragedies. In France Emile Zola, well-read in the medical literature on degeneration, described the pitiful deterioration of several generations of an entire family, the Rougon-Macquarts, owing to the hereditary degenerative effects of alcoholism and neurosis. Catalepsy, homosexuality, blood-lust, and nymphomania were some of the manifestations of this hereditary taint. In America Zola's disciple, Frank Norris, probed the veneer of his huge, dim-witted but well-meaning hero, McTeague: "Below the fine fabric of all that was good in him ran the foul stream of hereditary evil, like a sewer. The vices and sins of his father and of his father's father, to the third and fourth and five hundredth generation, tainted him. The evil of an entire race flowed in his veins." Jack London, avid self-taught exponent of scientific materialism, penned a terrifying portrait of Captain Wolf Larsen, "the perfect type of the primitive man, born a thousand years or generations too late and an anachronism in the culminating century of civilization." Larsen, added London, was "a magnificent atavism, a man so purely primitive that he was of the type that came into the world before the development of the moral nature."[26]

These fictive renderings were not, or not solely, imaginative constructs; they were based on the researches of biologists and anthropologists in Europe and America. Scientists were groping for a theory of the still mysterious processes of heredity. Darwin was himself as much in the dark as anyone else. For some time he considered a theory of heredity—that is, a theory of the origin of variation—to be essential to his explanation of evolution by natural selection. In the end he realized rightly that his mechanism could stand on its own, but he was uncomfortable with the obvious gap in his argument. During the 1860s he worked out a provisional theory he called pangenesis, much influenced by some speculations of

Herbert Spencer and the anatomist Richard Owen. Pangenesis supposed the existence of "gemmules," particles that were thrown off by all cells of the body and that circulated through the bodily fluids and eventually came to rest in the sexual organs, where they were combined into the sex cells. This theory would explain why, for example, characters common to one sex might suddenly appear in the opposite sex, or how reversion to ancestral traits (atavism) occurred. In the first case, the gemmules giving rise to sex-specific traits could be imagined as present but dormant in the opposite sex. In the second, the gemmules might pass through several generations without expression, only to give rise to ancestral characteristics in a later descendant. Though entirely speculative, and not very enthusiastically received even by many of Darwin's supporters, pangenesis was a serious attempt at explaining a scientific enigma. As Michael Ruse puts it, "Darwin's theory of pangenesis was therefore not some aberrant extravaganza of a brilliant mind, but was in harmony with (not to say a product of) the most respectable of beliefs."[27]

One of the features that Darwin believed intelligible upon the hypothesis of pangenesis was the inheritance of acquired characteristics. A bodily change, such as increased strength in the blacksmith's arm (Darwin's own example), could affect the gemmules thrown off by the cells of that arm. These, gathering in the reproductive organs, would alter the muscularity of offspring. Darwin's mechanism of natural selection functioned as an alternative to Lamarck's hypothesis of organic variation as a response on the part of the organism to a felt need triggered by some change in the environment. But Darwin was far from denying a role to the Lamarckian inheritance of acquired characteristics, and indeed he expanded that role as time went by. The real controversy over Lamarckian inheritance awaited the vigorous criticism of August Weismann, a cytologist at the University of Freiburg and a firm supporter of Darwinian natural selection, in the late 1880s and 1890s, and extended over a period of at least two decades. As late as 1907 the eminent geneticist Thomas Hunt Morgan treated the theory seriously, although he concluded that "the best evidence, viz. that from experiment, that we have at present does not show that acquired somatic characters are inherited through the germ cells." The absence of clarity on this issue, crucially important for establishing what could and could not be passed on from parents to children, left the field open for the most diverse speculation as to how heredity worked, or, more frighteningly, miscarried.[28]

How Nature Failed

Atavism, or reversion, perhaps the simplest of these concepts, had its roots in Darwin's *Descent of Man,* which referred to "the principle of reversion, by which a long-lost structure is called back into existence." As an example, Darwin noted the prominent size of the canine teeth in some human beings as a reversion to "an ape-like progenitor." And in a neat offensive maneuver, he blocked potential criticism of this idea:

> He who rejects with scorn the belief that the shape of his own canines, and their occasionally great development in other men, are due to our early forefathers having been provided with these formidable weapons, will probably reveal, by sneering, the line of his descent. For though he no longer intends, nor has the power, to use these teeth as weapons, he will unconsciously retract his "snarling muscles" (thus named by Sir C. Bell), so as to expose them ready for action, like a dog prepared to fight.[29]

Because atavism always implied a skipping of generations—the appearance of a parental trait in an offspring was normal and not atavistic—it was sometimes referred to as "discontinuous heredity." But the discontinuity could be large or small, extending over one or two generations or several millennia. Paolo Mantegazza, for example, an Italian anthropologist who invented the term *psychic atavism* to designate regressive mental phenomena, described an instance of two skipped generations: he himself, though not at all resembling his paternal great-grandmother, had nevertheless inherited "her marked *penchant* for gardening." At the other extreme, G. Stanley Hall found in women's preference for committing suicide by drowning evidence of humanity's "pelagic origin," for women, like children, were "phyletically older and more primitive . . . [Havelock] Ellis thinks drowning is becoming more frequent, and that therein women are becoming more womanly." One writer even suggested that human cyclopean "monsters" (one of whom he helpfully included in a photograph) might be regarded as reversions to the single-eyed sea squirts who were possibly the ascidian precursors of the vertebrates.[30]

To an age immensely concerned about the meaning of evolution for the human race, the call of the atavism was spellbinding. A great deal of nonsense masquerading as scholarship can be found in the chapter on "The Child as Revealer of the Past" in *The Child: A Study in the Evolution of Man* by Alexander F. Chamberlain. Chamberlain catalogued atavisms at exhaustive length: physical atavisms, water-atavisms, monkey-atavisms, psychic, alimentary, dirt, genital, and cruelty atavisms, fear and anger atavisms, and a grab bag category of miscellaneous atavisms. In the search for genetic echoes nothing was too farfetched to include. The taste for raw oysters among people of all races and civilizations pointed to that period of prehistory when "the race enjoyed a diet of raw, uncooked flesh before the invention of fire and the gradual rise of gentler instincts made the art of cooking possible." Love-bites, common "in Germany and England among the uneducated classes," recalled the cannibalistic origin of kissing, and the "scents, sniffs, smells, smacks and bites of the beast of prey at its victim." "The light shawl on the arm of the opera-goer" recapitulated "the Semito-Hamitic girdle or sash." The principal importance of the concept of atavism, however, lay not in these imaginative exercises but in its utility, shortly to be discussed, for the new field of criminal anthropology.[31]

Degeneration first became an important hereditary concept in the writings of a French psychiatrist, Benedict Morel, in 1857. Morel considered degeneracy a falling away from a more perfect form, a kind of retrograde evolution. Poor living conditions or vicious behavior—alcoholism, drug addiction, and the like—weakened the hereditary endowment of subsequent generations. This inferior inheritance expressed itself in typical patterns over time: "alcohol and neurosis in one generation might be followed by hysteria in the next, insanity in the third, then idiocy and sterility." Culminating as a rule in reproductive failure, this downward spiral had at least the virtue of terminating the tainted stock. The concept of degeneration found widespread acceptance in European psychiatry and anthropology. Besides Morel its proponents included influential figures like Henry Maudsley and Thomas Clouston in England, Cesare Lombroso and Richard von Krafft-Ebing on the Continent. The second generation of American somatic neurologists were receptive to degeneracy theory in the 1880s, and it gained wider importance in the diagnosis of criminality and insanity. The concept attracted attention most spectacularly when it was applied to Charles Guiteau, the man who assassinated President McKinley. Neurologists classified Guiteau as "a degenerate of the regicidal class," whose criminal behavior was caused by a breakdown of the higher nervous centers.[32]

Unlike atavism, degeneration required the Lamarckian impress of environment (as in poverty) or somatic change (as in alcoholism) on the reproductive cells of ancestors. So long as scientists accepted the inheritance of acquired characteristics, degeneracy theory therefore tended to encourage the belief that progressive deterioration was not irreversible, since it was responsive to external factors. Changes in the environment and preventive health measures could do much to reverse the downward trend. E. S. Talbot, devoting a chapter of his book *Degeneracy: Its Causes, Signs, and Results* (1899) to "the prophylaxis of degeneracy," called for governmental regulation of opium, alcohol, and sanitation and individual training in health care to prevent neurasthenia, seedbed of neurosis.[33]

In addition to atavism and degeneration, evolutionary imperfection might, finally and lastly, be ascribed to arrested development. The process by which organisms matured sometimes miscarried, freezing particular organs or entire organisms in eternal immaturity. Recapitulation afforded an explanation of fetal abnormalities as failures to complete development: "If different parts of the fetus can develop at different rates, then monstrosities will arise when certain parts lag behind and retain, at birth, the character of some lower animal." Even the distinguished founder of embryology, Karl Ernst von Baer, generally hostile to recapitulation, admitted its utility for teratology, the study of abnormal development. From teratology the concept of arrested development found its way into less specialized disciplines like anthropology and psychology. Paul Topinard's standard text *Anthropology* briefly noted the evolutionary significance of congenital defects: "Harelip, polydactilia [supernumerary digits], microcephaly, are, as it were, hesitations of the principles of evolution, attempts on its part to stop at points where it had rested in anterior forms, or to progress in other previously-followed directions."[34]

One example beloved of biologists and psychiatrists was the congenital idiot, whose brain exhibited convolutions fewer in number, less complex, broader and smoother than those found in the normal human brain. The idiot at birth had not acquired and could never hope to acquire the trappings of humanity:

> When we reflect that every human brain does, in the course of its development, pass through the same stages as the brains of other vertebrate animals, and that its transitional states resemble the permanent forms of their brains; and when we reflect further, that the stages of its development in the womb may be considered the abstract and brief chronicle of a series of developments that have gone on through countless ages in Nature, it does not seem so wonderful, as at the first blush it might do, that it should, when in a condition of arrested development, sometimes display animal instincts. Summing up, as it were, in itself the leading forms of the vertebrate type, there is truly a brute brain within the man's; and when the latter stops short of its characteristic development as *human*—when it remains arrested at or below the level of an orang's brain—it may be presumed that it will manifest its most primitive functions, and no higher functions.

Henry Maudsley, author of the above comments, pointed out that some idiots exhibited animal traits and instincts. He knew of one such, apelike in appearance and manner, who grinned, chattered, and screamed and who exhibited short hair on his face, a leaping walk, filthy habits, and a way of sitting apelike on the floor "with his genitals always exposed." Carl Vogt discerned in the idiot a kind of link between primate and human: the idiot was "a mixture of human and simious character, the latter being produced by an arrested development of the foetus *in utero,* forming thus an intermediate stage between ape and man."[35]

Most common during embryonic growth, arrest of development could also take place considerably later, especially, in the human race, at puberty, as happened with Negroes and women. Heredity might or might not be to blame; no one could be sure. Indeed, the lack of a universally accepted theory of inheritance made it very difficult to distinguish among the various types of evolutionary miscarriage. Could anyone say with assurance whether the grinning idiot was an atavistic reversion to the ape, or whether he had simply failed, as Maudsley indicated, to develop fully? Max Nordau, who wielded degeneracy as a critical category against contemporary literature and art of which he disapproved (Wagner, Nietzsche, Ibsen, Verlaine, Mallarmé, and more), muddled the categories of evolutionary misfortune completely. He identified degeneracy both with atavism (the degenerate who suffered from an excess in the number of fingers was reverting to "the multiple-rayed fins of fishes") and with developmental arrest (if, for example, the nervous centers controlling the unconscious were arrested in their development, "the degenerate lose the instincts which, in normal beings, find expression in nausea and disgust at certain noxious influences").[36]

Frederick Howard Wines, American minister and penologist, made a valiant effort to distinguish among the terms: atavism was "a line turned back upon itself," degeneration, "a line bent downward at an angle," and arrested development, "a line abruptly terminated." But these lines could not be traced in the flesh. In practice, sharp distinctions could not be insisted upon, and no one seemed overly concerned about precision.[37]

Biology Defines the Criminal

Nowhere did recapitulation loom larger than in the young science of criminal anthropology and in the work of its founder, Cesare Lombroso. Trained as a surgeon, an expert in the anatomy and physiology of the brain, Lombroso owed intellectual debts to the degeneracy theory of Morel, the moral insanity theory of James C. Prichard and Henry Maudsley, and the racism of Arthur de Gobineau. But above all he was indebted to Darwin, who "first furnished the atavistic key," and to Paul Broca. Lombroso viewed anthropometry, especially cranial anthropometry, as "an ark of salvation from the metaphysical, *a priori* systems dear to all those engaged on the study of Man." If criminals were set apart from normal human beings by perceptible biological differences, criminology could become a science, "the Natural History of the Criminal." This promising possibility burst upon Lombroso while he was examining the skull of a notorious criminal:

> At the sight of that skull, I seemed to see all of a sudden, lighted up as a vast plain under a flaming sky, the problem of the nature of the criminal—an atavistic being who reproduces in his person the ferocious instincts of primitive humanity and the inferior animals. Thus were explained anatomically the enormous jaws, high cheek-bones, prominent superciliary arches, solitary lines in the palms, extreme size of the orbits, handle-shaped or sessile ears found in criminals, savages, and apes, insensibility to pain, extremely acute sight, tattooing, excessive idleness, love of orgies, and the irresistible craving for evil for its own sake, the desire not only to extinguish life in the victim, but to mutilate the corpse, tear its flesh, and drink its blood.[38]

Following up this clue, Lombroso examined a great many criminals and mental defectives as well as normal human beings. He became convinced that the criminal was a pathological type, a kind of special species, or subspecies, of man with distinct physical and mental characteristics. The born criminal was an atavism, a savage in the midst of civilization: "His emotions and desires, his responsibilities and religion are those of an autochthon, born dead centuries and decades of centuries ago." Evidence of the criminal's atavistic nature was his resemblance to the savage. Physically, he exhibited a far greater proportion of anatomical abnormalities than could be found among the ordinary European population, an excess characteristic of lower races. Psychically, criminals "constantly reproduce the features of savage character—want of forethought, inaptitude for sustained labor, love of orgy, etc." Lombroso was particularly struck by the propensity of criminals, like savages, to adorn themselves with tattoos, frequently of an indecent or lawless nature. (Some of Lombroso's evidence as to the lewdness of criminal tattoos was admittedly inconclusive. Stephen Jay Gould cites one example: "Long live France and french fried potatoes.") Primitive peoples, whether living in the nineteenth century or at the dawn of history, were themselves lawless and unprincipled by contemporary standards, since law-abiding behavior and the moral sense were recent acquisitions of the race. George E. Dawson, a student of G. Stanley Hall, argued, for example, that the predatory instinct of the thief was a normal instinct among savages and semi-civilized peoples. It was left to the French sociologist Gabriel Tarde to give this comparison classic form in his study *La Criminalité Comparée* (1886), when he observed of members of the criminal class: "Some of them at least would have been the ornament and the moral aristocracy of a tribe of Red Indians."[39]

Consonant with recapitulatory parallelism, criminal anthropologists recited the resemblances between criminal and child. The adult criminal in effect never outgrew his childhood. Did this mean that children had a natural capacity for evil? It emphatically did. One of the most striking instances of the rejection of early-nineteenth-century romanticism is the hardheaded revaluation of childhood that took place among scientists of Lombrosian persuasion in the later part of the century. No longer "trailing clouds of glory," the child was born into the world egoistic, cruel, and unscrupulous, a criminal in the cradle. "The child," wrote Havelock Ellis, "is naturally, by his organization, nearer to the animal, to the savage, to the criminal, than the adult." Herbert Spencer pronounced children naturally given to cruelty, thieving, and lying, and remarked that "the popular idea that children are 'innocent' " would not survive "half an hour's observation in the nursery." Henry Maudsley agreed: "The thoughts, feelings, and habits of boys or girls when they are together and not under suspicion of supervision are hardly such as a prudent person would care to discover in order to exhibit proof of the innate innocence, though he might watch them curiously as evidence of the innate animality, of human nature." Fortunately children were weak and timid, for "What terrific criminals would children be if they had strong passions, muscular strength, and sufficient intelligence!" This echo of seventeenth-century Calvinist orthodoxy (an atavistic reversion, perhaps, to an earlier conceptual frame) did not, however, invoke disciplinary measures. Children were ontogenetically upward bound; in due course they would naturally acquire the blessings of a civilized conscience. Criminals and savages never would. As Lombroso wrote of born criminals, "Theoretical ethics passes over these diseased brains, as oil does over marble, without penetrating it."[40]

The Lombrosian school quite consistently extended the re-

capitulatory parallel of criminality to women. Against the back-
drop of the Victorian canonization of true womanhood, it is curious
to listen to their voices, shrill though few, dissecting the female soul
to discover it festering with revenge, jealousy, and cruelty. Women
harbored "evil tendencies more numerous and more varied than
men's," though usually latent. Inside the normal woman lurked
"the innocuous semi-criminal," rendered harmless for the most
part by "piety, maternity, want of passion, sexual coldness, by
weakness and an undeveloped intelligence." Loose these checks just
once and slumbrous criminality, aroused, transformed woman into
"a born criminal more terrible than any man." The female criminal
combined the worst of both sexes. Psychologically more male than
female, "excessively erotic, weak in maternal feeling, inclined to
dissipation, astute and audacious," she often added to these un-
lovely traits "the worst qualities of woman: namely, an excessive
desire for revenge, cunning, cruelty, love of dress, and untruth-
fulness, forming a combination of evil tendencies which often
results in a type of extraordinary wickedness." When she was good
she was good out of weakness, but when she was bad she was
horrid. One bright note was sounded in this melancholy concert:
Dr. Antonio Marro in *I Carratteri dei Delinquente* (1887) affirmed
that women most strongly marked by degenerative stigmata and
hence prone to criminality were likely to be "masculine, unsexed,
ugly, and abnormal." They would find no mates, thus bear no
children, and their wickedness would die with them.[41]

In the time-worn grooves of jurisprudence and penology the
Lombrosian school of criminal anthropology set up new and exciting vibrations. All previous systems, so it was said, had studied an
abstraction, crime; modern criminal anthropology would study
instead the criminal, and would do so in the light of post-Darwinian
science. No longer need crime, pauperism, and insanity be viewed
uncomprehendingly as acts of God or chance or fate. Scientific
sociology would bring them within the domain of law: "These
things cease to be accidents in nature or the result of satanic inter-
ference. They happen, as virtue, health, intelligence and prosperity happen, because some antecedent conditions have produced
them."[42]

In America the new doctrine was greeted with enthusiasm as a normal and natural adaptation of Darwinian anthropology. G. Stanley Hall praised Lombroso's "great and epoch-making significance." Social reformers approved the humanitarian message of the new criminology, which refuted the notion that the criminal was a normal individual who chose to commit crime out of perversity: "It is as illogical to execute Guiteau," wrote a journalist, "as it is to kill a cave fish for not seeing." The criminal could not help himself; defective through birth or illness he was victim as much as victimizer. Punishment henceforth would be tailored to fit the criminal, not the crime. [43]

But American criminologists, though in general welcoming Lombroso's approach, were not blind to his speculative excesses, to his notion, for example, that crime could be traced back to the consumption preferences of carnivorous plants. In the category of excess they appear also to have placed Lombroso's theory of female criminality, which was conspicuously ignored. Whatever might be the case on the Continent, in England and America very few men of science were willing to view women as "innocuous semi-criminals," still less as "born criminal[s] more terrible than any man." The Anglo-American scientific community preferred to continue paying conventional tribute to true womanhood.

Women Without Beards

Scientists in England and America did agree with their European colleagues, however, that woman was a developmental anomaly. Though she might not be evil she was most certainly flawed. Like the Negro, woman stopped growing too soon. Her sex pronounced her destiny unmistakably at puberty. Rightly viewed, woman was, as Harry Campbell announced in a chapter heading, "Undeveloped Man." Von Baer had shown that development proceeded from the simple to the complex, or from the general to the special. Von Baer's law of increasing individuation stated that "the developmental history of the individual is the history of the growing individuality in every respect." Lower forms, then, remained closer to their embryonic type. So it was with women, of whom Johann Friedrich Meckel, professor of anatomy at Halle, had observed as early as 1821 that they were less differentiated from the common, primitive, embryonic type. Endowed with a lesser measure of individuality, women resembled one another more than men did. Woman's nature was "more generic and less specific," as G. Stanley Hall noted. "Each woman is a more adequate representative of her sex than a man is of his." (In modern idiom: "If you've seen one, you've seen them all.") The psychological correlate of uniformity was conformism: "Women go in flocks, and in social matters are less prone to stand out with salient individuality."[44]

Woman's developmental arrest was especially marked with respect to secondary sex characteristics, such as body size and musculature, the pitch of the voice, and beard growth. W. K. Brooks, prominent Johns Hopkins zoologist and teacher of several eminent geneticists, quoted from the *Cyclopaedia of Anatomy and Physiology* a passage asserting that "in assuming at the age of puberty the distinctive secondary peculiarities of his sex, the male, so far as regards these secondary peculiarities, evidently passes into a higher degree of development thàn the female . . . physiologically at least, we ought to consider the male type of organization to be the more perfect, as respects the individual, and the female as respects the species." The female, failing to develop to the full the characteristics of the race, was "an arrested male." For the human race, then, "possession of a beard must be regarded as a general characteristic of our race . . . when a female, from disease or mutilation or old age, assumes a resemblance to the male, the change is an advance."[45]

Many scientists noted the curious fact that women and the lower races exhibited marked precocity when young. Girls attained physical and intellectual maturity earlier than boys, frequently outstripping their male classmates at school. Hall described the adolescent girl as "riper in mind and body than her male classmate, and often excelling him in the capacity of acquisition, nearer the age of her full maturity than he to his." This developmental superiority foreshadowed not brilliance but arrest. Precocity, in late-nineteenth-century parlance, was a physiological dead end: rushed too quickly into maturity, the precocious individual, like the harsh young wine from grapes picked too soon, never mellowed into greatness. James McGrigor Allan perceived in this difference of the sexes the working of a great natural law:

> In the animal and vegetable kingdoms we find this invariable law—
> rapidity of growth inversely proportionate to the degree of perfec-

tion at maturity. The higher the animal or plant in the scale of being, the more slowly does it reach its utmost capacity of development. Girls are physically and mentally more precocious than boys. The human female arrives sooner than the male at maturity, and furnishes one of the strongest arguments against the alleged equality of the sexes. The quicker appreciation of girls is the instinct, or intuitive faculty in operation; while the slower boy is an example of the latent reasoning power not yet developed. Compare them in after-life, when the boy has become a young man full of intelligence, and the girl has been educated into a young lady reading novels, working crochet, and going into hysterics at sight of a mouse or a spider.[46]

One wonders if Mr. McGrigor Allan was married, and if his sardonic reflections resulted from bitter experience with a vapid Victorian wife. One wonders too at his choice of words. That girls were "*educated* into . . . reading novels, working crochet, and going into hysterics at sight of a mouse or a spider" (my italics) was precisely the burden of contemporary feminist complaint.

Be that as it may, McGrigor Allan articulated one strand of the recapitulatory fabric that clothed a great deal of scientific discourse in the late nineteenth century. The very phylogeny that raised the white races up to global supremacy at the same time predestined the humbler fates of all who were yellow, brown, or black. The ontogeny that dowered the Caucasian male child with gifts of wisdom and dominion uttered, like the spiteful fairy in Sleeping Beauty, a curse over the cradle of his sister. But such a message was scarcely compatible with the traditional nineteenth-century veneration of womanhood. The most extreme writers—among them the Lombrosian school, the French anthropologist Gustave Le Bon, and James McGrigor Allan—made no attempt to reconcile the two ideologies. On the contrary, they seem to have gloried in flouting the conventional pieties. Listen to Henry Maudsley on that holy of holies, maternal love: "Looking at the matter objectively in the dry light of reason, could anything be more ridiculous than all this affectionate fuss about what is essentially an excretory product and comes into the world by excretory ways? Moreover, there is nothing nice in the process of parturition nor in the base services which the child exacts of [the mother], much on the contrary to provoke disgust, were it not for the strength and sanctity of the maternal instinct."[47]

Most students of sex difference were more discreet; they were careful to balance women's disabilities with their strengths. The favored concept to describe the natural relationship of the sexes was not superiority and inferiority, but complementarity. On this topic writers showed more delicacy, or more prudence, than they felt it necessary to bring to the description of racial differences. However insignificant as individuals, women were acknowledged to be splendid en masse. Like St. Paul, they might glory in their infirmities, secure in their collective identity as "magnificent organ[s] of heredity." Unlike the lesser peoples of Asia and Africa, who were dispensable, women bore, quite literally, the future of the race.[48]

CHAPTER 3

Hairy Men and
Beautiful Women

In regard to the general hairiness of the body, the women in
all races are less hairy than the men . . .

Man is more powerful in body and mind than woman, and
in the savage state he keeps her in a far more abject state of
bondage, than does the male of any other animal; therefore it
is not surprising that he should have gained the power of
selection . . . As women have long been selected for beauty,
it is not surprising that some of their successive variations
should have been transmitted exclusively to the same sex;
consequently that they should have transmitted beauty in a
somewhat higher degree to their female than to their male
offspring, and thus have become more beautiful, according
to general opinion, than men.

—Charles Darwin (1871)

Recapitulation told a story with a clear message: women lagged
behind men. But how had it happened, and why? What
purpose was served by differences between the sexes? Why were
men more pugnacious and women more nurturant? Why did men
get beards and women get beauty? Recapitulation described, but it
could not explain, these curious facts. Somehow they must be
bound up with the reproduction of the species, but the mechanisms
of reproduction and inheritance were largely unknown.

The individual who saw these issues with greatest clarity was,
not surprisingly, Charles Darwin. Even before publication of the
Origin, Darwin had been fascinated by certain physical features—
present in one sex and not the other—that did not lend themselves
gracefully to explanation in terms of natural selection. He had
therefore introduced into the *Origin* a supplemental principle he
called sexual selection, which depended "not on a struggle for
existence in relation to other organic beings or to external condi-

tions, but on a struggle between the individuals of one sex, generally the males, for the possession of the other sex." So intriguing did Darwin find this concept that when twelve years later he published his reflections on "how far the general conclusions arrived at in my former work were applicable to man," sexual selection threatened to run away with the book: Darwin covered *The Descent of Man* in 202 pages (in the 1874 edition, including an Appendix by Thomas Henry Huxley comparing the brain in men and apes), while needing 410 pages to do justice to *Selection in Relation to Sex*.[1]

The Mating Game

Sexual selection referred to "the advantage which certain individuals have over others of the same sex and species solely in respect of reproduction." The characters that conferred this advantage were those that did not seem to be of aid in the universal struggle for existence, "such as the weapons of offense and the means of defense of the males for fighting with and driving away their rivals—their courage and pugnacity—their various ornaments—their contrivances for producing vocal or instrumental music—and their glands for emitting odors, most of these latter structures serving only to allure or excite the female." These attributes could not have been gained by natural selection because they did not enhance the animal's chances for survival. Had they possessed survival value they would have been developed in both sexes, yet "the females who are unarmed and unornamented, are able to survive and procreate their kind."[2]

Far from conferring an advantage in the struggle for existence, some traits appeared downright detrimental: "The development . . . of certain structures—of the horns, for instance, in certain stags—has been carried to a wonderful extreme; and in some cases to an extreme which, as far as the general conditions of life are concerned, must be slightly injurious to the male." Many male birds found their movements actually impeded by the beautiful plumage with which they charmed their mates. Stags, their heads laden with branching horns to defeat their sexual rivals, "in escaping from beasts of prey are loaded with an additional weight for the race, and are greatly retarded in passing through a woody country." But these same horns and feathers would be of service in wooing and winning a mate.[3]

Darwin envisaged a dual mechanism of sexual selection: male battle and female choice. The latter process he thought particularly characteristic of birds, and some of the most delightful pages of the *Descent* describe the courtship displays and dances of lyre-birds and bower-birds and Argus pheasants. Darwin was uncomfortably aware that despite a lengthy correspondence he had failed to win Wallace to his way of thinking about sexual selection. Wallace preferred to explain the lack of female ornament by the need for females, as guardians of nests and young, to remain inconspicuous. Other contemporary naturalists found the concept of aesthetic preference in the avian kingdom ludicrously anthropomorphic. The idea that the female bower-bird, for example, gave her heart to the male who decorated the most attractive enclosure appeared to some scientists to be an illicit transference of Victorian romanticism from the boudoir to the bush. Darwin stood firm against his critics, however.

Darwin did admit that "the law of battle" appeared to overshadow "the display of . . . charms" in mating among the mammals. Still he insisted on the existence of female choice here too: "In the fourteenth chapter of Birds, a considerable body of direct and indirect evidence was advanced, showing that the female selects her partner; and it would be a strange anomaly if female quadrupeds, which stand higher in the scale and have higher mental powers, did not generally, or at least often, exert some choice." Given this reasoning and his obduracy about female choice in the face of the skepticism of his peers, it is interesting that Darwin awarded the power of sexual choice among human beings to the males. Men had "gained the power of selection" because they were "more powerful in body and mind" than women. It was true, Darwin allowed, that even in savage societies women had some limited freedom of choice: "They can tempt the men whom they prefer, and can sometimes reject those whom they dislike, either before or after marriage." But clearly the primary selector was the man.[4]

Why this situation did not represent a "strange anomaly" as it would have among the quadrupeds, Darwin did not explain. One may suspect that the answer lies in Darwin's assertion of greater male strength not just in body but also in mind. It was true, and not insignificant, that the male physique excelled the female: "Man on average is considerably taller, heavier, and stronger than woman, with squarer shoulders and more plainly-pronounced muscles." But the greater massiveness of the human male was a characteristic he shared with the males of many mammals. What set the human race apart from the other mammalia was the sexual disparity in intellect. Firmly denying Mill's twin assertions on the subject— first, that the inherent qualities of womanhood could never be known in the artificial conditions under which women lived and, second, that women's failure to produce female Aristotles and Homers was no more than a negative fact which left the question uncertain—Darwin confidently affirmed the inferiority of the female mind. This was not a conclusion he could have arrived at as he arrived at differences in temperament between the sexes, on the basis of analogy with the lower animals. There was no evidence that female dogs were any less intelligent than male dogs, or female lions than male lions. Hence Darwin's resort, as we saw earlier, to the social argument from the lack of female achievement.[5]

What biological mechanisms triggered this intellectual disparity? Ignorance of the laws of heredity made real understanding out of the question, but Darwin made some extremely shrewd guesses. In general, he believed, equal transmission of characters to offspring of both sexes was the commonest form of inheritance. To this rule there was an important exception: "variations which first appear in either sex at a late period of life tend to be developed in the same sex alone." Darwin reasoned that masculine intelligence was crucial to success in adult life: "to avoid enemies, or to attack them with success, to capture wild animals, and to fashion weapons, requires the aid of the higher mental faculties, namely, observation, reason, invention, or imagination. These various faculties will thus have been continually put to the test and selected during manhood; they will, moreover, have been strengthened by use during this period of life." They would therefore tend in accordance with Darwin's rule to descend in the male line alone.[6]

Did a sex-linked transmission of intelligence actually occur? On this critical issue it can only be said that Darwin waffled. Never doubting that men were brighter than women, he clearly had difficulty explaining how this could be so. On the one hand, he rejoiced that the law of equal transmission prevailed with mammals; "otherwise it is probable that men would have become as superior in mental endowment to women, as the peacock is in ornamental plumage to the pea-hen." This statement implies that daughters as well as sons possessed a birthright share in the intellectual capacities of their fathers. On the other hand, since men honed their intellectual faculties whether in combat with rival males or in the general struggle for life when they were grown, one might expect that sharpened wits descended to sons alone. Darwin thought this hypothesis supported by the fact that young boys and girls received the same early education yet grew up to manifest unequal intelligence. Something happened to these children as they arrived at maturity to quicken the minds of young men and not of young women.[7]

Sex-entailed inheritance of at least some aspects of intellect was therefore very much involved in Darwin's recommendation for eliminating the sexual disparity in mental powers: "In order that woman should reach the same standard as men, she ought, when nearly adult, to be trained to energy and perseverance, and to have her reason and imagination exercised to the highest point, and then she would probably transmit these qualities chiefly to her adult daughters." Alas, the results of this training were far from assured: first, because these energetic women would have to produce more offspring than did untrained women in order for the superior new type to spread throughout the population; and second, because in any event men would still have their powers sharpened at the grindstone of struggle for subsistence, "and this will tend to keep up or even increase their mental powers, and, as a consequence the present inequality between the sexes."[8]

The tacit premise of this conclusion is worth noting: men labored for subsistence, women did not. Darwin was perfectly cognizant of the fact that, as he himself wrote, "the women in all barbarous nations are compelled to work at least as hard as the men." He used this fact to argue the implausibility of man's greater size having been caused through more strenuous labor. But he assumed that such was not the case with "civilized people," among whom "the men, as a general rule, have to work harder than the women for their joint subsistence." So devoutly did Victorian intellectuals cherish the exemption of women from labor that Spencer and other theorists made it the touchstone of high civilization. Yet that very exemption relegated women to intellectual inferiority. Only if women engaged in the struggle to survive along with men could they narrow the mental gap. This was a supposition more radical than a good Victorian gentlemen like Darwin could contemplate, let alone recommend.[9]

Do Female Lions Hunt?

Darwin's discussion of sexual differences in intellect, admittedly speculative, necessarily lacks the authoritative ring of his best work. Yet its inconclusiveness stems from more than a laudable unwillingness to dogmatize; it is rooted in two problematic aspects of his argument. First is the complex shifting back and forth between natural and sexual selection. In his explanation of the intellectual disparity between the sexes Darwin invoked both kinds of selection, though purporting to discuss sexual selection alone. The activities cited by Darwin as testing and strengthening adult male intelligence—"to avoid enemies or to attack them with success, to capture wild animals, and to fashion weapons"—are activities that fall under the domain of natural, not sexual, selection. Their successful prosecution leads to survival, not to enhanced reproductive efficiency relative to one's peers. Darwin had to call on natural selection when he admitted that men no longer engaged in combat for mates: "the arbitrament of battle for the possession of the women has long ceased," and thus "this form of selection [i.e., sexual] has passed away." No longer a factor in human evolution, sexual selection could not explain what Darwin was certain he saw—great mental inequality between the sexes.[10]

The introduction of natural selection into the analysis was not without difficulty, however. Natural selection, it must be remembered, was a universal principle; it did not admit exceptions. Female animals were as much under its sway as were males. If developed intellect were an advantage in the struggle for survival, then female gorillas stood as much in need of it as their mates. The only exception to this rule of identical need would be cases of "different structure between the two sexes in relation to different habits of life," cases, that is to say, where the two sexes inhabited different environments. Darwin seems to be saying just this with reference to human beings in a state of advanced civilization like his own where the men worked and the women did not. Men lived at the cutting edge of the struggle for existence. Women, removed from that struggle, led lives so sheltered as to amount to life in a different environment altogether. The needs of the two sexes, and therefore their capacities, were not the same.[11]

Putting to one side the question of whether or not this assumption was correct, it is worth observing that on Darwin's own terms it marked a rather startling reversal in the trend of evolution. For Darwin had pointed out at the commencement of his discussion of sexual selection that sexual differences connected with different habits of life were generally confined to the lower animals. He elaborated on this assertion at a later point:

> As variations occurring late in life and transmitted to one sex alone, have incessantly been taken advantage of and accumulated through sexual selection in relation to the reproduction of the species; therefore it appears, at first sight, an unaccountable fact that similar variations have not frequently been accumulated through natural selection, in relation to the ordinary habits of life. If this had occurred, the two sexes would often have been differently modified, for the sake, for instance, of capturing prey or of escaping from danger. Differences of this kind between the two sexes do occasionally occur, especially in the lower classes. But this implies that the two sexes follow different habits in their struggle for existence, which is a rare circumstance with the higher animals.[12]

Indeed it was a rare circumstance, and one that some feminist writers were to exploit with great effect. One of the most effective of these dissenters was the American feminist and socialist Charlotte Perkins Gilman, who used Darwin's findings to arrive at a most un-Darwinian conclusion. Gilman pounced on the discrepancy between the animal realm, where females were forced equally with their males to win subsistence from nature, and the human realm, where, alone, women were kept by their mates: "Whereas, in other species of animals, male and female alike graze and browse, hunt and kill, climb, swim, dig, run, and fly for their livings, in our species the female does not seek her own living in the specific activities of our race, but is fed by the male." With all other mammals natural selection, far from augmenting the effect of sexual selection, acted as a check on it, preventing excessive sex distinction.

> If the peacock's tail were to increase in size and splendor till it shone like the sun and covered an acre,—if it tended so to increase, we will say,—such excessive sex-distinction would be so inimical to the personal prosperity of that peacock that he would die, and his tail-tendency would perish with him. If the pea-hen, conversely, whose sex-distinction attracts in the opposite direction, not by being large and splendid, but small and dull,—if she should grow so small and dull as to fail to keep herself and her young fed and defended, then she would die; and there would be another check to excessive sex-distinction.

In human beings, alone among the higher animals, natural selection no longer acted as a brake on the action of sexual selection, but reinforced it. Hence, Gilman was convinced, there arose an intense and excessive sex distinction, the feminine delicacy and weakness of the refined nineteenth-century woman.[13]

Looked at somewhat differently, the "sexuo-economic relation," as Gilman called it, grew out of Darwin's perception that a funny thing had happened on the way up the ladder: among humans, the female no longer chose but was chosen. Woman's dependence on man for subsistence nullified any genuinely free choice. In the marriage market, the prospective husband shopped for a likely bride: "He is the market, the demand, She is the supply." This transaction, Gilman observed, was remarkable for its ingenious cruelty. It was the woman who needed marriage—"The girl must marry: else how live?"—yet she was forbidden to seek it. Tragic as this situation was, however, it represented only an especially invidious aspect of the root problem, the economic dependence of women on men. So long as women were kept by men, so long as "all that she may wish to have, all that she may wish to do, must come through a single channel and a single choice," so long would human progress languish, mired in a vicious and unwholesome social system.[14]

The solution to this unhappy situation was implicit in Gilman's analysis: set women to work in the world beyond the home. Economic independence was the philosopher's stone that would dissolve the sexuo-economic relation and free women to make their rightful contribution to the future of the race. In the final sentences of *Women and Economics,* Gilman fairly glowed at the prospect: "Where our progress hitherto has been warped and hindered by the retarding influence of surviving rudimentary forces, it will flow on smoothly and rapidly when both men and women stand equal in economic relation. When the mother of the race is free, we shall have a better world, by the easy right of birth and by the calm, slow, friendly forces of social evolution."[15]

The discrepancy between what happened in the rest of the animal world and what happened among human beings, this discrepancy that Gilman had seized upon as unnatural, implied an awkward break in evolutionary continuity that Darwin was, perhaps, loath to admit. The import of his theorizing appeared obvious and inescapable: civilization had put an end to selective pressure on half the human race by exempting women from the struggle for survival, remanding them to the stagnation of home and hearth. Their intellects softened by disuse, women could be trained to acquire "robust virtues" to some extent, but intellectual parity would continue to elude them without occupational parity, and this Darwin could not conceive.

Darwin's treatment of sex in intellect suffered from a second and graver defect rooted in the confusion between biology and culture pervading late-nineteenth-century thought. Explicitly in Herbert Spencer and Auguste Comte and a host of lesser social theorists, implicitly in most of the rest, the study of society was seen as a kind of extension of biology to be pursued according to the methods and concepts of the natural sciences. Pride of place was given to the organic analogy, which explained society, "the social organism," by means of its resemblance to the living biological organism. Within such an understanding of society the transmission of culture could only be construed as a physical process, a question of human heredity not widely different from that of the inheritance of blue eyes or short stature. Cultural traits descended from parent to child through Lamarckian use-inheritance, the acquisitions of adults during their lifetimes being passed on to their offspring.[16]

Darwin shared this general disposition to treat mind and culture in biological terms. Indeed, he had particularly strong reasons for doing so. For one thing he was deeply influenced by what he had learned about artificial selection from his voluminous correspondence with plant and animal breeders. This led him to construct a breeder's model of human evolution in which civilization was analogous to a process of domestication, whereby small individual differences in populations might be nudged and encouraged in certain directions to produce change. Such a model would make sense of Darwin's supposition that the Lamarckian transmission of strengthened mental powers from trained mothers to their daughters could effect permanent improvement. But the breeder's model also required controlled reproduction, in order that the modification not be swamped by the greater number of the unmodified. In this instance, superior women had to outbreed their inferior sisters, and Darwin thought this outcome dubious.[17]

Far more important to Darwin's position than the influence of a breeder's model of evolution was his theoretical commitment to a naturalistic explanation of mind. It was crucial to Darwin's entire evolutionary strategy that human beings be integrated into the animal economy, that the differences between humans and animals be seen as differences of degree and not of kind. In the case of intellectual and moral qualities, Darwin had to argue particularly strenuously against the partisans of human uniqueness, but he did so with the conviction that his entire argument hung in the balance. Once admit a break in the evolutionary web, and the supernaturalists would begin to creep through.

The passion behind Darwin's commitment to naturalism is evident in his bitter disappointment at Wallace's defection in the late 1860s. Under the influence of spiritualism, Wallace had by this time become convinced of the need to invoke a "Higher Intelligence" to account for some aspects of human evolution. In 1870, in an article entitled "The Limits of Natural Selection as Applied to Man," Wallace rejected specifically the possibility that the moral sense could be explained by natural selection. Wrote Darwin in response to this change of heart: "But I groan over Man—you write like a metamorphosed (in retrograde direction) naturalist, and you the author of the best paper that ever appeared in the *Anthropological Review*! Eheu! Eheu! Eheu!—Your miserable friend." So also Darwin disputed Mill's contention that mental and moral qualities were acquired rather than innate. Asserting that "on the general theory of evolution this is at least extremely improbable," Darwin registered his dissent in strong terms: "The ignoring of all transmitted mental qualities will, as it seems to me, be hereafter judged as a most serious blemish in the works of Mr. Mill."[18]

The biological understanding of mind and culture exacted its price. Among reform-minded natural and social scientists, the attack on Lamarckian inheritance initiated by August Weismann in the 1880s and 1890s set off an alarm bell. If parental gains were not passed on to children, of what use was education or environmental improvement? The support Lamarckianism afforded to cherished notions of social progress was one reason for the tenacity with which American social scientists continued to embrace it even after its intellectual foundations had been severely damaged. In a sense, nonetheless, the intuition of the Lamarckians was ultimately validated: the transmission and diffusion of culture does seem to follow a Lamarckian pattern, though we now know it to be a social rather than a biological phenomenon. We really are born into the cultural heritage of our ancestors. We do not have to recreate for ourselves the achievements of a Plato or a Shakespeare, or a Darwin. Their legacy is ours to appropriate.

In Darwin's case, a better understanding of the social nature of intellectual development might have led him to a more optimistic appraisal of the benefits of education for women. He might then have been less concerned about the need for a small group of highly trained Portias to outbreed the mediocre mass, and more concerned about the provision of effective education for all. Mothers of trained and disciplined intellect do indeed do a service to their offspring, not, however, by way of the enlarged capacities they transmit but by way of the enhanced environments they provide. Absorbed in a breeder's model, Darwin's vision was both highly individualistic and highly elitist: female minds would improve not by large-scale instruction of the many, but by selective breeding of the few.

Sexual Selection under Attack

Sexual selection, despite its impeccable credentials, does not appear to have won the minds of the majority of biologists by the turn of the century. Even natural selection had by then gone into eclipse as neo-Lamarckians, mutationists, and orthogenesists, among others, rejected it for what they saw as logical and empirical deficiencies. The failings of sexual selection were of several kinds. Some biologists insisted that sexual selection was merely a particular form of natural selection and not a separate agency at all. Others balked at the attribution of highly developed aesthetic taste to female birds and mammals. Still others, like Alfred Russel Wallace in his later work and W. K. Brooks, ascribed secondary sexual characteristics to constitutional maleness and femaleness. The best-known embodiment of this last view was an influential book entitled *The Evolution of Sex* by Patrick Geddes and J. Arthur Thomson.[19]

Patrick Geddes, a Scotsman who received his early training in zoology under Darwin's self-styled "bulldog," Thomas Henry Huxley, taught zoology and botany at the University of Edinburgh until 1919, after which time he concentrated on his second career as town planner and student of urban civilization. But throughout his professional life he was deeply concerned with the meaning of biological ideas for social thought. Both as a biologist and as a sociologist and city planner Geddes exerted considerable influence on some prominent American intellectuals, including Jane Addams and the young Lewis Mumford. *The Evolution of Sex* was the outcome of Geddes's decade-long inquiry into sex differences in nature and their implications for human society. In this enterprise Geddes was joined by his former student J. Arthur Thomson, who, as professor of natural history at the University of Aberdeen, showed the influence of his mentor by reaching out beyond the confines of the scientific community to instruct a large popular audience in the meaning of biology for ethical values and social

welfare. The two men's first joint venture in scientific popularization, *The Evolution of Sex* (1889) found an appreciative audience; it
was widely read and frequently cited.[20]

Geddes and Thomson could not believe that Darwin's concept of
sexual selection had penetrated the mystery of sex differences.
Secondary sexual characteristics, the authors asserted, "are not and
can not be (except teleologically) explained by sexual selection, but
in origin and continued development are outcrops of a male as
opposed to a female constitution." Darwin had explained brilliancy
of color, superfluity of hair, activity of the scent glands, and so on,
as features useful to masculine reproductive success. Not so. Secondary sex characteristics were not functional but expressive, indicators of "exuberant maleness." Signs rather than instruments,
they bore witness to the essence of maleness, which was activity.
The male organism was physiologically active, destructive, or
katabolic, the female organism passive, constructive, and anabolic.[21]

In introducing the terms *anabolic* and *katabolic,* Geddes and
Thomson were appealing to one of the great accomplishments of
nineteenth-century physiology, the establishment of the concept of
metabolism. Modern physiologists, they noted, envisioned organisms as undergoing continuous chemical change, on the one hand
being built up by an influx of nutritive material into entities increasingly complex and unstable, on the other hand breaking down into
more and more stable compounds, and finally into waste products.
The metabolic model conceived of organisms as heat machines
engaged in energy transformation, and thus amenable to analysis
by physical and chemical methods. Geddes and Thomson associated anabolism with large size, placidity (or "sluggishness"), and
conservatism; katabolism with small size (except with most birds
and mammals), activity, and variability. As the ovum typified the
passively quiescent, large, well-nourished anabolic cell, so did the
sperm typify the small, active, flagellate, katabolic cell. This difference expressed itself in characteristic masculine and feminine mental traits. The more active male, encountering a wider range of
experience, possessed a bigger brain and greater intelligence. The
quiescent female excelled in altruistic emotions—constancy of affection, sympathy, and patience. "Man thinks more, woman feels

more. He discovers, but remembers less; she is more receptive, and less forgetful."[22]

The difference between this view of sexuality, static and essentialist, and that of Darwin, dynamic and functionalist, is dramatic. Darwin thought always in terms of the functional contribution any given trait made to the survival and reproductive success of the organism. Sexuality, and specifically the secondary sexual characteristics, had to be seen not as hypostatized essences, but as attributes needed to negotiate the everyday hurly-burly of life. The gulf between Geddes and Thomson and Darwin on this score can perhaps best be appreciated in the juxtaposition of two quotations. The first is from Harry Campbell, *Differences in the Nervous Organisation of Man and Woman,* a book that appeared two years after *The Evolution of Sex.* Campbell explicitly rejected the theory of Geddes and Thomson. More, he was prepared to push the functionalist implications of sexual selection even further than Darwin himself. To suppose that sexual selection explained secondary sexual characteristics, he argued, was to suppose that the sexual constitution was not fixed: "woman is not what she is, and man is not what he is, simply because the one has ovaries and a uterus, and the other testicles; and it [sexual selection] at least strongly suggests that *all* the secondary sexual characteristics in men and women might be transposed—that the strength, courage, and fire of the man might be transferred to the woman; the weakness and timidity of the woman, to the man." Surely an extraordinary assertion for the times, this statement needs to be set beside the second quotation, taken from the close of Geddes and Thomson's discussion of the permanence of sexual types: "What was decided among the prehistoric *Protozoa* can not be annulled by Act of Parliament." Here there could be no question of change or transposition, for sex, a constitutional fact of metabolism, was insulated from the environment. Obliterating psychic differences between men and women would therefore require having "all of evolution over again on a new basis." Queen Victoria might rule an empire with feminine patience and common sense, but originality and verve would have to be supplied by another, masculine, mind. What Geddes and Thomson had done was, in effect, to construct an argument for the biological necessity of Benjamin Disraeli.[23]

Lurking behind the appeal to the prehistoric protozoa, it must be said, was a certain perceptible apprehension in the authors' tone. They were at pains to insist that in defining the province of one sex as thought and of the other as emotion they did not mean to suggest any hint of superiority or inferiority in the one or the other. In the great human symphony male and female played in harmonious counterpoint. Each higher in its own way, the two sexes were complementary and mutually dependent. It was unfortunate that modern women had begun to tinker with the sexual score. A new and discordant note of "intersexual competition for subsistence" threatened "complexly ruinous results" for men and women alike, and for their families. Obviously discomfited by the militant tone of contemporary feminism, Geddes and Thomson extolled a better way, "that complex and sympathetic cooperation between the sexes in and around which all progress past or future must depend."[24]

Males Vary, Females Conserve

In the general scientific onslaught on Darwin's concept of sexual selection one incidental aspect of the analysis not only survived but won almost universal acceptance, the notion of the greater variability of the male. Rising from the ashes of sexual selection, male variability and its concomitant, female conservatism, went on to become part of the accepted scientific wisdom about sex differentiation, a part so entrenched that it remained in the literature long after virtually every other vestige of nineteenth-century sex theory had been superseded. It can be argued that male variability presented the most sophisticated challenge to the case for equality of the sexes. It could not be dismissed by feminists as a product of masculine prejudice, for it appeared to be empirically well-founded. Nor could it be effectively attacked on its own terms: the statistical information needed to do so was not to be had at the turn of the century, not, indeed, until the 1920s and 1930s.

Though Darwin did not originate the notion of greater male variability, his name was regularly invoked as the authoritative source. Darwin did use the concept as an aid to understanding why, in cases where the sexes differed in appearance, the males were more modified than the females, that is to say, differed more from the young and from other males. We have seen that some writers, among them Herbert Spencer and W. K. Brooks, taught that woman was underdeveloped man. Darwin, by contrast, taught that man was evolved woman. Man's secondary sexual characteristics arose because of his greater sexual passion, as an instrument furthering reproductive success. Darwin added that "the development of such characters would be much aided if the males were more liable to vary than the females," and he could confidently assert, on the basis of his own research and scraps of evidence from others, that such was the case. But Darwin's discussion referred only to physical characteristics. Nor did Darwin attribute to male variability anything like the significance it was to acquire in the writing of Havelock Ellis and others. The elaborate edifice of female conservatism and male progressivism, female mediocrity and male genius, that was presently erected on the foundations of variability does not derive immediately from *The Descent of Man*.[25]

W. K. Brooks provided one of the clearest discussions of variability in *The Law of Heredity* (1883). Alluding to "one of the most remarkable and suggestive of the laws of variation," that parts exclusively male or of greater importance in males were "very much more variable" than parts confined to or more important in females, Brooks derived a general corollary, "that males are as a rule more variable than females." Indeed Brooks believed that unlike Darwin, who professed ignorance ("the cause of the greater general variability for the male sex, than for the female is unknown"), he could offer a hereditary explanation for male variability in the differing functions of the sex cell. The male cell had developed "a peculiar power to gather and store up germs." Hence, when new variations arose in the male and were transmitted to the reproductive organs (Brooks accepted pangenesis), they would aggregate in the male cell and be transmitted by impregnation. Critical to this theory was the assumption that the transmission was sex-linked, so that variations accumulated exclusively in the male line: "Gemmules which are formed in the male body are vastly more likely to be transmitted to descendants than those which are formed in the female body." Brooks could not, of course, provide evidence, but the message was at any rate clear: "According to this

view, the male element is the originating and the female the per-
petuating factor; the ovum is conservative, the male cell progressive."[26]

By the time Havelock Ellis took up variability and enshrined it
at the heart of his exceedingly influential *Man and Woman,* he
felt entitled to state, "Since Darwin wrote the evidence has accumulated and the greater variational tendency of males has never
been questioned." There was indeed much evidence, new since
Darwin's time, in Ellis's catalogue: statistics collected by the Anthropometric Committee of the British Association; Harry Campbell's figures on deaths from congenital defects; studies of super-
numerary digits, of ear anomalies like the Darwinian tubercle
(though the significance of one study showing "the proportion of
normal ears to be 28 per cent in men and 41 per cent in women" is
not self-evident), of insanity and idiocy and sexual perversion. As
to intellect, Ellis was content simply to state that genius, defined as
"an organic congenital abnormality," was "undeniably" more
common in men than in women. Ellis still accepted some connection between brain size and intellect ("It is probable that great
thinkers generally have large brains"), but he did not need the
evidence of man's greater brain weight to make his case. His real
argument rested on the twin bases of observation (among women
intellectual and artistic accomplishment was a "rarity") and analogy (if men varied more at the low end of the intellectual spectrum—and everyone agreed that there were more male than female
idiots—then they must also vary more at the top).[27]

"Women of Genius Are Men"

It is probably safe to assume that the question of which sex had the
greater number of normal ears would never have generated much
controversy. That the theory of male variability did become a
storm center by the turn of the century was owing to its bearing on
the vexed issue of sex in intellect, and to its part in interpreting the
different contributions of men and women to race progress. Masculine variability closed off to women the higher ranges of the
mind. Though women possessed "as great an aptitude in dealing
with the immediate practical interests," they could not, by and

large, aspire to the intellectual empyrean. This was because in mind as in body women clustered around the midpoint of a normal bell-shaped curve. If they were less likely to suffer from idiocy, so also were they strangers to the realm of excellence. Cesare Lombroso recorded their destiny: "In the history of genius women have but a small place. Women of genius are rare exceptions in the world . . . Even the few who emerge have, on near examination, something virile about them. As Goncourt said, "there are no women of genius, the women of genius are men." Harry Campbell put the case more temperately. In admitting that the world at large had undervalued the female mind, Campbell argued that there was "greater intellectual equality between the sexes than is generally supposed." But that equality ceased at the upper ranges of intelligence. Campbell, indeed, found it necessary to emphasize the point: *"when we pass into the region of genius . . . we see the intellectual disparity of the two sexes unmistakably revealed.* Genius of the highest order is practically limited to the male sex."[28]

Related to the issue of genius was the sexual dichotomy that gave to women custody of the heritage of the past, to men the winning of new frontiers. Brooks waxed especially eloquent on the significance of this division of labor:

> if the female organism is the conservative organism, to which is intrusted the keeping of all that has been gained during the past history of the race, it must follow that the female mind is a storehouse filled with the instincts, habits, intuitions, and laws of conduct which have been gained by past experience. The male organism, on the contrary, being the variable organism, the originating element in the process of evolution, the male mind must have the power of extending experience over new fields, and, by comparison and generalization, of discovering new laws of nature, which are in their turn to become rules of action, and to be added on to the series of past experiences.[29]

One would expect to find greater uniformity in female minds, since they hoarded the past experiences of the race as codified in laws of conduct. Male minds, fermenting with new ideas, differed more markedly from one another. Brooks appended an interesting corollary. Women, better able to predict the conduct of others, were skilled in influencing and persuading, as opposed to convincing, "for to convince is to innovate and place matters in a new light, but the secret of influence is a vivid appreciation of the motives and incentives to conduct." Brooks's conclusions earned the admiration of G. Stanley Hall, who, on the basis of their acquaintance at Johns Hopkins, tried unsuccessfully to woo Brooks for Clark University. Crediting Brooks as his source, Hall wrote of woman's mind as "more than that of man, essentially an organ of heredity." Woman might sometimes appear "volatile and desultory" but she could not help herself: "the fact that her processes seem to be unconscious emancipates her from nature less than is the case with men."[30]

Havelock Ellis thought that female conservatism could even be traced in the lineaments of the body. He turned to anthropology for confirmation of the proposition that primitive racial elements in a population were more distinctly preserved among the women. Such evidence was forthcoming from many countries, including Italy, where "at Cortona and Chiusi the women recall the ancient Etruscans, and at Albano the ancient Romans, more than do the men." Ellis himself rejoiced in this sexual distinction in one of his most lyrical passages:

> A large part of the joy that men and women take in each other is rooted in this sexual difference in variability. The progressive and divergent energies of men call out and satisfy the twin instincts of women to accept and to follow a leader, and to expend tenderness on a reckless and erring child, instincts often intermingled in delicious confusion. And in women men find beings who have not wandered so far as they have from the typical life of earth's creatures; women are for men the human embodiments of the restful responsiveness of Nature. For every man, as Michelet has put it, the woman whom he loves is as the Earth was to her legendary son; he has but to fall down and kiss her breast and he is strong again.[31]

The theory of greater male variability did not go entirely unchallenged. Karl Pearson, the biometrician (and also, apparently, Ellis's rival for the affections of the South African writer Olive Schreiner), made a passionate assault on the theory. Proposing "to lay the axe to the root of this pseudo-scientific superstition," Pearson denied the validity both of Ellis's choice of variations, which he branded "pathological," and of his statistical methods. His own figures showed no masculine predominance, but rather a slight tendency toward greater female variability. Ellis, in turn, issued a fierce rebuttal to the Pearson article, which he appended to subsequent editions of *Man and Woman*. Giving not one inch of ground, he amplified and strengthened his earlier conclusions and would appear to have prevailed, partly because Pearson's treatment, statistically sophisticated, was not well adapted to a popular audience.[32]

Feminists Praise the "Middle Virtues"

Even feminists accepted male variability. Charlotte Perkins Gilman, working within her particular variant of Darwinism, theorized that the subjection of women had been essential to evolutionary progress. For in the period of female ascendancy before woman's subordination society was stationary. "Since the female had not the tendency to vary which distinguished the male, it was essential that the expansive force of masculine energy be combined with the preservative and constructive forces of female energy." In Gilman's all-female utopia, Herland, there were no geniuses but many diligent workers. "Art in the extreme sense," Gilman supposed, "will perhaps always belong most to men."[33]

The feminist pacifist Anna Garlin Spencer expressed her understanding of the law of variability in a popular collection of essays, *Woman's Share in Social Culture,* published in 1912:

> Speaking generally, the feminine side of humanity is in the "middle of the road" of life. Biologically, psychologically and sociologically, women are in the central, normal, constructive part of the evolutionary process. On the one side and on the other, men exhibit more geniuses and more feeble-minded, more talented experts and more incompetents who cannot earn a living, more idealistic masters of thought and action and more "cranks" and ne'er-do-wells who shame their mothers.

Spencer saw this distinction as benevolent, since women were the child-rearers and could give children what they needed most for their healthy development, "the conserving weight of the middle virtues and the mean of powers." Only later should the highly specialized variations of men, leading to human progress on the one side, human degeneracy on the other, enter the educational process "as example or warning."[34]

Some will wonder on what grounds Spencer considered herself a feminist. It was, however, common for turn-of-the-century feminists to assert temperamental and intellectual differences between the sexes as the very reason for greater feminine participation in public life. In taking this tack, feminists like Antoinette Brown Blackwell, Eliza Burt Gamble, and the editors of the *Women's Journal* admitted that the battle for female equality would be won or lost on the fields of scientific inquiry. Accepting the recent findings of Darwin and others as to important differences between the sexes, they tried to turn such research to their own uses by stressing that different did not mean inferior. The sexes, they argued, had complementary and strictly equivalent strengths. These feminists sought what might be termed a theory of differential equality.[35]

Yet the insecure grounding of this argument is well illustrated in the work of Spencer, whose brief for women amounted in practice to a praise of mediocrity. However golden the mean might be as a guide to conduct, when it came to intelligence the mean was made of baser stuff. Karl Pearson exposed the romanticizing of Spencer's "middle of the road" in expressing the eugenicist's contempt for "the average man":

> Greater interest is attached to individuals who occupy positions towards either of the ends of a marshalled series than to those who stand about its middle. An average man is morally and intellectually an uninteresting being. The class to which he belongs is bulky and no doubt serves to help the course of social life in action. It also affords, by its inertia, a regulator that, like the fly-wheel to the steam-engine, resists sudden and irregular changes. But the average man is of no direct help towards evolution, which appears to our dim vision to be the goal of all living existence. Evolution is an unresting progression; the nature of the average individual is essentially unprogressive.

So long as scientists associated the average with the unprogressive, and the feminine with the average, women were not likely to be taken seriously as leaders, as thinkers, or indeed as participants in the majestic forward movement of the human race.[36]

Conscious of their responsibility to inform the public, those writers who, with Havelock Ellis, saw the immeasurable significance of the law of variability ("The whole of our human civilization would have been a different thing if in early zoological epochs the male had not acquired a greater variational tendency than the female") felt duty-bound to share the social implications of their labors with the uninitiated. To that end they wrote books designed for a lay audience and placed articles in the popular press (above all, in the United States, in that organ of scientifically respectable popularization, *Popular Science Monthly*). It is of course very difficult to know how far the homilies of scientists influenced social policy. Certainly the authors intended them to have an effect, and the women and men who opposed their views, and who favored expanding women's educational and occupational opportunities, clearly feared the influence of scientific pens. Time and again they felt it necessary to challenge the scientific and medical wisdom. When, for example, Edward Clarke exposed the deterioration of female health consequent upon women's attainment of higher education, his book "brought down a storm of protest" that included four or five books and a host of essays.[37]

The variability hypothesis was unfortunately a great deal more difficult to counter effectively than the simple physiological argument of Clarke. It could, perhaps, be shown that women's bodies did not decay from attending college. It could not so readily be shown that women's minds were equal to the challenge of original thought. In America, the variability hypothesis quite naturally entered into the youthful testing movement in psychology. One of the most eminent exponents of this movement, the Columbia psychologist Edward Thorndike, used variability as had Ellis and Campbell to explain male predominance at the highest levels of intelligence. With the results of a great many mental measurements at his fingertips, Thorndike was able to document with much more precision the great similarity of the sexes in average intelligence. Masculine superiority emerged clearly only at the top of the scale. A review of the second edition of Thorndike's authoritative *Educational Psychology* described his message succinctly: "Comparative tests of the sexes have failed to show large differences on the average, and the dominant position of the male in intellectual and executive pursuits should be laid, apparently, in part to social conditions, in part to the fighting instinct and zeal for mastery of the male, and, very likely in largest part, to a greater variability of the male, which would cause the observed preponderance of males among idiots and also among individuals of the highest ability."[38]

In a popular article Thorndike spelled out the social and educational implications of greater male variability. "Of the thousand most eminent intellects of history 97 per cent are men," Thorndike noted, a fact which impelled him to refer to a masculine "monopoly of genius," caused by variability. That women "depart less from the normal than men" was a datum of tremendous significance: "This one fundamental difference in variability is more important than all the differences between the average male and average female capacities." Women might become engineers and scientists but never Edisons, voters but not senators, and priests but not popes. Since, then, they were restricted "to the mediocre grades of ability and achievement," Thorndike thought it behooved the educational establishment to plan accordingly:

> The education of women for such professions as administration, statesmanship, philosophy or scientific research, where a few very gifted individuals are what society requires, is far less needed than education for such professions as nursing, teaching, medicine or architecture, where the average level is the essential. Elementary education is probably an even better investment for the community in the case of girls than in the case of boys; for almost all girls profit by it, whereas the extremely low grade boy may not be up to his school education in zeal or capacity and the extremely high grade boy may get on better without it. So also with high school education. On the other hand post-graduate instruction, to which women are flocking in great numbers, is, at least in its higher reaches, a far more remunerative social investment in the case of men.

From a latter-day perspective the relegation of medicine and architecture to minds of "the average level" may appear amusing, but the import of this article, for women, was anything but amusing. Thorndike was flatly recommending that the graduate school gates be shut against them. And there was, at the time that he wrote, painfully little that women could say by way of rebuttal.[39]

Conclusion: Darwinism, Function, and Essence

As a concept, variability can be traced back to Charles Darwin. It should by now be evident, however, that Darwin was not responsible for all the uses to which it was put by later writers. *Darwinism* has in the past been a popular term to apply to certain social and ethical theories; the phrase *social Darwinism* has become for modern sensibilities a label of opprobrium. But social Darwinism is a term altogether too vague and misleading to be useful. Rosalind Rosenberg wittily entitled her fine dissertation "The Dissent from Darwin," yet that title is in a sense misleading: the "dissent from Darwin" was much more a dissent from a host of other scientists and scientific popularizers, many of whose views were far more seriously at odds with the emancipation of women from traditional restraints.

How did Darwin himself feel about the sexual allocation of roles in Victorian society? We cannot be entirely certain, but there is no reason to suppose that his attitude was not that of a conventional Victorian gentleman. As a young man he hoped to find a "nice soft wife" who would be his "constant companion," but he did not envision that companionship as intellectual. In Emma Wedgwood he found everything he had wished for in a wife. She devoted herself to his well-being, no small task as he rapidly declined into invalidism. He, in turn, "worshipped" her (the word was his) and commended her to their daughter as "twice refined gold." Charles and Emma were, in short, an extraordinarily devoted couple who in no way contravened the normal gender-role conventions of their society. Darwin's personal life appeared to confirm his theoretical perspectives on the sexes.[40]

At the same time, though Darwin's discussion of sex differences was assuredly stereotypic, it was also open to change. One striking aspect of his analysis—one that set him apart from the majority of commentators on male and female nature—was the tentativeness of his conclusions and the cautiousness of his recommendations. Darwin was not a dogmatist. If change was the essence of evolution, he did not propose to elaborate theories that foreclosed change. With the flexibility afforded by his functional analysis Darwin was able to imagine enhancing the intellectual capacities of women through training and selective reproduction. He did not, it is true, appreciate the social nature of the cultural process, but he certainly believed in the improvement of humanity, and he held that it could be furthered by better education of its feminine half. "Educate all classes," Darwin had written in his notebook in 1838, "avoid the contamination of caste, improve the women (double influence) & mankind must improve." When, many years later, women were admitted to the "Little-Go" and Tripos Examinations at Cambridge, Darwin was enthusiastic. "You will have heard," he wrote his son George, "of the triumph of the Ladies at Cambridge . . . Horace [another Darwin son] was sent to the Ladies' College to communicate the success and was received with enthusiasm."[41]

Much more hostile to feminist aspirations were the many variants of the "essentialist" conception of sexual divergence, which cast sex in the leading role in the drama of human differences. "Sex modifies every drop of blood in the veins, and every thought and act in the life," according to one such account. So pervasive was it that a person could be made less masculine or less feminine only "through being maimed in limb or dwarfed in mind." Short of such drastic measures, sex, a fact of the organic constitution, was immutable. This view, best represented by the anabolism-katabolism distinction of Geddes and Thomson, rejected the possibility of real change in the sexual division of labor. Essentially ahistorical, it invoked evolution in the name of a static conception of human nature.[42]

Darwin's model of the interaction of organism and environment pointed in the direction of a functional analysis of mind as instrumental to adaptation. Geddes and Thomson's depiction of the individual as "but the bye-play of ovum-bearing organisms" focused attention away from the environment and toward contemplation of "internal constitution" or Platonic essence. Organic progress was a question "not . . . of mechanism but of character, to which incident is accessory but not fundamental,—not of details put together, but of aggregate organic life or temperament." When all was said and done, woman was an overgrown ovum, about whose nature nothing more need be known. Time might go by, nations rise and fall, she would remain true to the constancy, sympathy, and patience of the egg awaiting in joyful expectation the dynamic embrace of the sperm.[43]

Charles Darwin will never be elevated to a niche in the pantheon of feminism. He did not challenge the conventional wisdom of his era with regard to women; he was profoundly skeptical of Mill's attempt to do so. The legacy of his insistence on the sufficiency of biological explanation haunted feminist attempts to develop an environmentalist perspective on mental traits. Yet it is well to remember that in the context of Victorian science Darwin was among the most gentle and moderate of men. Far worse as enemies of feminine aspiration were the outright misogynists like Gustave Le Bon, the romantic paternalists like G. Stanley Hall, the sexual essentialists like Geddes and Thomson, and the dogmatists of every persuasion. *The Descent of Man* did not validate the oppression of women.   ?, ??

CHAPTER 4

The Machinery of the Body

Only that mental energy is normally feminine which can coexist with the production and nursing of the due number of healthy children. Obviously a power of mind which, if general among the women of a society, would entail disappearance of the society, is a power not to be included in an estimate of the feminine nature as a "social factor."

—Herbert Spencer (1873–1874)

The Indian squaw, sitting in front of her wigwam, keeps almost all of her force in reserve; the slow and easy drudgery of the savage domestic life in the open air—unblessed and uncursed by the exhausting sentiment of love; without reading or writing or calculating; without past or future, and only a dull present—never calls for the full quota of her available force; the larger part is always lying on its arms.

   The sensitive white woman—pre-eminently the American woman, with small inherited endowment of force; living indoors; torn and crossed by happy or unhappy love; subsisting on fiction, journals, receptions; waylaid at all hours by the cruellest of robbers, worry and ambition, that seize the last unit of her force—can never hold a powerful reserve, but must live and does live, in a physical sense, from hand to mouth, giving out quite as fast as she takes in . . .

—George Beard (1884)

M*en*," Miss M. A. Hardaker wrote emphatically in 1882, *"will always think more than women."* Aside from the novelty of the author's sex, the conclusion was utterly predictable. The reasoning, however, was arresting: men thought more because they ate more. The idea that great thinkers are hearty eaters may strike the modern reader as whimsical, particularly given the abstemious or dyspeptic natures of many intellectual giants—think, in Miss Hardaker's own day, of William James, Thomas Carlyle, Charles Darwin. But Hardaker was attempting, however naively, to apply to the woman question an important and recently established principle of science, "the conclusion," as she wrote, "that the human body is subject to the same laws of the conservation and transformation of energy which pertain to the whole material universe." That being so, the body could be viewed as an input-output system; food was taken in, energy (including thought) emerged, and the energy was "an exact equivalent of the amount of food assumed and assimilated." In Hardaker's crudely quantitative universe bigger was definitely better, and men were bigger: "the factor of size has given man a superiority over woman, which he will always retain while he retains his larger body and brain . . . Unless woman can devise some means for reducing the size of man, she must be content to revolve about him in the future as in the past."[1]

men's size

Prospects for cutting men down to size did not, needless to say, look good. And in any case physiology offered Miss Hardaker a further argument for deflating women's intellectual pretensions. Even supposing woman's energy level equal to man's, perhaps twenty percent of it between the ages of twenty and forty was diverted "for the maintenance of maternity and its attendant exactions." The author invited her readers to consider what it would be like were that not so: all food, in women as in men, would go into thought, none into reproduction. Women then might (still supposing their energy equal to men's) challenge the intellectual supremacy of men, but the cost would be catastrophic: "The necessary outcome of an absolute intellectual equality of the sexes would be the extinction of the human race." Presumably that would give even feminists pause.[2]

Enter the First Law

Hardaker's article did not go unanswered. The next volume of the *Popular Science Monthly* included a "Reply to Miss Hardaker on the Woman Question," which rather effectively demolished the arguments of this "professed enemy of her sex." But Hardaker's thesis, though cruder than most, nicely illustrates the attraction of that great achievement of physical theory in the midnineteenth century, the law of the conservation of energy. Taking shape in the work of physicists in Germany and England at about the same time that Charles Darwin was pondering the origin of species, conservation theory was a principle of even greater scope than the principle of evolution. Though less humanly engaging, perhaps, than the evolutionary perspective, the law of energy conservation evoked its own share of poetic responses. Herbert Spencer based his entire philosophic system upon it. Spencer's American disciple, Edward Youmans, editor of a book of essays entirely devoted to the new law, rhapsodized over its universality:

> Thus the law characterized by Faraday as the highest in physical science which our faculties permit us to perceive, has a far more extended sway; it might well have been proclaimed the highest of *all* science—the most far-reaching principle that adventuring reason has discovered in the universe. Its stupendous reach spans all orders of existence. Not only does it govern the movements of the heavenly bodies, but it presides over the genesis of the constellations; not only does it control those radiant floods of power which fill the eternal spaces, bathing, warming, illumining and vivifying our planet, but it rules the actions and relations of men, and regulates the march of terrestrial affairs. Nor is its dominion limited to physical phenomena; it presides equally in the world of mind, controlling all the faculties and processes of thought and feeling. The star-suns of the remoter galaxies dart their radiations across the universe; and although the distances are so profound that hundreds of centuries may have been required to traverse them, the impulses of force enter the eye, and impressing an atomic change upon the nerve, give origin to the sense of sight. Star and nerve-tissue are parts of the system—stellar and nervous forces are correlated. Nay more; sensation awakens thought and kindles emotion, so that this wondrous dynamic chain binds into living unity the realms of matter and mind through measureless amplitudes of space and time.[3]

In its simplest form the principle of the conservation of energy, also known as the First Law of Thermodynamics, states that the energy of a system remains always constant, although its usefulness for work may diminish, because energy can neither be created nor destroyed. Apparent loss of energy, such as takes place when a steam engine produces less work than the potential energy of the coal fueling it, is actually a transformation into another form of energy (in this case, heat). A variety of types of energy exist—heat, electricity, magnetism, and mechanical motion, for example—but all are convertible into one another. Thus heat can be transformed into work, and work into heat, but in all cases the quantity of energy remains the same. Platitudinous as this concept may now seem, when initially formulated it contradicted the wisdom of common sense. The reduction of work output in a machine caused by friction certainly appeared, after all, to be an uncompensated loss, or destruction, of the potential energy of the coal.[4]

A number of physicists shared in establishing the conservation theory, but the German physicist and physiologist Hermann von Helmholtz first enunciated it mathematically in its most general form in the late 1840s. Significantly, Helmholtz, one of a school of German biologists committed to studying organic functions as strictly physico-chemical phenomena, expected to provide mechanical explanations for the process of life. He and his colleagues scorned the notion that living things had some mysterious essence that set them quite apart from the realm of physics. In the words of the renowned physiological psychologist Wilhelm Wundt, "Physiology thus appears as a branch of applied physics, its problem being a reduction of vital phenomena to general physical laws, and thus ultimately to the fundamental laws of mechanics."[5]

For purposes of this reduction the conservation principle provided a vital link between the realms of living and nonliving matter. It offered to the Berlin school and other like-minded materialistic physiologists a paradigm for the study of animal metabolism: organisms could be viewed as animate engines, transforming food into heat, muscle power, and nerve force. Julius Mayer, a German physiologist who, like Helmholtz, arrived at the notion of energy conservation because of an interest in animal heat, asserted its importance to physiology in a paper in the early 1850s: "As the power to work is without question the most important of the products of animal life, the mechanical equivalent of heat is in the very nature of things destined to be the foundation for the edifice of a scientific physiology." By extending the concept of the correlation of forces to include vital as well as physical force, scientists laid the foundation for an experimental physiology based on the study of metabolism.[6]

In England a prominent figure in this development was William B. Carpenter, author of numerous standard works on plant, animal, and human physiology and one of the best-known physiologists of his day. As early as 1838 Carpenter was questioning the need to posit a special vital principle in living things and arguing instead that vitality was a property of a certain kind of organized matter quite comparable to gravitation or electricity. The force that originated in the Divine Will, he affirmed in an influential paper of 1850, expressed itself in inorganic matter as "electricity, magnetism, light, heat, chemical affinity, and mechanical motion"; in organisms as "growth, development, chemico-vital transformation" and ultimately "nervous agency and muscular power."[7]

The Human Engine

The fascination of this new view of the body as a heat- and work-producing machine like any man-made mechanism is evident in an article in the *Popular Science Monthly* entitled "The Human Body as an Engine." Its author, E. B. Rosa, who taught at Wesleyan University, noted that while the obedience of the body to the laws of chemistry was thoroughly accepted, its obedience to "the fundamental law of physics, namely, the law of the conservation of energy," was not so fully recognized. To further that recognition, Rosa drew a parallel between a locomotive, that "complex inanimate engine of iron and steel," and the human body, "a still more complex living engine of flesh and bone and blood." Beginning the day, like the locomotive, with an intake of fuel and water, the body converted these into tissue and heat and mechanical work. Oxidizing its fuel in combustion, converting heat into work, eliminating its wastes, the bodily engine, in close parallel to the steam engine, conformed to the working of the First Law.[8]

Rosa carefully sidestepped the immensely controversial area of mind-body interaction to which the logic of the First Law inexorably pointed. Asking the reader to consider the human body only as "a living engine," Rosa hastened to add, "That man is more than matter is, of course, conceded. But we here regard only the animal body, guided by the brain as its engineer." The engineer at the controls of the engine—it was an attractive metaphor that suggested an intellectual mastery over the material flesh. Yet it did little to resolve that question of questions haunting nineteenth-century psychology, the relation of mind to body. Once accept the convertibility of physical and vital forces, and it was impossible to resist the extension of the principle to the less tangible realm of the nervous and mental.[9]

The integration of mind into nature, what L. S. Jacyna has called "the naturalization of mind," was clearly visible long before Darwin, although it took on an evolutionary cast after 1860. In England its origins date back to the phrenology of the early part of the century, which offered a physical account of the mind. Many of the important figures in the development of a biological psychology, men like Thomas Laycock, Herbert Spencer, and Alexander Bain, were deeply influenced by the phrenological dictum that the brain was the organ of the mind. The old dichotomy between mind and body gave way to a new view in which, however uneasily, body and mind became integrated: in the words of Alexander Bain, "the law of mental sequence is . . . not mind causing body and body causing mind, but mind-body giving birth to mind-body; a much more intelligible position." Intelligible, perhaps, but scarcely self-explanatory: the exact nature of their relationship set the terms of neurological research down to and beyond the end of the century. The focus of psychological inquiry was definitively reshaped away from introspective contemplation and toward an analysis of the material brain and nervous system. On this, scientists from all across the philosophical spectrum could agree: "whether in health or disease, the mind is to be studied from a purely material standpoint, and not as a mysterious principle to be looked upon with awe as something entirely beyond our reach."[10]

The entry point for a physical analysis of mind was the concept of nerve force. Carpenter interpreted nerve force as one of the modes of vital force, transmitted by means of chemical changes taking place between the substance of the ganglionic center and the oxygenated blood. Nerve force occupied a kind of middle ground, mediating between the mind and the physical forces of nature. In the words of Bain, nervous power was "a certain flow of the influence circulating through the nerves, which . . . has for its distinguishing concomitant the MIND." There was a definite equivalence between mental manifestations and physical forces, Bain continued, such that "the mental manifestations are in exact proportion to their physical supports." More, they were dependent upon physical changes: the psycho-physiologist had to look to some change in the substance of the brain as "the immediate Physical antecedent" of mental activity.[11]

Such reasoning entered deep philosophical waters. Pondering the significance of this transformation "from physical to psychical energy," John Cleland, professor of anatomy at the University of Glasgow, asked, "Has then the energy the conservation of which has become one of the greatest laws for the physicist a larger circuit here than the mere material universe?" He answered in the affirmative: the First Law applied to mental as well as material phenomena, and "thought and physical energy are mutually convertible." The new intimacy signaled in this notion of convertibility fairly demanded of scientists that they confront the nature of the relationship. Most of them sensibly opted for a kind of philosophical agnosticism, following the lead of Thomas Laycock and especially John Hughlings Jackson, who announced, "I do not concern myself with mental states at all, except indirectly in seeking the anatomical substrata. I do not trouble myself about the mode of connection between mind and matter. It is enough to assume a parallelism." This doctrine of concomitance, or psycho-physical parallelism, was Hughlings Jackson's declaration of independence from metaphysics, adopted explicitly to enable neurologists and physiologists to get on with their materialist researches into the functioning of the nervous system. It implied a methodological materialism that insisted on finding physical causes for psychical states, though it did not deny the reality of psychic phenomena. Hughlings Jackson emphasized that to argue that the mind caused some physiological event would be to introduce an alien element into a closed system, and thus to "imply disbelief in the doctrine of the conservation of energy." Every mental state appeared in conjunction with a correlative nervous state, but neither interfered with the other.[12]

Psycho-physical parallelism intentionally evaded the ultimate metaphysical question of the nature of mind and its relation to the body. But no such self-denying ordinance marked the work of scientific radicals like Thomas Henry Huxley and W. K. Clifford, the "enfant terrible" of scientific naturalism. Huxley flatly challenged the notion of parallel and independent systems, one physiological and one psychical. Rather, he asserted, "all states of consciousness . . . are immediately caused by molecular changes of the brain-substance"; human beings are "conscious automata." The very same year (1874) that Huxley uttered the inflammatory sentence, "We are conscious automata," his friend, the brilliant and corrosive W. K. Clifford, threw down the gauntlet to dualism equally aggressively. Arguing, like Hughlings Jackson, that the nervous system was a closed circuit in which sensory impulses sufficed to produce motor responses, Clifford went on, quite unlike Hughlings Jackson, to conclude that states of consciousness were epiphenomena. Neither the will nor any other conscious state could affect activity. In fact, what we call mind and what we call matter were at bottom one. There was, then, no immaterial mind, no free will, and no supernatural divinity.[13]

Most British psycho-physiologists were horrified by these assertions, for they had pledged a dual allegiance to both science and religion. On the one hand, they had committed themselves to a naturalistic exploration of the phenomena of mind; on the other hand, they were anxious to construe the facts thus obtained in such a way as to leave room for human free agency and a transcendent spiritual order. Thus John Cleland, who confessed that he found the conclusions to which he had been driven "startling," hastened to add that "the statement that thought is a form of physical energy cannot possibly convey any meaning," and comforted himself and his readers with the belief that "Spirit is the one substratum of everything." And another stout defender of divinity, William Carpenter, refused to relinquish the efficacy of the will, coming close, indeed, to rebuilding the wall between different kinds of forces that he himself had done so much to break down. "Though the spheres of *moral* and *physical* Causation impinge (as it were) upon one another," wrote Carpenter, "they are in themselves essentially distinct . . . The Moral power of the 'thoughts that breathe, and words that burn' in the utterances of the Poet, cannot be correlated, like the mechanical Energy exerted by his muscles in the writing of his verse, with the quantity of food he may have consumed in their production." Acknowledging that his own research had established "the intimacy of that *nexus* between Mental and Bodily activity, which, explain it as we may, cannot be denied," Carpenter emphatically rejected mechanism as ultimate in the order of nature: "the Man of Science cannot dispense with the notion of a Power always working throughout the Mechanism of the Universe; . . . on scientific grounds alone this Power may be regarded as the expression of Mind." Such perorations occur with frequency in the literature of British psycho-physiology. They point to the metaphysical anxiety which accompanied the rise of an empirical neurophysiology and which joined with the more generalized apprehension over the meaning of evolution to create a groundswell of spiritual insecurity.[14]

The Bodily Economy

The concept of correlated forces and its extension to the mind had immediate practical as well as philosophical repercussions. Scientists and medical men seized on it to give a semblance of concreteness to intangible and poorly understood entities like the mind and the nerves. The new description of mental activity in terms of forces gave promise of a better insight into the workings of the brain and nervous system. This was important in itself, as an addition to scientific knowledge, but doubly so in that it offered the basis for a new therapeutics of mental health. From the late 1860s onward physicians elaborated a theory of mental health defined as the prudential conservation of nerve force. Health depended upon moderation in the expenditure of energy, while nervous exhaustion or worse threatened the profligate spender.[15]

Nerve force and mind force, it was believed, became comprehensible to the degree that they could be likened to some better-known correlative force. For this purpose far and away the favored analogy was to electricity. Psychologists and neurologists with one voice identified nerve force with electricity. According to William Carpenter nerve force was transmitted just as an electric current is transmitted along the telegraph wire through "chemical Changes taking place between the metals and the exciting liquid of the Galvanic battery." For the author of *Nervous Exhaustion and the Diseases Induced by It*, every bodily and mental effort involved "a discharge of nervous force, much as a Leyden jar discharges its charge of electricity." George Beard, alerting his compatriots to their liability to "American nervousness," likened the nervous system to "Edison's electric light."[16]

Nerve force and brain force did not arise *de novo,* but were products of oxidation just as muscular exertion was. Psychologists established an economy of the body, in which the nutrition a person took in created a definite quantity of force to be divided among a number of activities, including digestion, the maintenance of heat, and muscular and mental effort. If energy conservation implied, as E. B. Rosa noted, that "energy can be measured, stored up and expended, just as truly as merchandise or money," an energy calculus could be reckoned up for the mind and nerves. Nerve force became a measurable quantity, and thought could perhaps be quantified.[17]

The calculus of vital energy required recognition that all the functions of the body competed, as it were, for the available energy. Intense effort in any one area, by making an excessive draft on a limited fund of energy, temporarily enfeebled the others. Thus, "in high mental excitement, digestion is stopped; muscular vigor is abated except in the one form of giving vent to the feelings, thoughts, and purposes; and if the state were long continued or oft repeated, the physical powers strictly so called would rapidly deteriorate." Balfour Stewart reckoned that at times of intense mental excitement, perhaps one-third to one-half of all the oxidation of the body went into "keeping up the cerebral fires." Conversely, "the digestion of a dinner calls force to the stomach, and temporarily slows the brain." Great accomplishment in one area, then, entailed correspondingly lesser attainment elsewhere, since, in the words of the American evolutionist Joseph LeConte, "all development takes place at the expense of decay—all elevation of one thing, in one place, at the expense of corresponding running down of something else in another place."[18]

The cost of brain work not surprisingly engaged the particular interest of writers. It cannot be said that their conclusions offered much encouragement to would-be intellectuals. Of all human endeavors, thinking involved probably the greatest drain on bodily energies:

> Anything like a great or general cultivation of the powers of thought, or any occupation that severely and continuously brings them into

play, will induce such a preponderance of cerebral activity, in oxidation and in nerve-currents, as to disturb the balance of life, and to require special arrangements for redeeming that disturbance. This is fully verified by all we know of the tendency of intellectual application to exhaust the physical process, and to bring on early decay.

Cesare Lombroso had some such idea in mind when he invoked "the law of conservation of energy which rules the whole organic world" to explain why the man of genius so often showed abnormalities like "precocious grayness and baldness, leanness of the body, and weakness of sexual and muscular activity." The neurologist J. Leonard Corning agreed that intellectuals were apt to suffer severe loss of fatty, and especially muscular, tissue. They were of course all the more at risk if they dared combine "inordinate intellection" with athleticism, thereby "burning the candle at both ends." Loving relationships also withered under the energy drain of excessive thought. One whose life was devoted to cultivation of the mind could give only "abated support" to affairs of the heart; hence, "great intellect as a whole is not readily united with a large emotional nature."[19]

For their part, the emotions were scarcely less exigent, and the wise individual carefully computed the cost of emotional outlays. It was not enough simply to avoid pain, one had to ration pleasure as well. Pointing out that "every throb of pleasure costs something to the physical system, and two throbs cost twice as much as one," Balfour Stewart warned, "of this . . . there can be no reasonable doubt—namely, that a large amount of pleasure supposes a corresponding large expenditure of blood and nerve-tissue, to the stinting, perhaps, of the active energies and the intellectual processes." While a precise cost-benefit computation might be impossible, Stewart urged his readers to take these considerations into account: "It is a matter of practical moment to ascertain what pleasures cost least, for there are thrifty and unthrifty modes of spending our brain and heart's blood." As an emotional ideal Stewart recommended "a moderate surplus of pleasure—a gentle glow, not rising into brilliancy or intensity, except at considerable intervals (say a small portion of every day), falling down frequently to indifference, but seldom sinking into pain."[20]

Stewart's recommendation of emotional continence illustrates

Barbara Sicherman's contention that "the husbanding of resources was a central metaphor in nineteenth-century America," one that represented a restrictive model of mental health. Through the psychological literature of the period runs a refrain of limitation, depletion, and potential breakdown. An article in the *Popular Science Monthly* described the nervous system in terms of a "physiology of limitations" in which "thinking and feeling exhaust the mechanism." Cesare Lombroso warned of the certainty of being "severely punished on the other side" for every extravagant expenditure of energy. No one, it seems, ever enjoyed a comfortable energy surplus. Hugh Campbell explained that "nutrition, however perfect, cannot be carried on beyond a certain point"; hence "the supply of nerve force must have a certain limit, and if more demand is made on brain and nerve than they are calculated to meet, the strength and quality of the forces must eventually suffer."[21]

The very conditions of modern civilization—the printing press, the railroad, the steam engine, the telegraph—conspired against health by quickening the pace of life and making greater demands on one's attention. So pervasive were these dangers that neurologists elaborated an entire etiology of a disease which they dubbed neurasthenia, defined as nerve exhaustion or a failure of nerve force. Though induced by the tensions of modernity, neurasthenia did not strike at random. Its victims tended to come from the urban middle class, to be slight of frame, delicate, and soft-haired. They were also likely to have inherited a defective or weak nervous constitution that predisposed them to fall victim to disease. Attempting to pin down a disease with no organic manifestations and a bewildering variety of symptoms, George Beard, the pioneer in the field, indulged in an orgy of metaphor:

> The neurasthenic is a dam with a small reservoir behind it, that often runs dry or nearly so through the torrent at the sluiceway, but speedily fills again from many mountain streams; a small furnace, holding little fuel, and that imflammable [*sic*] and combustible, and with strong draught, causing quick exhaustion of materials and imparting unequal, inconstant warmth; a battery with small cells and little potential force, and which with little internal resistance quickly becomes actual force, and so is an inconstant battery, evolving a force sometimes weak, sometimes strong, and requiring fre-

quent repairing and refilling; a dayclock which, if it be not wound up every twenty-four hours, runs utterly down; an engine with small boiler-power, that is soon emptied of its steam; an electric light attached to a small dynamo and feeble storage apparatus, that often flickers and speedily weakens when the dynamo ceases to move.[22]

It is interesting that neurasthenic collapse was frequently described in economic terms; it was bankruptcy, physical and mental, "a species of insolvency, to be dealt with according to the sound method of readjusting the relations of expenditure and income." The improvident neurasthenic overdrew his (or more frequently her) account of nerve force, and there ensued "what always happens if great expenses are met by small incomes; first the savings are consumed, then comes bankruptcy."[23]

The Divided Force of Females

Against this background of fragility, the particular problems of women stand out as doubly jeopardizing. For to all the normal drafts of bodily energy common to both sexes women added a singular expense of their own—the development and maintenance of a highly complex reproductive system. This system, that "delicate and extensive mechanism within the organism—a house within a house, an engine within an engine," exacted "an extraordinary expenditure of vital energy" at puberty, when it was first becoming established. Failure to develop the ovaries and their accessory organs properly and to regularize the "periodical functions" would lead to a lifetime of weakness and disease.[24]

Easily the most famous work in this vein was Edward Clarke's *Sex in Education; or, A Fair Chance for the Girls* (1873). Clarke, a former professor at the Harvard Medical School, built his case against identical education of the sexes explicitly on the limited-energy model of conservation theory. "The system," he wrote, "never does two things well at the same time . . . The digestion of a dinner calls force to the stomach, and temporarily slows the brain. The experiment of trying to digest a hearty supper, and to sleep during the process, has sometimes cost the careless experimenter his life. The physiological principle of doing only one thing at a time, if you would do it well, holds as truly of the growth of the organization as it does of the performance of any of its special functions." Adolescent girls, then, needed to abate brain work during the years of reproductive development. "It is . . . obvious that a girl upon whom Nature, for a limited period and for a definite purpose, imposes so great a physiological task, will not have as much power left for the tasks of the school, as the boy of whom Nature requires less at the corresponding epoch."[25]

Clarke offered his readers a series of affecting morality tales about young women who had transgressed against these principles of female health. Miss A., for example, had attended a New York state seminary for girls, and graduated at the age of nineteen, "the first scholar, and an invalid." When she consulted Dr. Clarke some three years later with symptoms of "prolonged dyspepsia, neuralgia, and dysmenorrhoea," he had no trouble arriving at a diagnosis:

> She was well, and would have been called robust, up to her first critical period. She then had two tasks imposed upon her at once, both of which required for their perfect accomplishment a few years of time and a large share of vital force: one was the education of a brain, the other of the reproductive system . . . The school, with puritanic inflexibility, demanded every day of the month; Nature, kinder than the school, demanded less than a fourth of the time . . . The schoolmaster might have yielded somewhat, but would not; Nature could not. The pupil, therefore, was compelled to undertake both tasks at the same time . . . She put her will into the education of her brain, and withdrew it from elsewhere . . . Presently . . . the strength of the loins, that even Solomon put in as a part of his ideal woman, changed to weakness . . . Doubtless the evil of her education will infect her whole life.[26]

The reproductive system exacted its greatest prolonged toll during puberty. Maturity moderated the energy drain but did not eliminate it. Comparing the respective fitness of men and women for intellectual labor meant raising, in the words of Clarke's English counterpart Henry Maudsley, "not a mere question of larger or smaller muscles, but of the energy and power of endurance of the nerve-force which drives the intellectual and muscular machinery; not a question of two bodies and minds that are in equal physical conditions, but of one body and mind capable of sustained and regular hard labor, and of another body and mind which for one quarter of each month during the best years of life is more or less sick and unfit for hard work." Under the best of circumstances women lived at the nervous edge. They had, generally, a lesser endowment of nerve force than men. George Beard wrote that women were unlikely to be numbered among the "millionnaires [*sic*] of nerve-force" who never knew nervous exhaustion, and were consequently "more nervous, immeasurably, than men, and suffer more from general and special nervous diseases." Nervousness was, apparently, synonymous with female sexuality. Harry Campbell thought woman's physiological predisposition to nervous ailments was clearly shown by her improved nervous health after menopause: "Her nervousness is, in fact," as he put it, "more or less co-extensive with her sexual life." It is true that neurasthenia struck down individuals of both sexes, among them eminent male sufferers like William James, Charles Darwin, and Herbert Spencer, but it was much commoner in women than in men. Summing up the best information available, Havelock Ellis in *Man and Woman* cited a figure (which admittedly he personally believed excessive) of fourteen neurasthenic women to every neurasthenic man.[27]

Women were enjoined against strenuous labor during their fertile years not alone for their own sake, but for the sake of the race. Energy spent in cerebration was of course lost to reproduction, and the intellectual maiden became a sterile matron. Such a conclusion flowed directly from a fixed-energy conception of the human body, and received its classic and oft-cited incarnation in the work of Herbert Spencer. Spencer first developed his theory of the antagonism between individuation and genesis (or individual development and fertility) in an early article on population in the *Westminster Review,* and incorporated it into his synthetic philosophy thereafter. As evidence of this antagonism Spencer pointed to "the fact that intense mental application, involving great waste of the nervous tissues, and a corresponding consumption of nervous matter for their repair, is accompanied by a cessation in the production of sperm-cells." (Was Spencer, himself a disciplined thinker and lifelong bachelor, perhaps an example of this?) Conversely, "undue production of sperm-cells involves cerebral inactivity. The first result of a morbid excess in this direction is headache, which may be taken to indicate that the brain is out of repair; this is followed by stupidity; should the disorder continue imbecility supervenes, ending occasionally in insanity."[28]

Scholars and Spinsters: The War between Books and Babies

Evidently Spencer did not at this point have women primarily in mind, and in fact he was not certain "how the antagonism affects the female economy." Over time he arrived at certitude. Young women, he concluded, stopped developing both physically and mentally at a stage somewhat less advanced than that attained by young men. This developmental arrest was the cost of reproduction: "Whereas, in man, individual evolution continues until the physiological cost of self-maintenance very nearly balances what nutrition supplies, in women, an arrest of individual development takes place while there is yet a considerable margin of nutrition: otherwise there could be no offspring." Adolescent girls, arriving at maturity earlier than boys, missed out on the final refinement of the nervo-muscular system. Their minds had "somewhat less of general power or massiveness"; in particular they lacked "those two faculties, intellectual and emotional, which are the latest products of human evolution—the power of abstract reasoning and that most abstract of emotions, the sentiment of justice."[29]

Spencer was here alluding to his evolutionary conception of mental development, according to which the highest centers of thought and feeling emerged latest in both the individual and the race. Savages, for example, could "readily receive simple ideas but not complex ones," because their minds remained at a lower level of development. Up to a point the African child actually excelled the white child in intellectual quickness, but, according to Sir Samuel Baker, an explorer and administrator in the Nile region who had observed them closely, "the mind [of the Negro child] does not expand—it promises fruit but does not ripen." So also with judgment: "from the comparatively-judicial intellect of the civilized man we pass to the intellect of the uncivilized man, sudden in its inferences, incapable of balancing evidence, and adhering obstinately to first impressions."[30]

These very same differences, though smaller in degree, obtained between the minds of men and women, and they explain why

Spencer viewed proposals to alter the political status of women with apprehension. In women a "less developed sense of abstract justice" joined with a maternal fondness for the helpless to create citizens who responded "more readily when appeals to pity are made than when appeals are made to equity." Spencer's own social philosophy rested on a concept of equity that rigidly excluded compassion. Admitting women to a greater share in government could only mean, from a Spencerian perspective, substituting sentimentalism in public policy for justice.[31]

Despite these deficiencies and despite what many scientists considered the very plain mandate of nature, some women persisted in training their minds to the detriment of their bodies, especially in America. These were the "mannish maidens" who, in the words of Edward Clarke, "graduated from school or college excellent scholars, but with undeveloped ovaries. Later they married, and were sterile." Worse, they might become so enamored of self-development that they refused to marry at all. G. Stanley Hall upbraided the New Woman who forsook marriage and maternity:

> Despairing of herself as a woman, she asserts her lower rights in the place of her one great right to be loved . . . Failing to respect herself as a productive organism, she gives vent to personal ambitions; seeks independence; comes to know very plainly what she wants; perhaps becomes intellectually emancipated, and substitutes science for religion, or the doctor for the priest, with the all-sided impressionability characteristic of her sex which, when cultivated, is so like an awakened child.

Such a woman, living her own life rather than living for others, might be a splendid friend, intellectually stimulating, "at home with the racket and on the golf links," but she was not a mother:

> The bachelor woman is an interesting illustration of Spencer's law of the inverse relation of individuation and genesis. The completely developed individual is always a terminal representative in her line of descent. She has taken up and utilized in her own life all that was meant for her descendants, and has so overdrawn her account with heredity that, like every perfectly and completely developed individual, she is also completely sterile. This is the very apotheosis of selfishness from the standpoint of every biological ethics.[32]

Perhaps the harshest expression of "biological ethics" came from Henry Maudsley. Maudsley is a pivotal figure in the development of an evolutionary science of mind, and in the interpretation of its meaning to the educated public. He possessed formidable credentials: superintendent of the Manchester Royal Lunatic Asylum, editor of the *Journal of Mental Science,* Fellow of the Royal College of Physicians, and professor of medical jurisprudence at University College, London. Yet success brought him little joy. Whether because of an unhappy childhood (his mother died when he was young and his father, a stern Yorkshire farmer, withdrew into himself) or because of some quirk of constitution, Maudsley seems to have been incapable of happiness. In the world of Victorian psychiatry he was an acknowledged leader, yet bitterness and arrogance isolated him from his colleagues; nor could he summon any compassion for the mentally afflicted whose ills he diagnosed. Much influenced by Herbert Spencer, he was far from sharing Spencer's cosmic optimism. He viewed human nature with a deep pessimism, although Aubrey Lewis, his admiring biographer, has described his attitude as skeptical rather than despairing. Biology had revealed to him the iron determinism of nature and the inequality that was its direct result. The metaphysical doctrine of equal mental capacity was, he insisted, erroneous, and "as cruel as it is false":

> What man can by taking thought add one cubit either to his mental or to his bodily stature? Multitudes of human beings come into the world weighted with a destiny against which they have neither the will nor power to contend; they are the step-children of Nature, and groan under the worst of all tyrannies—the tyranny of a bad organization. Men differ, indeed, in the fundamental characters of their minds, as they do in the features of their countenances, or in the habits of their bodies, and between those who are born with the potentiality of a full and complete mental development, under favorable circumstances, and those who are born with an innate incapacity of mental development, under any circumstances, there exists every gradation.[33]

A modern writer has described Maudsley as "consistently . . . the defender of the prevailing order against the threats of degeneration and savagery," a man of "deep social commitment" whose work was "in good part . . . not science at all but a scientific ideology of social control." Among the groups in need of control were women, who seemed to be in danger of forgetting that, like the feeble-minded, they could not "rebel successfully against the tyranny of their organization." Maudsley ridiculed those philosophers (unidentified, but certainly including Mill) who believed that once women were educated identically with men their minds would be revealed as essentially the same: "To my mind it would not be one whit more absurd to affirm that the antlers of the stag, the human beard, and the cock's comb, are effects of education, or that, by putting a girl to the same education as a boy, the female generative organs might be transformed into male organs." Until education could transform a woman into a man, their spheres remained distinct. Because "there is sex in mind . . . there should be sex in education."[34]

Maudsley's message, scarcely novel, commended to educators a training that would focus on women's "foreordained work as mothers and nurses of children." What separates his lecture to women from the large number of similar endeavors is its lack of sentimentalism. Most writers, even as they encouraged women to devote themselves to maternity, made of that vocation a holy calling. Hall's readiness to worship the Madonna is representative of the characteristic Victorian idealization of motherhood. Mauds-ley, by contrast, not only refused to grant women this compensa-tory reverence but even denigrated their maternal role. The duties of motherhood, he wrote, were after all "somewhat mean and unworthy offices in comparison with nobler functions of giving birth to and developing ideas." Yet women could not be absolved of their responsibility for these offices, however mean: "For it would be an ill thing, if it should so happen that we got the advantages of a quantity of female intellectual work at the price of a puny, enfeebled, and sickly race."[35]

The obsessive concern among scientists and medical men that woman be mindful of her biological function gains perspective in the context of contemporary demography: marriage- and birth-rates were declining in the late nineteenth century, particularly among the middle classes. By 1904, when G. Stanley Hall sum-marized the literature, studies of the health and fertility of college women were numerous and mostly negative. Under the headings "Nubility of Educated Women" and "Fecundity of Educated

Women," Hall reviewed this material at some length and added his own findings from research on Vassar, Smith, and Wellesley graduates. The data were calamitous: in 1900 the percentage of married women among the female graduates of eight leading colleges founded before 1885 varied between 16.5 and 35.1 percent. Even excluding recent graduates who might still marry the figures were not encouraging. Of the 323 women who had graduated from Vassar between 1867 and 1876, only 179, or 55.4 percent, had married by 1903. Nor were those who did marry keeping up to the mark reproductively: 58 of the 179 had no children at all, and the total number of children was only 365, an average of 2.03 per married woman. The comparable figures for Smith and Wellesley graduates were 1.99 and 1.81 children per married member. Herbert Spencer's dictum that "absolute or relative infertility is generally produced in women by mental labor carried to excess" appeared, thought Hall, to be confirmed.[36]

In the face of statistics like these, educated women came under sustained and sometimes vituperative attack. Women, it seemed, had no right to self-fulfillment that could stand for a moment against the claims of society on their wombs. Some of the very individuals who at other times championed the expansion of opportunities for women, men like Havelock Ellis and Karl Pearson, were harsh on the issue of maternity. Ellis had a history of feminism. He once told his dear friend, the South African feminist writer Olive Schreiner, that he had had "ever since I can remember such a deep feeling of the equality of men and women in every respect." And when he married it was to a woman who wrote, in an article about marriage, "The very root of the whole sex question is the absolute economic and social independence of woman." Pearson, also Schreiner's friend and a professor of applied mathematics and later of eugenics at the University of London, trained, hired, and collaborated with a number of academic women despite the skepticism of his mentor Francis Galton about the intellectual capacity of women. Ellis's biographer tells us that Pearson assailed Ellis's variability hypothesis in part because of "the tacit assumption that somehow Ellis's theory cast a slur upon women."[37]

Yet both men viewed feminism through the prism of maternity, ever more so as each became caught up in the developing eugenics movement. In *The Task of Social Hygiene* (1912) Ellis praised the

German feminist movement, which "so far from making as its ideal the imitation of men, bases itself on that which most essentially marks the woman as unlike the man." German feminism focused on "the demands of woman the mother." The 1929 edition of *Man and Woman*, unlike the first edition of 1894, mapped out a social space firmly divided by gender: "When women enter the same fields as men, on the same level and to the same degree, their organic constitution usually unfits them to achieve the same success, or they only achieve it at a greater cost. Woman's special sphere is the bearing and the rearing of children, with the care of human life in the home."[38]

Karl Pearson similarly illustrates the biological imperative that insisted that women be breeders first and foremost before any talk of their putative rights. The first question for feminists to settle, he wrote in an early article on "The Woman Question," was "what would be the effect of [woman's] emancipation on her function of race-reproduction . . . The higher education of women may connote a general intellectual progress for the community, or, on the other hand, a physical degradation of the race, owing to prolonged study having ill effects on woman's child-bearing efficiency." Not surprisingly, this enemy of individualism had no use for a feminism that invoked John Stuart Mill: "What advocate of 'women's rights' has once and for all thrown John Stuart Mill's *Subjection of Women* overboard, and measured women's as well as men's 'rights' by the touchstone of general social efficiency?" If Pearson and Ellis were friends of woman, she hardly needed enemies.[39]

It is fair to ask whether the exhortations to replenish the earth did not apply equally to both sexes. Men as well as women were obviously required for the great work. Men's bodies, like women's, operated within a universe of strictly limited energy. The birthrate among male college graduates was, like that of women, a cause for concern. These are points worth making. Men *were* admonished to do their part in creating the next generation. G. Stanley Hall, for example, lamented the days when "marriage and children were felt to be religious, if not also patriotic, duties," and suggested that "many, but not all, bachelors who shirk it without adequate excuse should perhaps be taxed progressively beyond a certain age."[40]

Yet there is no question but what the burden of concern and

opprobrium fell disproportionately on women. It did so for several reasons. In the first place, it was women's traditional role, not men's, that was being questioned by feminists and that was, in fact, beginning to change in the late nineteenth century. Men had been attending college for generations, but women were just beginning to taste the delights of higher education. It was not surprising, then, that the blame for the troublesome decline in middle-class fertility was laid at the feet of educated women rather than educated men. They were a new phenomenon, and their advent undeniably coincided with fertility's fall. Second, although energy conservation governed the physiological lives of both sexes, it bore with far greater severity on women. What Ely Van de Warker called the "penalty of sex" and Herbert Spencer referred to as the "physical tax which reproduction necessitates," requiring "a certain obligation to pay this tax and to submit to this sacrifice," was gender-specific:

> Those who advocate the equal treatment of the sexes must bear in mind that great culture in a man does not unfit him for paternity, but, on the contrary will help him in the struggle for existence to maintain a family. For women, on the contrary, exceptional culture will infallibly have the tendency to remove the fittest individuals, those most likely to add to the production of children of high class brainpower, from out of the ranks of motherhood.

Finally, men were considered to have other important roles to play besides that of fatherhood; they were the thinkers and doers who shaped and enriched civilization, moving it forward to ever higher levels. The gift of the genius to society was worth his possibly impaired fertility. But woman was mother—that and that alone; motherhood was, in essence, her sole contribution to society as that part of the race "told specially off for the continuance of the species." She had no other gift to offer but her healthy—and numerous—offspring.[41]

The Body at Bay

Women would undoubtedly have been charged with reproductive negligence whether or not a scientific theory was ready at hand to explain their diminished fertility. The charge gained gravity, however, from the negative implications attached to contemporary bodily energy theories. A vocabulary of "penalty," "tax," and "sacrifice," of limitation and exhaustion and disease, did not encourage a sanguine view of the potential of any human being, regardless of sex. If on top of the "tyranny of one's organization" science superimposed the special disabilities of the female sex, the outlook for simple health, let alone achievement, appeared faint.

The emphasis on weakness and liability is puzzling because it conflicts with the metabolic model that underlay the new understanding of human energy. The body, physiologically considered, regularly replenishes itself by taking in nutriment from outside. It engages in continuous interaction with its environment. This steady-state maintenance is what the physiologist means by the term *homeostasis*. As the biologist Ludwig von Bertalanffy has pointed out, the study of metabolism leads to a conception of the living organism as an open system, continuously engaged in the exchange of material with its environment. Open systems import free energy from outside; at the very least this process suggests a measure of resilience in the face of stress. Weary bodies rest and eat and are replenished. Energy is renewable. More, organisms grow; capacities expand and flower. The metabolic model provides a brief for an expansive, rather than restrictive, reading of human potential.[42]

Yet this is certainly not the interpretation adopted by scientists and physicians describing the human nervous system. Human beings, in their eyes, came into the world endowed with a certain fixed quantity of nervous energy. The luck of the hereditary draw determined whether one was a "millionnaire of nerve-force" or a pauper, and there was little one could do about it. Such an interpretation is much more akin to the closed-system model of physics than to the open system of biology.

It is true that some writers mentioned the possibility of renewing and even augmenting nervous resources. George Beard, the "father" of neurasthenia, noted that "the human body is a reservoir of force constantly escaping, constantly being renewed from the one center of force—the sun." That being so, "the force in this nervous system can be increased or diminished by good or evil influences, medical or hygienic, or by the natural evolutions—growth, disease, and decline." Balfour Stewart conceded the possibility of combining physical and mental exertion by increasing the quality and quantity of food, ensuring good air and exercise, and avoiding "all excesses and irregularities" of mind and body. But the stress was overwhelmingly on the likelihood of exhaustion rather than the possibilities of enhancement. J. Leonard Corning, a New York neurologist, made the disconcerting (unnerving?) assertion that cerebral exhaustion could occur even when the brain was abundantly nourished, and Beard came close to suggesting that neurasthenia was the birthright of every civilized person:

> when new functions are interposed in the circuit, as modern civiliza-
> tion is constantly requiring us to do, there comes a period, sooner or
> later, varying in different individuals, and at different times of life,
> when the amount of force is insufficient to keep all the lamps actively
> burning; those that are weakest go out entirely, or, as more fre-
> quently happens, burn faintly and feebly—they do not expire, but
> give an insufficient and unstable light—this is the philosophy of
> modern nervousness.

Despite his image of the body as a reservoir of renewable force, Beard in the end proffered a starkly pessimistic message: "The constant and unwavering admission of the fact that the human brain, in its very highest evolution, is an organ of very feeble capacity indeed, is the preliminary truth."[43]

Why scientists and medical men set aside the positive implications of the metabolic model in favor of their own darker conclusions is not entirely clear. Presumably their perspective was related to the new intimacy of the relationship between the spiritual and the material within each human being. However exciting the scientific vistas opened up by neurophysiological research, the naturalization of mind caused shock and pain. It is not surprising that here as elsewhere (compare the fear of evolutionary miscarriage) this development engendered a pervasive sense of human frailty. Once the human spirit had soared free, "a separate Immaterial existence" completely independent of "the Bodily instrument"; now it was a caged eagle, a thing of nerve cells and circuits and ganglionic centers. The effort to give material shape to the intangible in the form of mental forces that could be measured and tabulated almost of necessity induced a preoccupation with organic bookkeeping. And this preoccupation, given a scientific climate that increasingly stressed the importance of heredity over environment, focused on limitation rather than potential.

In addition, it may well be that scientists in the latter part of the nineteenth century were influenced by the pessimistic overtones of the Second Law of Thermodynamics. Emerging from studies on the efficiency of steam engines, the Second Law, as generalized by William Thomson in 1852, announced the existence of "a universal tendency in nature to the dissipation of mechanical energy." Whereas the First Law had stated that energy could not be destroyed, the Second Law insisted that the energy thus conserved became less and less useful; in the modern terminology coined by Clausius in 1865, the entropy of the universe tended constantly to increase. The dissipation principle suggested that at some time in the future when all mechanical energy had been transformed into heat at a uniformly low temperature life on earth would cease, and "the universe from that time forward would be condemned to a state of eternal rest." Such a scenario, dubbed "the heat death of the universe," chilled the speculative climate of the period. Behind the comforting stability of conservation, the specter of dissipation could now be seen to lurk. The realization stunned even such a resolute cosmic optimist as Herbert Spencer. When his friend, the eminent physicist John Tyndall, told Spencer that complete physical equilibrium meant omnipresent death, Spencer responded worriedly, "Regarding, as I have done, equilibrium as the ultimate and *highest* state of society, I have assumed it to be not only the ultimate but also the highest state of the universe. And your assertion that when equilibrium was reached life must cease, staggered me . . . I still feel unsettled about the matter." By the 1890s, under the spell of the Second Law, Henry Adams was collecting evidence of degradation in many areas—physical, geological, biological, and social, and astronomer Camille Flammarion was writing *La fin du monde*. At a time, then, when physical theories seemed to offer only the prospect of a universal decline of useful energy, it is reasonable to suppose that they may have encouraged physiologists' and psychologists' preoccupation with human energy depletion. Many years would pass before philosophically inclined scientists rebelled against the closed-system implications of physical theory and articulated an interactive organic model that escaped the shadow of the Second Law.[44]

Meanwhile, in a landscape peopled by the neurasthenic and brain-weary and reproductively impaired, there was little chance that scientists would smile on the vaunting intellectual aspirations of women. Minds were now firmly situated in bodies, and bodies, as all the latest research confirmed, were pitifully liable to collapse under the multiplied burdens of modernity. The repositories of the next generation must be safeguarded, from themselves if necessary. Their slender store of force must be husbanded. These beings, "upon whom, more than upon men, rest the burdens and responsibilities of the generations," were "too sacred to be jostled roughly in the struggle for existence." Surely the world owed them, in the words of Iowa psychologist G. T. W. Patrick, "reverent exemption" from some of the duties shouldered by the (quite literally) more energetic male.[45]

CHAPTER 5

The Physiological Division of Labor

The development of the race has been a steady growth in
specialization; from the differentiation of tissues in the lower
forms of life, producing different organs with different functions; on through the division of labor which makes man an
important member of a community instead of an isolated
savage; up to the wonderful complexity of our modern life in
which each man or woman, filling his or her special niche,
has interests inextricably interdependent with those of countless other men and women.

—Mrs. Mary K. Sedgwick (1901)

Sexual dimorphism tends to become more frequent and more
conspicuous as we ascend the series. With growing dimorphism the essential functions of the males and the females
become more and more different, their habits of life diverge,
and to the primary contrasts of maleness and femaleness there
are added all manner of secondary expressions, which may
usefully be designated masculine and feminine. This contrast
of secondary sex-characters . . . saturates through and
through the organism, manifesting itself in mind as well as in
body, in intellect as well as in emotion.

—J. Arthur Thomson and Patrick Geddes (1912)

Victorian social theorists, like Victorian physical and biological
theorists (and they were sometimes one and the same person), loved the topic of woman's status. According to the British
social anthropologist E. E. Evans-Pritchard, "only religion competed with it for the interest of those puritanical unbelievers."
Unbelievers in orthodox religion these men may have been, but
they were devout in their admiration of contemporary Victorian
society and their conviction that the improved condition of women
through long ages of evolution demonstrated the upward progres-

sion of society. It became a commonplace of social theory that the treatment of women in any society was a prime indicator—perhaps *the* prime indicator—of that society's place in the evolutionary hierarchy. At the apex of the social order stood the societies of contemporary western Europe and America—whose distinguishing sexual characteristic (extensive evidence to the contrary notwithstanding) was the exemption of women from productive labor, that they might better devote themselves to the bearing and rearing of children. At the foot stood the primitive cultures of Africa, Asia, and the Americas, whose women, slaves to their men in all but name, toiled unceasingly at the most arduous physical tasks. The contrast was stark: on the one hand, the pampered Victorian woman, beloved wife and fond mother, safely supported in the confines of her comfortable home; on the other hand, the aboriginal female, perhaps only one among many wives, beaten and abused by a dictatorial spouse and charged with all the drudge work he would not lower himself to perform. Humanity had much to regret in the barbaric treatment to which it had subjected the female sex, but equally much to take pride in in its transcendance of barbarism: "Perhaps in no way is the moral progress of mankind more clearly shown," pronounced Herbert Spencer, "than by contrasting the position of women among savages with their position among the most advanced of the civilized."[1]

The exemption of women from labor did not take place higgledy-piggledy but, like all evolutionary social processes, in accordance with Law. The law in question was one already familiar to a generation and more of political economists—the law of the division of labor. It might be supposed that Herbert Spencer and those analysts of women's status who followed his lead would simply appropriate that concept from the literature of political economy, with which they were thoroughly familiar. Though it had Continental as well as English roots (in the work of Saint-Simon, Comte, and the German organicists), the concept of the division of labor had been most thoroughly elaborated in the English Utilitarian tradition of Paley and Malthus, and above all in the classic formulation of Adam Smith. Yet Spencer, and Darwin too, chose not to claim descent from Adam Smith and the political economists, but turned instead to the literature of biology, and specifically to the contributions of the eminent French zoologist Henri Milne-Edwards.

Writing in the first half of the nineteenth century Milne-Edwards had stressed again and again the increasing complexity, differentiation, and specialization of parts within organisms as one ascended the evolutionary scale. In 1834 he made the analogy between the works of nature and those of human beings, both of which depended for their improvement on these tendencies: "The principle which seems to have guided nature in the perfectibility of beings, is as one sees, precisely one of those which have had the greatest influence on the progress of human industry technology: the *division of labor.*" Milne-Edwards explored this theme at greatest length in his well-known *Introduction à la zoologie générale,* the third chapter of which opened with a declaration that "in the creations of nature, as in the manufactures of men, it is mostly by the division of labor that perfectibility is obtained." The Frenchman credited the term *division of labor* to the political economists, especially Jean Baptiste Say; he then adapted it to his own use by coining a new term, "the physiological division of labor."[2]

Milne-Edwards's *Introduction* came into Spencer's hands in the fall of 1851. G. H. Lewes had brought the book with him when the two friends went for a walk in Kent, and in it, says Spencer, "for the first time I met with the expression—'the physiological division of labour.' " Spencer adds that the concept was not new to him—he had in fact already written of society as developing from simplicity to complexity, and from independent like parts to mutually dependent unlike parts—but the manner of its formulation was. Spencer was much taken with the phrase, as, shortly thereafter, he was with the German embryologist Karl Ernst von Baer's formula for development—the change from the general to the special, or from homogeneity to heterogeneity. The greater generality of von Baer's formulation enabled Spencer to extend the concept to inorganic as well as organic phenomena. Taken together, this cluster of images gave focus to the vague evolutionary speculation taking shape in the mind of the "English Aristotle."[3]

Charles Darwin had a parallel experience at about the same time as Spencer's while he was reflecting on how species characters diverge in the course of evolution. He reread Milne-Edwards in 1852 and found that ideas he had already been entertaining now fell into place. Thenceforward, Darwin attributed his theory of divergence to the inspiration of the French scientist, even though he certainly owed a large debt to the English political economists as well.[4]

Darwin, Spencer, and Political Economy

Why were Darwin and Spencer so reticent about their ties to political economy? For both men, the natural sciences were far better guides to reality than were the social sciences—more empirical, more reliable, less speculative. In a real sense they were the most fundamental branches of knowledge, the sources whence all other branches flowed. Darwin held that political economy was a kind of subsection of evolutionary biology, "whose empirical laws were eventually to be explained by biological principles." Spencer's case is even more striking. As a cosmic philosopher Spencer was, after all, committed, in a way Darwin was not, to working out the fundamental principles underlying reality—"those highest generalizations now being disclosed by science which are severally true not of one class of phenomena but of *all* classes of phenomena." He genuinely believed that knowledge was strictly hierarchical— that as biology built on the foundation provided by physics, so the social sciences built on biology. Spencer therefore was powerfully motivated to utilize biological ideas in writing about society, and any reader of his *Principles of Sociology* can attest to the thoroughness with which he did so.[5]

There is more to the question than epistemology, however. In the case of Darwin, Silvan Schweber has offered insight into the complex linkage in his work between biological and social thought. Neither Darwin nor Spencer needed Henri Milne-Edwards to teach him about the division of labor. Darwin was familiar with Utilitarianism from his study of Paley at Cambridge and from his reading of other Utilitarian tracts during the years 1838–1840. He knew the work of Adam Smith as well, perhaps from encountering it while a student at the University of Edinburgh, and certainly as it was mediated through J. R. McCulloch's *Political Economy* (1830) and from conversations with his wife's uncle, Jean Charles Léonard Simonde de Sismondi, an eminent Swiss economist. McCulloch had expounded enthusiastically and at some length the advantages of the division of labor for industry: it increased the skill and dexterity of the workers; it saved time; and it encouraged development of further labor-saving machinery and techniques. Yet another source of the concept for Darwin was Charles Babbage's *On the Economy of Machinery and Manufactures* (1832), which identified the division of labor as "perhaps the most important principle on which the economy of manufacture depends."[6]

The concept, however, was not value-free. Utilitarianism "had a decidedly political flavor," and Adam Smith certainly believed that the division of labor was both competitively advantageous and socially beneficent. Others, of whom the most famous is Karl Marx, expressed emphatic dissent. Sismondi argued that the division of labor caused the workers to suffer: "man loses mental and bodily vigour, health, cheerfulness, all that renders life desirable."[7]

Sensitive to the partisan import of political economy, Darwin wished to keep biology free from ideology. Or it may be that he wished to cloak the ideology that inevitably clung to the concept in the respectable garb of science. Such appears to be the implication of Schweber's observation, "I do not doubt that when he [Darwin] adopted the maximum-minimum formulation of the Utilitarians and Adam Smith's insight into the competitive advantage of the division of labor, Darwin was aware that he was 'biologizing' the explanations political economy gave for the dynamics of the wealth of nations." It appears that Darwin was not neutral on the merit of the division of labor (he termed Sismondi's dissenting view "poor"), but preferred to legitimize and "decontaminate" the concept by locating its source in biology.[8]

Essentially the same considerations motivated Spencer's heavy reliance on Milne-Edwards and von Baer. Tracing the lineage of a concept to biology rather than to political economy satisfied his taste for ultimate principles while it removed any ideological taint or personal political bias. The entire organic world testified to the wonders of specialization. Spencer was but a transcriber of demonstrable law.[9]

Biologists traced the growth of structural differentiation and specialization in the organic economy from the lowliest single-celled organism to lordly Man. Milne-Edwards explained:

> [As] one rises in the series of beings, as one comes nearer to man, one sees organisms becoming more complicated; the body of each animal becomes composed of parts which are more and more dissimilar to one another, as much in their morphology, form and structure, as in their functions; and the life of the individual results from the competition of an ever greater number of "instruments" endowed with different faculties. At first it is the same organ that smells, that moves, that absorbs from the environment the needed nutrients and that guarantees the conservation of the species; but little-by-little the diverse functions localize themselves, and they all acquire instruments that are proper to themselves. Thus, the more the life of an animal becomes involved in a variety of phenomena, and the more its faculties are delineated, or the higher the degree to which division of labor is carried out in the interior of the organism, the more its structure is complicated.[10]

Whereas the organs and cells of a highly specialized animal or plant performed "definite, restricted functions exactly and efficiently," noted W. K. Brooks, each part of a low organism "fills many offices, but fills them all imperfectly." The animal, in other words, resembled a workshop in miniature, and the organs were the workers, each with a particular function to perform at which it was expert. In the single-celled organism one workman, in effect, produced the whole. The unicellular economy was a primitive, Robinson Crusoe affair. In the highly developed organism, by contrast, division of labor effected the manufacture of the finished product (the functioning organism) better and more efficiently by parceling out the work among many workers each skilled in one operation.[11]

One aspect of organisms that lent itself particularly well to this kind of analysis was reproduction. Reproductive mechanisms manifested a striking evolutionary progression from asexuality through hermaphroditism and parthenogenesis (which the authors of *The Evolution of Sex* labeled "degenerate sexual reproduction") to division into two sexes and a higher and higher degree of sexual dimorphism. Nothing could more clearly illustrate the law of increasing specialization and division of labor: "Among the humbler groups of the animal kingdom the whole reproductive task is performed by all members of the species. In other words hermaphroditism prevails. As we ascend to higher groups the sexes are separate, and the species becomes dimorphous . . . Among vertebrates, and especially in mankind, the function of the female sex seems limited to nurture—intra- and extra-uterine—of the young." The ungallant but safely anonymous author of this passage went on to conclude, "Were men immortal and nonreproductive, woman's *raison d'être* would disappear."[12]

What made the union of two separate and distinct sexes a higher form of reproduction than asexual reproduction or sexual variants like hermaphroditism and parthenogenesis? These latter forms had after all managed to perpetuate their species quite as well as the more familiar form of sexual mating. The specific utility of uniting two sexes was still something of a mystery to late-nineteenth-century science. Patrick Geddes and J. Arthur Thomson, in their compendium *The Evolution of Sex,* noted that some scientists, including Francis Galton, believed that fertilization imparted new vigor to a species, since asexual multiplication was liable to end in degeneration or death. August Weismann and W. K. Brooks preferred to stress the mingling of male and female elements as a source of variation, and this thesis was winning general acceptance.

Beyond biological utility, sexual union had enormous psychological and ethical import. As Geddes and Thomson wrote, "the vague sexual attraction of the lowest organisms has been evolved into a definite reproductive impulse . . . this again, enhanced by more and more subtle psychical additions passes by a gentle gradient into the love of the highest animals, and of the average human individual." Because of that love, a man labored for a lifetime not out of self-interest but for his mate, and she in turn labored at home for him and for her little ones. The two sexes were complementary and mutually dependent. Sex complementarity marked the triumph of evolution: "Virtually asexual organisms, like Bacteria, occupy no high place in Nature's role of honour; virtually unisexual organisms, like many rotifers, are great rarities. Parthenogenesis may be an organic ideal, but it is one which has been rarely realised. Males and females, like the sex-elements, are mutually dependent."[13]

So persuaded, Geddes and Thomson drew from their study of sexuality the happy lesson that competition and survival of the fittest did not tell the whole evolutionary story, nor should they be considered the essential mechanism of progress, "as economist and biologist have too long misled each other into doing." Rather, what shone forth from the history of reproductive sexuality was love and cooperation and self-sacrifice. These, the true heart of evolution, offered a distinctly non-Darwinian moral: "'creation's final law' is not struggle but love."[14]

Herbert Spencer: The Social Division of Labor

Geddes and Thomson's ennobling gloss on the sexual facts of life suggests a yearning to read out of biology some gentler social lesson than Darwinian (or Hobbesian) strife. For this purpose the concept of division of labor had much to offer. There can be little doubt that the vision of organic harmony and cooperation based on that concept exerted an enormous attraction on social theorists. Herbert Spencer, according to historian J. W. Burrow, looked forward to the ultimate establishment of a kind of renewed state of nature, a perfect industrial society in which all conflict had ceased and the state had withered away. Only the essential bonds of a perfected humanity continued to hold society together—and these, so Spencer fervently believed, were natural sympathy and the division of labor.[15]

Spencer founded his sociology on biology; it was really a social extension of biological principles. He was wont to refer to social development as "super-organic evolution," and as a social theorist he is perhaps best remembered for his extended analogy between society and the biological organism. It is clear that Spencer considered division of labor the linchpin of the social, as of the biological, organism: "This division of labour . . . is that which in the society, as in the animal, makes it a living whole." Division of labor implied two processes that Spencer called differentiation and integration, in other words, specialization and cooperation. As division of labor increased, "the agencies of different social actions while becoming in one respect more distinct, become in another respect more mutually ramified through each other." Greater differentiation led to greater integration, which in turn furthered still more differentiation. Thus an exchange of commodities initiated because localities varied in their capacity to produce different goods would lead to improved transportation, which would facilitate more trade, thus generating further improvements in production, and so on.[16]

Spencer had no doubt that the degree of division of labor was a measure of social worth. In this he was fully warranted by biologists' routine use of evaluative terms like *lower, higher, greater perfectibility, harmonious interaction,* and so on. At times Spencer's conviction about the virtue of complexity was merely amusing, as when, in a discussion of language, he remarked that "it is more especially in virtue of having carried this subdivision of function to a greater extent and completeness, that the English language is superior to all others." At other times his judgments were more blatantly offensive, as when he commented that the civilized European departed further from the "vertebrate archetype," thanks to his greater differentiation, than did the savage: the Papuan, for example, had small legs not very different from his arms, thereby resembling the quadrumana, whose fore and hind limbs were similar. That the European's leg was longer and more massive than his arm meant that he had evolved further from the animal kingdom than the Papuan had. Spencer actually arranged human societies on a scale analogous to the forms of organic life, beginning with the Bushmen, who, like the Protozoa, lived like clusters of similar cells without any division of labor, and continuing through savages with some minimal differentiation at least in government (these resembled the Polyp), to those slightly higher primitive societies akin to the Hydra in which many functions continued to be performed in common, arriving eventually at the fully differentiated societies of western civilization.[17]

Division of labor also civilized the emotions. The more people worked together and relied on one another, the more sympathetic and loving they became. A social life marked by "abstinence from aggressive actions and a performance of those mutually-serviceable actions implied by the division of labour" encouraged "development of those gentle emotions of which inferior races exhibit but the rudiments. Savages delight in giving pain rather than pleasure—are almost devoid of sympathy." Clearly simplicity, versatility, and self-sufficiency compared poorly in Spencer's opinion to complexity, specialization, and interdependence. No contriving Robinson Crusoe, no isolated self-reliant pioneer, would ever be the cultural hero of a Spencerian utopia.[18]

Spencer indeed was sublimely uninterested in individual human beings. It is odd that this should be so. He has come down to us as perhaps the arch-individualist, so concerned with championing the individual against the encroachment of the state that he doubted the wisdom of municipal (as opposed to privately operated) sewer systems. Repeatedly he asserted the primacy of the individual over society: "Society exists for the benefit of its members; not its members for the benefit of society." Society could in fact be known only "by enquiring into the nature of its component individuals." Yet Spencer had little sense of individuals as historical actors influencing the course of events, and was at pains to debunk the "Great Man Theory of History." In his sociology individuals remain abstractions, the essential stuff of society yet hardly creatures of flesh and blood. His eyes fixed steadily on the cosmos, he inhabited an intellectual universe of systems and processes, into which the individual entered not in his or her own right but only as part of a larger social aggregate.[19]

This indifference to persons helps explain why emotion plays so little part in the great sweep of Spencerian social evolution. Even supposing the path of social progress to have been overwhelmingly beneficial, one looks almost in vain for any sign that progress might exact losses as well as gains, or that some individuals might suffer even as others prospered. The cries of those sacrificed on the altar of progress (colonialized primitives, for example, or women in gilded cages) failed to penetrate the aura of bland satisfaction in which Spencer's cosmic process unfolded. He was not alone in this satisfaction, it should be said. One of the most fervent tributes to the social division of labor was offered by the physiologist William B. Carpenter, who described "the most developed form of the Social State" as one in which everyone found just the work "for which he is best fitted, and in which he may reach the highest attainable perfection." This condition occurred when specialization and mutual dependence reached a maximum, and "every individual works for the benefit of all his fellows, as well as for his own." Only in such a society did "the greatest triumphs of human ability become possible."[20]

Neither in Carpenter nor in Spencer is there a whisper of concern at the possibility, so apparent to Marx, that greater and greater division of labor, far from always conferring social benefits, might alienate the worker from his work and further social inequality. Yet the latter outcome, at least, was a direct conclusion of Spencer's own analysis. These unexamined ambiguities surface with particular clarity in relation to sex. If increased differentiation was a clear social advance, then its first appearance in human society should have been a positive step. Yet we read in Spencer that the first division of labor led directly to a class division between masters and slaves. At a time when society was still primitive, only "a homogeneous aggregate of individuals having like powers and like functions," it was sex that provided the basis for the most elementary form of task division. Men's greater physical strength allowed them to coerce women into doing society's drudge work, and the only limit on the brutality to which they subjected their women was the latter's "inability to live and propagate under greater." This, then, was the primal phase of social progress: "The slave-class in a primitive society consists of the women; and the earliest division of labour is that which arises between them and their masters." Spencer's account has the virtues of forthrightness and clarity, but it certainly does not provide women with much cause for cheering evolution on.[21]

The Evolutionary Status of Women

Similar difficulties arise elsewhere in Spencer's discussion of women. Starting out from the principle that "diversity of relations to surrounding actions initiates diversity of social relations," Spencer pointed out that where women shared food procurement with their men, as among the Clatsop and Chinook Indians who lived on fish and roots, or where they fought as warriors side by side with the men, as in Dahomey, they enjoyed extraordinary prestige and influence. Where, on the contrary, men monopolized war and the chase, while women were restricted exclusively to gathering food and carrying burdens, the women were "abject slaves." Spencer inferred from this information that social status and political influence were more evenly divided between the sexes when men and women shared pursuits in common, rather than when they specialized according to sex. Shared pursuits were a historic aberration, however. Normally sex specialization held sway: "Men and women being by the unlikeness of their functions in life, exposed to unlike influences, begin from the first to assume unlike positions in the community as they do in the family." To the extent, in other words, that women's work differed from men's, women found themselves a subject sex. Again, women might find the siren song of advancing division of labor something less than irresistible.[22]

In America as in Europe gender specialization was the rule. Indeed it was all the more striking in a society which gave such free rein to its maidens to observe their domestic sequestration as matrons. Alexis de Tocqueville, that shrewd observer of American mores in the early nineteenth century, found the contrast between the freedom of the young American girl and her subsequent confinement once wed perhaps the most striking difference between European and American gender relations. In America, as nowhere else, had society taken the lesson of Adam Smith to heart:

> [Americans] think that nature, which created such differences between the physical and moral constitution of men and women, clearly intended to give their diverse faculties a diverse employment; and they consider that progress consists not in making dissimilar creatures do roughly the same things but in giving both the chance to do their job as well as possible. The Americans have applied to the sexes the great principle of political economy which now dominates industry. They have carefully separated the functions of man and of woman so that the great work of society may be performed.[23]

In this living laboratory of sexual specialization Herbert Spencer's American heir, the tough-minded Yale sociologist William Graham Sumner, and his younger colleague, Albert Galloway Keller, carried forward the Spencerian analysis in a massive collaborative work entitled *The Science of Society*. In earliest times, they wrote, men needed the help of women simply to get enough to eat. Gradually, as they obtained a steadier food supply through better techniques of hunting and herding, men no longer needed women's help, and the latter, once cooperators, were reduced to the status of slaves. Sex specialization led naturally to slavery. For Sumner and Keller, however, slavery posed no insuperable moral issues, since social equality was not an unequivocal social good. Indeed, "inequality is the very precondition of organization and progressive adjustment." Male domination was in any case a law of nature, and the two Yale professors suggested that those who felt it unfair should lodge their protest with the creator of human bisexuality.[24]

The ostensibly scientific and objective urbanity of Sumner and Keller is nowhere more evident than in their conclusions about women's status over time. Nothing was to be regretted, nothing deplored: "when it was expedient for society that woman should get rights, she got them, and without agitation, just as children did." Expedience was the key to their interpretation; always throughout social evolution the sexual division of labor represented an "expedient adjustment," although the authors were willing to admit that it may at times have been "repellent to cultured taste." *The Science of Society* provides food for thought about the evolutionary progress of the discipline of sociology from Spencer to Sumner. Under the banner of Darwinian adjustment Sumner and Keller were able to discount any humane qualms about the ruthless treatment of weak or disadvantaged social groups in times past. Whatever happened was written in the mores. Qué será, será. Yet even Spencer, caught up as he was in the vision of advancing social perfection, held to definite standards of societal good and was at least sporadically aroused by moral issues. He loathed militarism, for example, and was convinced that society was evolving away from militarism toward the peaceful industrial state. In addition he clearly deplored brutality in the treatment of women. "In the history of humanity as written," he lamented, "the saddest part concerns the treatment of women, and had we before us the unwritten history we should find this part still sadder." It is open to question whether Sumner and Keller's twentieth-century scientific objectivity is to be preferred to Spencer's Victorian sentimentality when it comes to sensitive social judgment.[25]

Spencer's view of primitive women as degraded and servile

expressed the general consensus of Victorian social theorists about the "barbarian status of women" (a view, it should be noted, to which iconoclastic thinkers like Marx and Engels and Thorstein Veblen took strong exception). Primitive women, it was assumed, were oppressed to the degree that they were made to labor, and since their tasks were constant and onerous, their degradation was profound. Arrogating to themselves the strenuous but intermittent and prestigious pursuits of war and the hunt, barbarian males had time in the intervals between these endeavors to take their ease beside the village campfire. Their women, meanwhile, carried all the burdens, gathered the food, cultivated the crops, tended the fires, cooked the meals, made the clothing, and cared for the children. Downtrodden and reviled, they occupied a secondary and shadowy status bereft of authority or influence in their families (where indeed they might be only one of several wives) and in society at large. Life for the primitive woman, from the perspective of the gentleman anthropologist, appeared unrelievedly dismal.

It is true that women have been rudely treated in some tribal societies, that they have appeared to do more than their fair share of the communal labor, that among some cultures they have been barred from exercising power, and that they have, indeed, led unenviable lives. But this is so far from being the universal pattern, and so far from being the whole truth even in most of the societies that appear to treat their women badly, that the question arises how nineteenth-century theorists could have gotten things so wrong. The answer, unsurprisingly, is that they could not see through the veil of their preconceptions. As E. E. Evans-Pritchard nicely puts it, "Liberals and rationalists, they believed above all in progress, the kind of material, political, social, and philosophical changes which were taking place in Victorian England . . . Consequently the explanations of social institutions they put forward amount, when examined, to little more than hypothetical scales of progress, at one end of which were placed forms of institutions or beliefs as they were in nineteenth-century Europe and America, while at the other end were placed their antithesis." With the possible exception of sexual laxity, female labor represented the most striking difference in gender relations between savage societies and their own. Savage women toiled; civilized women did not. It was self-evident, therefore, that the path of progress for the feminine half of humankind involved an increasing emancipation from productive labor. Children, the family, and all of society benefited from a sexual division of labor by virtue of which men provided the family bread and women provided its love and nurturance.[26]

Guglielmo Ferrero, son-in-law of the criminal anthropologist Cesare Lombroso, elevated this exemption of women from labor into what he termed the "Law of Non-Labor," the essential condition of feminine existence. Biologists, he pointed out, had found that in the animal kingdom the female who lacked help and sustenance from a male was forced to accomplish the work of reproduction at top speed and then quickly die. Here was a lesson for the human species: "the physiological prosperity of species depends on the division of labor between the sexes, for in exact ratio to this is the duration of life." Hence the slave labor of primitive women was a "very dangerous aberration," and women's work in civilized countries, while less arduous than that of primitive women, was still deleterious to society, throwing men out of work, endangering women's health, and lessening their grace.[27]

Divergence and Complementarity

Nature signaled the appropriateness of separate functions for the sexes in the appearance and function of the sex cells themselves. We have seen that Geddes and Thomson found significance in the relative size and motility of the sperm and egg cells. W. K. Brooks argued that such differences in size and form betokened a difference in role. The female sex cell transmitted the legacy of the past, the established hereditary features of the species. As the repository of "the conservative element in reproduction," it ensured race stability. The male sex cell, harbinger of change, stored up variations and transmitted them to the next generation, providing the basis for race progress. Secondary sex characteristics became increasingly conspicuous in the evolution from simpler to higher forms of life, and in the parallel evolution from lower to higher races of humanity. "The tendency of evolution is to make man more and more manly and woman more and more womanly," wrote Joseph Le-Conte in an unpublished manuscript. Theorists believed men and women were more nearly alike mentally and physically among primitive cultures where everyone worked. As the two sexes developed specialized functions over time, they lost that uniformity: "The continued devotion of the sexes to separate functions in the social organism has been followed by their better adaptation to those functions and their increasingly greater difference of structural characters. Thus the sexes have become more and more useful, and more and more interesting to each other."[28]

This increasing divergence was tangible. It appeared in the skeletal measurements made by Broca and other anthropologists, and more importantly in their cranial measurements. According to Broca, "the superiority of the man's cranial capacity is fifty per cent. more among the French in general, and a hundred and twenty-one per cent. more among the Parisians, than it was in the Cro-Magnon race." Broca's colleague Gustave Le Bon found that the difference in average cranial capacity of modern Parisian men and women amounted to nearly double the difference between the male and female skulls of ancient Egypt. So also "it is easy to observe in our cities how much more the men differ from the women among the richer than among the poorer classes."[29]

Modern readers may well be struck by the unconscious class bias of these visions of social evolution. Even as the scientists wrote, thousands of women in England, on the Continent, and in America were productive workers in factories and on farms. To be sure, the conditions of their labor were often exploitative, yet the reality of these women's lives went largely unacknowledged in evolutionary social theory. In fact, the productive role of primitive women was not so far removed from that of a great many contemporary rural women in the advanced western societies. E. E. Evans-Pritchard shrewdly notes that the Victorian anthropologists judged the status of savage women from their perspective as middle-class gentlemen, using as their benchmark not "the agricultural and industrial laborer's wife and daughter but their own mothers and sisters." Had they consulted statistics, they would have discovered that, far from diminishing, the numbers of gainfully employed women were expanding by the year, and there was no sign that this trend would be reversed. In light of that hard fact, any theory that identified the course of human evolution with the removal of women from the workplace was clearly more prescriptive than descriptive.[30]

However tenuous the fit of their conclusions with social reality, Victorian scientists drew from their scrutiny of nature's ways an unambiguous moral: the sexes were meant to be complementary, not competitive. Each sex had a distinctive function for which it was best suited, neither could prosper alone, and social harmony as well as social progress were best served when the boundaries that separated their respective domains were observed. A few, but only a few, scientists described the distinctive missions of the two sexes quite bluntly in terms of superiority and inferiority. Delauney, for example, believed that species evolution moved in all cases from female supremacy through sexual equality to male supremacy. Female superiority, he argued, characterized inferior species and races and children of the higher races. Equality of the sexes reigned among races and species a bit more advanced, as well as "youth, aged persons, and the lower classes." Evolution reached its apex in "the pre-eminence of the male over the female" that was typical of "superior species and races, the adult age, and the higher classes."[31]

Delauney's straightforward inegalitarianism did not, however, set the fashion for most discussions of the sexual division of labor. The majority of scientists preferred to exalt the beauties of complementarity. There was grandeur in their vision of a "cooperation of dissimilars" leading to "a united effort for the improvement of the mass." All members of society benefited when each man and each woman filled "his or her special niche." They benefited economically, to be sure ("The jack-of-all-trades is proverbially master of none"), but more important, they benefited morally, growing in intersexual sympathy and respect. Complementarity extended dignity to both sexes, and avoided individious sexual ranking. That was one of its most attractive features; it circumvented altogether the need to dwell on feminine incapacity, something that a Victorian gentleman-scientist might find distasteful. Here there was no question of better or worse. As Brooks suggested, "The sexes do not naturally stand in the relation of superior and inferior, nor in that of independent equals, but are the complemental parts of a compound whole." The goal of social policy should be to play up sexual differences and to sharpen the separation of sexual functions. "We should cultivate the difference of the sexes, not try to hide or abolish it," urged Edward H. Clarke, continuing the argument he had begun in *Sex in Education*. "The best quality, noblest power, and supreme beauty of the two sexes, grows out of their dissimilarity, not out of their identity."[32]

What this meant in practice with reference to higher education is suggested in the work of Brooks and G. Stanley Hall. The retentiveness of the feminine mind, Brooks believed, fitted it for an education in general culture, while the originality of the masculine mind adapted it to a more intensive, technical training. It is not easy to be precise about Brooks's interesting bifurcation of knowledge into culture and technical training because his exposition is exceedingly vague, but the gist of the argument is sufficiently clear: women were to assimilate the intellectual progress of past generations, men were to forge the intellectual progress of their own time. The distinction seems to be not so much between disciplines as between levels of understanding—the broad general familiarity of the educated layperson versus the detailed familiarity of the expert. Culture was

> thorough acquaintance with all the old and new results of intellectual activity in all departments of knowledge, so far as they conduce to welfare, to correct living, and to rational conduct . . . Culture is concerned only with results, not with demonstrations, and it does not look to new advances; while technical training is concerned with methods and proofs; and it values the results of the methods and investigations of the past only as they contribute to new advances . . . By culture we hold our own, and by technical training we advance to higher levels.[33]

Women, it was evident, ought to beware of competing with men. Although the male mind reached an apex in those men with ability "to pursue original trains of abstract thought, to reach the great generalizations of science, and to give rise to the new creations of poetry and art," even ordinary men were gifted with some powers of generalization from new experience that gave them an edge over women in professions "where competition is closest, and where marked success depends upon the union of the knowledge and skill shared by competitors, to the inventiveness or originality necessary to gain the advantage over them." Women would be well advised to lead from their strengths, seeking out occupations "where ready tact and versatility are of more importance than the

narrow technical skill which comes from apprenticeship or training, and where success does not involve competition with rivals."[34]

Taking his cue from Brooks, Hall issued a plea to the leaders of
women's education to remain true to the special genius of femininity and take a stand against "premature specialization" in higher
education. Young women needed above all a truly humanistic
education. So too did young men, who, however, eventually
passed beyond the humanistic stage to that of "expertness and
specialization without which their individuality is incomplete."[35]

Hall liked to imagine that his educational prescription laid to rest
old shibboleths about men's dislike of intellect in women and
women's demand for intellectual superiority in husbands. Nature
taught interdependence in marriage, the technical expertise of the
man giving him leadership in certain areas, the woman's appreciation of culture allowing her to humanize her mate:

> In his chosen line he would lead and be authoritative and rarely seeks
> partnership in it in marriage. This is no subjection, but woman
> instinctively respects and even reveres, and perhaps educated woman
> is coming to demand, it in the man of her whole-hearted choice. This
> granted, man was never more plastic to woman's great work of
> creating in him all the wide range of secondary sex qualities which
> constitute his essential manhood.

Hall summed up the ideal relationship between the sexes in the
highly educated classes in an appropriately educational simile: "The
relation of the academically trained sexes is faintly typified by that
of the ideal college to ideal university, professional or technical
school." Woman was to man as Vassar was to Harvard.[36]

Women and Work

Clear as nature's message appeared to the biologists, it was undeniably under attack by some disgruntled women. Herbert Spencer
professed bewilderment at this: "When we remember that up from
the lowest savagery, civilization has, among other results, caused
an increasing exemption of women from bread-winning labour,
and that in the highest societies they have become most restricted to
domestic duties and the rearing of children; we may be struck by the
anomaly that in our days restriction to indoor occupations has come

to be regarded as a grievance, and a claim is made to free competition with men in all outdoor occupations." Spencer could only suppose that women's restiveness arose from a failure of understanding: "If women comprehended all that is contained in the domestic sphere, they would ask no other." Other experts sounded a darker note. Women who sought to work and to vote were promoting "*anti-differentiation*—if we may use the expression," and moving society "a step backwards toward savagery." The old reciprocal solidarity of the sexes was being replaced by an "intersexual competition for subsistence" with its "complexly ruinous results" for both sexes and for family life. G. Stanley Hall begged that woman's soul not be "sown with the tares of ambition or fired by intersexual competition." Paraphrasing British neurologist Sir James Crichton-Browne, Hall observed of the sexes, "In union they are strong; in competition mutually destructive." And in a curious and rather obscure passage comparing "the New Woman . . . who has gone out to labour in the world" to the worker bee, Geddes and Thomson warned dourly that such women "have highly developed brains, but most of them die young."[37]

From a modern perspective it is easier to understand women's perverse refusal to accede to the Victorian division of labor than to understand why, given what they themselves had written, social theorists assumed that they would do so. If the sexual division of labor had originally condemned women to a life of servitude, what reason had women to suppose that the selfsame division of labor would in modern times become their salvation? Spencer's treatment of the issue appears inconsistent not only with logic but also with the very evidence that he himself provided that women fared better when they worked side by side with men. A few of the fiercer scientific spirits of Spencer's day, those who most insistently affirmed female inferiority, obviated this inconsistency by an open espousal of inequality. The French writer G. Delauney, we have seen, traced social evolution from an original condition of female superiority to a future condition of male superiority. Far from minimizing the disparity in status between the sexes, civilization and education increased it: "The equality of the sexes dreamed of by the philosophers is, then, not near being realized . . . The pre-eminence of men over women . . . is rather increased by instruction, the effect of which . . . is to assure definitively the supremacy of man." The same triumphalism pervaded the pages of the *Anthropological Review,* which linked women and blacks as lesser participants in the grand march of civilization and hailed inequality as the direct result of specialization and division of labor. A social caste system represented "the predominance of the more over the less morally and intellectually gifted members of a community." Caste, one anthropologist mused, might even be construed in Darwinian terms as a transmissible variety, "preparing to become a species, and perhaps ultimately even a genus!"[38]

But this frank avowal of hereditary caste was a fringe phenomenon, certainly not palatable to Spencer and the writers who took their sociological cues from him. One of the hallmarks of Spencerian social science was a marked distaste for societies of hereditary rank and fixed social status. Spencer and Sumner were prominent among those social theorists who called favorable attention to the shift in social organization from status to contract, from ties of birth, rank, and guild that "endured as long as life lasted" to ties of contractual agreement based on reason and enduring "only so long as the reason for [them] endures." Modern society, in this analysis, had no place for a caste system that established a permanent status hierarchy. But if forthright approval of caste was withheld by any but the most intransigent conservators of traditional status distinctions, how to deal with the inferential link between division of labor and inequality? One way was simply to ignore it, as Spencer was wont to do, by reveling in the benefits of diversity and specialization for the system as a whole, and not looking closely at its effects on individuals. Another way was to emphasize that whatever niche an individual might occupy in the industrial system, it was after all the result of the person's free choice. In medieval society the accident of birth had determined one's adult role, but that was no longer the case. Modern societies provided an ever-increasing number of vocational options among which individuals were at liberty to choose on the basis of their aptitudes and tastes. The physiologist William B. Carpenter, it will be remembered, extolled the society based on division of labor as one in which "every individual finds the work—mental or bodily—for which he is best fitted, and in which he may reach the highest attainable perfection."[39]

Here an obvious discrepancy arises in the case of women, for it could hardly be argued that all women had freely chosen marriage and maternity or, indeed, that all could attain them even if they had. The very existence of a literature exhorting women to renounce worldly ambition testifies to their unwillingness en masse to do so and confirms their exclusion from the cheerful scenario of freely selected labor conjured up by Carpenter. The hard truth is that the sexual division of labor did not operate on the basis of freedom of choice, and efforts to make it appear as if it did were by the late nineteenth century foundering on women's refusal to accede to the myth any longer.

Charlotte Perkins Gilman Rides the "Friendly Force of Evolution"

Yet the division of labor, artfully interpreted, held out to women not merely a positive but a downright revolutionary potential. The individual who demonstrated this potential and, in the process, turned the use of the principle upside down, was Charlotte Perkins Gilman. As much as Herbert Spencer, Gilman gloried in the organization of the modern economic system: "By the division of labor and its increasing specialisation we vastly multiply skill and power . . . The solitary savage knew neither specialisation nor organisation—he 'did his own work.' This process gives the maximum of effort and the minimum of results. Specialised and organised industry gives the minimum of effort and the maximum of results. That is civilised industry." But civilized industry, triumphant everywhere else, had not yet penetrated that bastion of conservatism, that "little ganglion of aborted economic processes," the home. Gilman could hardly control her indignation at the primitive level of household labor: "Just consider what any human business would be in which there was no faintest possibility of choice, of exceptional ability, of division of labor. What would shoes be like if every man made his own, if the shoemaker had never come to his development? What would houses be like if every man made his own? Or hats, or books, or waggons [*sic*]? To confine any industry to the level of the universal average is to strangle it in its cradle. And there, forever, lie the industries of the housewife."[40]

In *Women and Economics* (1898), Gilman pointed to the obvious solution: the professionalization of housework and child care. The harried housewife, Jill-of-all-trades and expert in none, would give over her manifold tasks into the trained and competent hands of a bevy of specialists—cooks, cleaners, launderers, child nurses. Each specialist would do one thing well, rather than all things poorly, at a great saving of time and human energy: "where now twenty women in twenty homes work all the time, and insufficiently accomplish their varied duties, the same work in the hands of specialists could be done in less time by fewer people; and the others would be left free to do other work for which they were better fitted, thus increasing the productive power of the world." Perhaps the most arresting passage in this arresting book depicted Gilman's vision of the ideal urban home of the future:

> if there should be built and opened in any of our large cities today a commodious and well-served apartment house for professional women with families, it would be filled at once. The apartments would be without kitchens; but there would be a kitchen belonging to the house from which meals could be served to the families in their rooms or in a common dining-room, as preferred. It would be a home where the cleaning was done by efficient workers, not hired separately by the families, but engaged by the manager of the establishment; and a roof-garden, day nursery, and kindergarten, under well-trained professional nurses and teachers, would insure proper care of the children.[41]

It is tempting to imagine the elderly Herbert Spencer reading these words (in reality he would never have done so; he made it a principle not to read books with which he disagreed). Surely he would have exclaimed that such a bold break with Victorian domesticity was not a legitimate inference from his beloved division of labor. And yet of course it was. Gilman had merely taken that principle to its logical conclusion by applying it to the one area of labor that had yet to be touched by modernization—women's work in the home. In so doing she categorically denied that all women were suited to the same kind of work, or that human welfare required the sacrifice of women's individuality. On the contrary, she claimed for women that emancipation from hereditary status which would permit them entry into the modern system of free contractual choice.

The division of labor, Gilman knew, was never applied to men as a class, but rather to individual men—some of whom would be tinkers, others tailors, and still others merchants and financiers. Why then should it apply to women as a class? Gilman had no desire to ignore the fact that women bore the children—indeed she celebrated maternity—but she vehemently resisted the notion that bearing babies was all a woman could do. Insisting that women, like men, be viewed as individuals rather than as one undifferentiated class meant, of course, making a complete break with the old sexual division of labor. Gilman was more than ready to let it go. In the misty beginnings of human evolution it had served a purpose, but now it was obsolete. Gilman flatly denied the biological determinism that saw constitutional differences between the sexes so profound ("A man is a man to his very thumbs and a woman is a woman down to her little toes") that they all but obscured their common humanity. It was not biology that drew exaggerated and unwholesome distinctions between boys and girls, men and women; it was society. And what society had done, society could undo.

Gilman held to a sublime evolutionary faith that human institutions responded, if at times tardily, to the needs of the particular moment. So endowed, she could afford to be confident about the role of women in the future, knowing that change had to come and would come: "This change is not a thing to prophesy and plead for. It is a change already instituted, and gaining ground among us these many years with marvellous rapidity . . . The time has come when it is better for the world that women be economically independent, and therefore they are becoming so."[42]

But if confidence in the "calm, slow, friendly forces of social evolution" is a hallmark of Gilman's work, it is noticeably absent from the work of the male social theorists from whom she dissented. The plaintive tone of much of the sociological literature suggests a concern rather incongruous in true believers in biology as destiny. Surely a division of labor that was given in nature should not have required so many exhortations to women to be mindful of it. The truth is that the concept failed in logic as in life. Those who used it to keep women in their place had always practiced a semantic sleight of hand: they applied it to men as individuals but to women as a group. This linguistic double standard signaled the intellectual weakness of the entire structure of argument and metaphor.[43]

Reality too was unkind to the concept. In the waning years of the nineteenth century a Spencerian tragedy was being enacted: a beautiful theory was being killed by an ugly fact.[44] Far from moving toward greater specialization by sex, society was moving toward role convergence. Far from respecting the sexual division of labor, women were breaching it in ever-increasing numbers. Time was on the side of Charlotte Perkins Gilman, not of Herbert Spencer. In the end, the sexual division of labor proved to be less an artifact of physiological reality than of human faith.

CHAPTER 6

The Victorian Paradigm Erodes

> There is perhaps no field aspiring to be scientific where flagrant personal bias, logic martyred in the cause of supporting a prejudice, unfounded assertions, and even sentimental rot and drivel, have run riot to such an extent as here.
>
> —Helen Thompson Woolley (1910)

> No man can quite emancipate himself from his age and country, or produce a model in which the education, the religion, the politics, usages, and arts, of his times shall have no share. Though he were never so original, never so willful and fantastic, he cannot wipe out of this work every trace of the thoughts amidst which it grew.
>
> —Ralph Waldo Emerson (1841)

This study originated in an observation and a question. The observation was that scientists in the late nineteenth and early twentieth centuries spoke with remarkable uniformity about the nature of womanhood and the differences between the sexes. The question was what body of evidence supported this striking agreement. The question posed itself because so little of the data we would consider germane existed at the time. Were we today to undertake an exhaustive study of gender differences in intellect and temperament, we would look at information supplied by genetics, endocrinology, and neurophysiology. We would examine the influence of heredity, the genetic and hormonal components of sex determination, and the effect of hormones, both pre- and postnatal, on intellect and personality formation. We would check for evidence of sex differences in the structure and function of the brain—in the synaptic connections among neurons in the hypothalamus, for example, or in hemispheric lateralization. We would consider what Freud and his successors have had to say about male and female psychosexual development, and what might be learned from comparative tests of intelligence and temperament. Yet with the exception of a neurophysiology that was in its infancy, not one of these disciplines, nor any of this information, was available to scientists in the late nineteenth century.

Empirical data on this topic began to be generated in the first decades of the twentieth century, and, as it did so, the nature of the scientific discourse on gender difference changed. The sciences themselves were in flux. Biology underwent rapid specialization governed by critical discoveries about heredity and reproduction and the nature of cellular structure. Psychology took the first steps toward establishing itself on an empirical basis. Sociology and anthropology proclaimed their independence of biology, and repudiated biological determinism. These developments directly affected the study of differences between the sexes.

At the turn of the century biology was becoming increasingly experimental, as evidenced in the flourishing of subspecialties such as embryology, genetics, cytology, and endocrinology. Much of the experimental work sought clues to that great enigma, still unsolved forty years after the *Origin of Species,* the mechanism of inheritance. The rediscovery of Mendel's work on inheritance in 1900 and the research of the Dutch botanist Hugo De Vries on mutation theory were the twin lodestars in the genetic firmament. The renowned physiologist Jacques Loeb noted in 1904 that "the work of Mendel and De Vries and their successors marked the beginning of a real theory of heredity and variation."[1]

Americans were responsible for much of the progress on the genetic frontier—men like Edmund B. Wilson and Thomas Hunt Morgan at Columbia and William E. Castle and Edward M. East at Harvard, together with their collaborators and students. This development signaled a geographic sea change in the life sciences—the emergence of American biology to international prominence. During these years scientists elaborated the chromosomal theory of heredity and established the gene as the unit of heredity. One highlight of this progress came with the strong evidence presented independently by Edmund Wilson and the Bryn Mawr geneticist Nettie Stevens in 1905 that the "accessory chromosome" first described fourteen years earlier actually determined sex.[2]

That same year in England Ernest Starling coined the term *hormone* for the chemical messengers manufactured in the ductless glands that control specific metabolic processes. Endocrinologists now joined the search for a fuller explanation of the mechanism of sex determination. Convinced that the geneticists did not have the complete answer, they found confirmation in a study by Frank Lillie that affirmed the existence of a powerful blood-borne chemical, the sex hormone, that directed the development of sex characters in the higher animals.[3]

By about 1920, then, the chromosomal theory of inheritance was accepted, as was the role played by the sex chromosome. Though hormonal control of normal sex determination was not at all understood, its existence was given credence by increasing numbers of embryologists and endocrinologists. This progress toward unraveling the mysteries of heredity and sex had enormous significance for the current theories about how and why the human sexes differed.

The Decline and Fall of Recapitulation

In the first place, the new experimentalism and the rise of Mendelian genetics undermined the foundations of recapitulation theory. The theory had been largely based on perceived connections, analogies, and the reconstruction of ancestral trees, but this kind of armchair natural history was no longer in fashion. More important, Mendelian genetics disproved the mechanism of recapitulation, terminal addition. According to the recapitulationists, evolution took place by the addition of new stages of development to the end of ancestral ontogenies, but genetics showed that all traits were governed by genes present in the animal from the moment of conception. Hence there was no reason to suppose that new traits would necessarily appear at the end of ontogenetic development; they could express themselves at any point. Evolutionary change occurs, we now know, not from something "added on" but from mutational substitution.[4]

Ontogenies are not caused by phylogenies, nor do they recapitulate them exactly. Gill slits in the human embryo do not necessarily testify to a common ancestry with the fishes; they may only be necessary precursors to the eustachian tube and inner ear canal, into which they eventually develop. There is, however, some relationship between the two structures. Jane Maienschein has argued for the validity of an updated biogenetic law that would define ontogeny as the product of heredity and adaptation to present conditions which reflects but does not recapitulate phylogeny. This new understanding of the relationship between ontogeny and phylogeny existed by 1908; she traces it to the work of six American embryologists at Woods Hole. It certainly informs the writing of a zoologist like Thomas H. Montgomery, Jr., at the University of Texas. In *The Analysis of Racial Descent in Animals* (1906), Montgomery flatly asserted that "the recapitulation hypothesis is scientifically untenable, and when there has been transmutation of species, the embryogeny, neither in whole nor in part, exactly parallels the racial history. The relation between the two is always that of an inexact parallelism."[5]

The fall of recapitulation meant that the conception of woman as midway between the child and the man, together with all those parallels among children, women, and savages beloved of nineteenth-century anthropology, was discredited. It is true that news of recapitulation's downfall did not immediately reach the world beyond the borders of embryology—G. Stanley Hall continued to fashion his imaginative myth of human development during these years—but the heyday of the creative analogizing that saw woman as child and as savage was clearly over.

Another theory put on the defensive by the new understanding of heredity was neo-Lamarckianism, with its conviction that acquired characteristics were transmissible. Challenges to the Lamarckian theory were not new by the turn of the century; they dated from Weismann's work in the 1880s and 1890s. But these views did not immediately prevail, in America least of all. Neo-Lamarckianism predominated among American scientists into the twentieth century, and was only gradually displaced thereafter. So strong was its identification with this country that its promulgators were known collectively as "the American school."[6]

Neo-Lamarckianism eventually crumbled before the onslaught of Mendelism and the chromosomal theory of heredity. In the face of accumulating evidence that heritable traits were passed on by way of the genes located on the chromosomes of the germ cells, the neo-Lamarckians could provide no good evidence that traits acquired in the lifetime of the parents reached the reproductive cells, nor any plausible mechanism by which they might do so. Never actually disproven, neo-Lamarckianism succumbed through failure of proof. The effect of its decline on the issue of sex differences was not, however, entirely clear-cut. On the one hand, it rendered less likely the hypothesis proposed by Darwin, among others, of the sex-entailed inheritance of mental traits. Darwin had surmised that male intelligence, sharpened in both the struggle for mates and the struggle for survival, descended in its enhanced form, as a kind of secondary sex characteristic, to male offspring alone. A similar conception governed the belief, widespread among anthropologists, that men and women were becoming more and more differentiated as civilization progressed. Differences between the sexes could accumulate over time only if traits descended from mothers to daughters and fathers to sons exclusively. But evidence that the father and mother each contributed exactly half of the genetic endowment of their children of both sexes called all such interpretations into question.

The psychologist Leta Stetter Hollingworth addressed precisely the possible utility, in a Darwinian sense, of differential intelligence in men and women when she wrote, "It might be supposed that natural selection would have evolved an intellectual (or unintellectual) type in women, which could find its complete natural satisfaction in the vocation of child-bearing and child-rearing." But this had not in fact taken place, because "no mental trait has ever been proved to be sex-limited in inheritance, or to exist as a secondary sex character. So far as we know, daughters inherit mental traits from fathers as well as from mothers, and sons inherit them from mothers as well as from fathers." Hollingworth added, a trifle sardonically, "Under such circumstances the law of natural selection can never become operative to solve the educational problems of women." She meant that biology in and of itself did not mandate and therefore could not be used to justify women's exclusion from intellectual pursuits.[7]

The discrediting of neo-Lamarckianism had, however, a less attractive implication for women. If acquired characteristics could not be inherited, then attempts to alter women's status by altering their environment—specifically, improving their education—in the expectation that daughters would benefit from the strengthened intellects of their mothers (Darwin's somewhat hesitant proposition) were doomed to futility. Neo-Lamarckianism's decline sharpened the distinction between innate biology and environment, making them seem mutually exclusive. Scientists were increasingly prone to stress the centrality of heredity in the making of personality and intelligence, and to emphasize their permanence rather than their amenability to change and development. Neo-Darwinism thus taught an ambivalent lesson. While it dispelled the notion that men and women were evolving in different directions, it also denied the hope of a shortcut to enhance feminine braininess through educating the maternal stock. In general, neo-Darwinism's fixation on biological endowment lent itself easily to an endorsement of the status quo and a hostility to environmental reform. Taken to an extreme, this attitude led to the eugenics movement of the 1910s and 1920s. Even short of that, it still fostered a complacency of caste based on irremediable biological difference and thus insensitive to the claims of marginal groups for intellectual equality.

Genetics and Endocrinology
Redefine the Lesser Man

The new information on sex determination also affected prevailing attitudes. The work of Darwin and Spencer and the physical anthropologists had reinforced what Helen Thompson Woolley called the "ancient idea" that the female was in essence an undeveloped male. Accordingly, when C. E. McClung suggested in 1902 that the accessory chromosome had some relation to sex, he simply assumed that it must make for maleness, since the male would surely have more chromosomes—being a more important production—than the female. Geneticists shortly discovered that if anything the opposite was true: in some lower organisms the female had one more chromosome than the male. In human beings, males and females had exactly the same number of chromosomes, but it took a larger sex chromosome to make a female than a male, the X chromosome being considerably more massive than the Y.[8]

This conception of the equivalence of the sexes was given a further boost by the work of the endocrinologists on sex hormones. Once again received wisdom assumed that masculinity would reveal itself in the possession of something extra—in this case, greater activity and chemical strength in the male hormone. And once again subsequent research established equality: male and female hormones were shown to be equally potent.[9]

Together, genetics and endocrinology made some of the headier nineteenth-century theories of sex difference no longer tenable. Woman was not a lesser man. She was not man arrested short of developmental perfection. She did not stand midway between the child and the man. Nor was sex a matter of metabolism: Geddes and Thomson's "exuberant maleness" failed as an explanation, and along with it the metaphor of sluggish egg and sportive sperm. The reality was less one-sided if also less colorful.

Physiology's iron dominion over the female mind waned, too, as researchers learned more about the female reproductive system—specifically, the tax menstruation exacted of the body—and about the energy resources of the human nervous system. As Mary Putnam Jacobi had been the first in 1891 to challenge the medical conviction that women were periodically disabled by menstruation, so her intellectual heirs, Clelia Duel Mosher and Leta Stetter Hollingworth, subjected that conviction to renewed scrutiny after 1910. Mosher, associate professor of personal hygiene and resident physician for women at Stanford, studied the menstrual records of four hundred healthy women, whom she regularly interviewed and who in addition were required to keep diaries. On the basis of data from more than 3,350 menstrual cycles, Mosher found that menstruation in and of itself did not incapacitate normal women. Rather, menstrual disability could be attributed to four factors that were cultural rather than physiological: restrictive clothing, inactivity, constipation resulting from poor diet and lack of muscle tone, and the general expectation that menstruation involved discomfort.[10]

Leta Hollingworth chose to approach the issue of periodicity not as one of general wellness or pain but as a factor in the performance of certain specific tasks. The subjects for her doctoral study took a series of mental and motor tests over and over again for a month (three months in the case of eight of her volunteers). The women also charted the occurrence of their menses. Examining the data Hollingworth, like Mosher, found they did not support menstrual disability. Her female students performed throughout their menstrual cycles with a steadiness that showed no sign of cyclical variation. Hollingworth concluded that the belief in women's periodic incapacity (which had, she noted, originated in the observations of male physicians about their ailing female patients) was scientifically unwarranted.[11]

Menstruation's cost to the female system was linked, it will be remembered, to the fixed-energy conception of the human body. Had nervous force been unlimited, presumably women could have drawn on this abundance to support the dual enterprises of reproduction and intellection. It was because nerve force was not in generous supply that women, whose physiological demands were so much greater, had been urged to eschew the life of the mind. But after 1900 views about the human body and its potential began to change. Increased information about the human nervous system resulted in a more positive assessment of human potential. Repeated experiments showed that the brain was sturdier, and less susceptible to fatigue, than had been thought. Columbia psychologist Robert Woodworth reported that subjects engaged in prolonged mental labor did indeed feel tired, but their fatigue was a feeling, a sensed weariness, rather than a physiological incapacity. They could continue their work when urged to do so, and continue it effectively. Far from being exceptionally liable to fatigue, the brain was surprisingly resilient. The physical limitations on intellectual work were apparently more expansive than had been assumed.[12]

The decline of the Spencerian paradigm of force can also be seen in the work of the social psychologists Charles Horton Cooley and George Herbert Mead, who questioned the validity of applying theories taken from the physical sciences to the activities of human beings. Thermodynamic laws, they argued, did not appear to make sense of psychological realities, nor was an emphasis on the slenderness of intellectual resources warranted. Wrote Cooley, "The physical law of persistence of energy in uniform quantity is a most illusive one to apply to human life. There is always a great deal more mental energy than is utilized, and the amount that is really productive depends chiefly on the urgency of the suggestions."[13]

The changed attitude after the turn of the century is eloquently revealed in the writings of William James. James, in 1904, wittily assailed Herbert Spencer's calculus of force, the basis of his entire synthetic philosophy. Deeper than concepts of matter and motion, space and time, force was "the ultimate of ultimates" in the Spencerian cosmos, and "the persistence of force" was the fundamental axiom of science, that "widest truth which can be merged in no other or derived from no other." James was having none of this. Denying that "persistence of force" had any definite meaning ("This law is one vast vagueness of which I can give no clear account"), he singled out for particular derision Spencer's use of the term *social force:*

> But what on earth is 'social force'? Sometimes he identifies it with 'social activity' (showing the latter to be proportionate to the amount of food eaten), and sometimes with the work done by human beings and their steam-engines, and shows it to be due ultimately to the sun's heat. It would never occur to a reader of his pages that a social force proper might be anything that acted as a stimulus of social change,—a leader, for example, a discovery, a book, a new idea, or a national insult; and that the greatest of 'forces' of this kind need embody no more 'physical force' than the smallest. The measure of greatness here is the effect produced on the environment, not a quantity antecedently absorbed from physical nature. Mr. Spencer himself is a great social force; but he ate no more than an average man, and his body, if cremated, would disengage no more energy.[14]

Three years later James was urging his readers to activate the "stored-up reserves of energy" lying latent within them; "few men," he insisted, "live at their maximum of energy." Yet they could learn to do so, and to do so in good health," for the organism adapts itself, and as the rate of waste augments, augments correspondingly the rate of repair." His message contrasts dramatically with what he had written in the early 1890s under the telling title, "The Gospel of Relaxation." At that time James had extolled husbanding "stores of reserved nervous force to fall back upon," rather than spending them, and had given high praise to a book called *Power through Repose*. Since power through repose was exactly the regimen women in particular had been enjoined to pursue, the new conviction that the organism could adjust the rate of repair to the rate of waste, could remain healthily balanced even when vigorously active, marked a significant improvement in the intellectual climate of opinion for women.[15]

The End of the Great Brain Theory

Of all the disciplines engaged in the debate over female potential, the most important was undoubtedly psychology. During the early years of the twentieth century psychologists were reshaping their discipline into a modern empirical social science and at the same time rejecting the long-standing somaticism of earlier theories of mind. Belief that the size, structure, and appearance of the brain were reliable indicators of the quality of intelligence was waning by 1905 under the impact of research that found such correlations spurious. It is true that skeptics had voiced doubts about the simple correlation of brain size with intelligence much earlier. Writing in the *Popular Science Monthly* in 1887, for example, a doctor named Joseph Simms observed that "any reflecting person who has studied the brain-weights of eminent men as compared with ordinary intelligence must arrive at the same conclusion—that a great mind may belong to a person who carries a very small, a medium-sized, or a very large brain, the size and weight neither adding to the mental power nor detracting from it, provided only that the encephalon is sufficient to give due support to the bodily life." Havelock Ellis, we have seen, having found the heaviest male brain weights to belong to an imbecile and a bricklayer as well as to Turgenev and Cuvier, doubted the cogency of the equation between brain mass and intelligence. But the most sophisticated attacks came after the turn of the century.[16]

One emanated from the biometric laboratory of Karl Pearson and was the work of one of his protégées, Alice Lee. Using the new statistical techniques pioneered by Pearson, Lee, in her doctoral thesis for the University of London, worked out a set of formulae for skull capacity. These she applied to a group of male anatomists who had had their skulls measured at a meeting of the Anatomical Society in Dublin in 1898. Differences in skull size were, she found, substantial, but "he would be a bold man who would assert that there is a substantial average superiority in the first half [of her ranking]. In fact, a number of the most capable men fall into the last nine, and J. Kollmann, one of the ablest living anthropologists, has absolutely the smallest skull capacity!" To clinch her point, Lee revealed an embarrassing fact: some of the women students of Bedford College, whose cranial capacities had also been recorded, possessed larger skulls than some of the male anatomists.[17]

Lee published her research in 1902. In the same year, Karl Pearson himself published a research note, "On the Correlation of Intellectual Ability with the Size and Shape of the Head," which reported the results of a study of Cambridge undergraduates whose skull measurements had been taken while at the university and whose degrees (whether honors or poll) and class rank were known. Citing Lee's study and its conclusion that "there is no marked correlation between skull capacity and intellectual power," Pearson remarked on the resistance the biometricians encountered: "We have found this result frequently contested and a very definite statement made that able men have large heads." But the later study reaffirmed the first. "Very brilliant men," concluded Pearson, "may possibly have a very slightly larger head than their fellows, but taking the general population there is really a very insignificant association between size of head and ability. For practical purposes it seems impossible, either in the case of exceptionally able men or in the bulk of the population, to pass any judgment from size of head to ability or *vice versa*."[18]

Some years later Franklin Mall, a Johns Hopkins anatomist, extended Lee's and Pearson's findings to other aspects of the brain deemed significant in the study of racial and sexual difference—the weight and size of the frontal lobe, and the complexity of its convolutions and fissures. His exhaustive study of the literature, together with extensive weighing and measuring of brains in the laboratory, yielded only negative results: neither race nor sex left palpable traces on the brain. Evidence did not sustain the concept of male and female brains, and "the general claim that the brain of woman type is foetal or of simian type is largely an opinion without any scientific foundation. Until anatomists can point out specific differences which can be weighed or measured, or until they can assort a mixed collection of brains, their assertions regarding male and female types are of no scientific value."[19]

The anthropologist Franz Boas attacked the typological thinking of the physical anthropologists about intelligence in yet another way. A cardinal tenet of those who judged human capacity on the basis of race or sex was the fixity of the brain type. Hottentot brains, Teutonic brains, female brains—all remained true to type. They had to, for otherwise they might be confused with one another. But in studies undertaken for the U.S. Immigration Commission between 1908 and 1910 Boas challenged the assumption of fixity. Measuring cephalic indices as well as other bodily traits in the great tradition of Broca, Boas found that the headform of the American-born children of immigrant parents differed markedly from that of their parents: among Jews from eastern Europe the children's heads lengthened and became less wide; among "long-headed Sicilians" the opposite was the case. These results pointed to "a decided plasticity of human types," Boas averred, a plasticity of mind as well as of body, for "if the bodily form undergoes far-reaching changes under a new environment, concomitant changes of the mind may be expected." After Pearson and Lee and Mall and Boas, the language of brain weight and brain type lost favor as a determinant of intelligence.[20]

The turn away from somaticism in the study of mind left an obvious void. If brains and skulls or the application of physiological laws could no longer be relied on to reveal the mind's powers, then other methods would have to be devised. Francis Galton offered one alternative. Galton was convinced that a continuum existed between the lower and higher powers of the nervous system, such that superiority in motor skills and sense perception indicated superiority in intelligence as well. Delicate powers of sense discrimination characterized high races, and most especially the males of high races. This conviction helps explain why Galton was interested in rather marginal phenomena like the predominance of males in the fields of tea and wine tasting and piano tuning. Men who could distinguish claret from Burgundy could presumably distinguish Kant from Comte. Women were unlikely to do as well, and

Galton advocated denying them admission to the universities and confining them to separate educational institutions of their own. (It is nice to know that Karl Pearson, though Galton's devoted disciple and friend, found his mentor's intransigence on the subject of women regrettable. When Galton joined the Anti-Suffrage Society, Pearson tactfully pointed out to him that the five female research workers out of fourteen in his laboratories, women whose work "is equal at the very least to that of the men," found themselves "a little tried . . . when your name appeared on the Committee of the Anti-Suffrage Society!")[21]

In America the Galtonian tradition was carried on by James McKeen Cattell, an experimental psychologist at Columbia who had worked with Galton as a student. Interested in mental measurement and individual differences, Cattell "laid the American foundations for the psychology of capacity." Believing with Galton in the inferior mental ability of women, Cattell also accepted Galton's correlation between lower and higher mental traits. Much of his early work centered on devising ever more refined tests of sense perception and motor ability and administering them to successive classes of Columbia undergraduates.[22]

Mental testing reached a broader public through the efforts of Joseph Jastrow of the University of Wisconson, an active popularizer of psychological ideas. Inspired, like Cattell, by Galton, Jastrow set up an anthropometric laboratory at the Chicago World's Columbian Exposition in 1893, where he tested thousands of curious visitors for a small fee. Interest in mental testing appears to have peaked during these middle years of the 1890s, symbolized by the appointment of a committee of the American Psychological Association, with Cattell as its head, to draw up a series of standard mental and physical tests.[23]

But the heyday of anthropometric testing, with its assumption that sensory and motor skills provided an index of intelligence, was drawing to a close. One of Cattell's own students, Clark Wissler, disputed the assumption that motor skills, sense perception, and intelligence were related. Wissler had learned the procedure of correlation, in which Cattell was untrained, from Franz Boas. He had himself administered Cattell's series of tests many times, and had access to the accumulated data in the Columbia laboratory.

When Wissler attempted to correlate test scores with the students' class grades, he was forced to conclude that no such correlation existed: "while the marks of students correlate with each other to a considerable degree, they show little tendency to do so with the mental tests of the psychologists." There seemed to be no connection between supple fingers and supple minds.[24]

Skulls and wine tasting thus began to appear increasingly dubious indicators of mental powers, and the psychology of sex differences remained unborn. At the University of Chicago a young graduate student named Helen Bradford Thompson surveyed the available literature and was unimpressed: "The biological theory of psychological differences of sex," she observed dryly, "is not in a condition to compel consent." Thompson determined to inaugurate a new era of empiricism in the discipline. She set fifty Chicago undergraduates to sorting different colored cards into piles, striking a target, testing for sweetness and sourness, indicating their pain thresholds, and performing other standard experimental procedures in the psychologist's arsenal. On some tests the men excelled, on others the women, but overall Thompson discovered that differences between the sexes were slight. As to the higher operations of the mind, Thompson agreed with Wissler's caveat against assuming a congruence between touching and tasting on the one hand and reasoning and abstracting on the other. So she devised her own tests—word associations, puzzles, and general information examinations. The word association test and the general knowledge exam did not uncover evidence of sex differences in intellectual ability. The Chicago men were, however, markedly superior to the women in the puzzle tests. But Thompson did not accept that the difference was biological; boys, she pointed out, were encouraged to independence and individuality, and were likely to receive mechanical training, while girls were trained to "obedience, dependence, and deference"—hardly the tools for effective problem-solving. Aware that the hereditarian persuasion was entrenched ("The suggestion that the observed differences of sex may be due to differences in environment has often," she conceded, "been met with derision"), Thompson urged that the environmentalist interpretation had at the least a claim to "unbiased consideration."[25]

Helen Thompson's study of *The Mental Traits of Sex,* as she entitled the published version of her dissertation, earned her a

Ph.D. *summa cum laude* and a niche in the history of mental testing. Crude though her measures and her statistical analyses were by later standards, she had pioneered the empirical study of sex differences in mind, and had cast serious doubt on those twin assumptions of nineteenth-century psychology—that men's and women's minds were significantly different, and that the difference was all in favor of men.

The advent of IQ tests eventually rendered Helen Thompson's tests and puzzles obsolete, but the IQ tests also tended to confirm her tentative conclusions. In 1905 the Frenchmen Alfred Binet and Théodore Simon published their scaled mental test, the prototype of the IQ test. In America Lewis Terman developed the standard revision of the Binet test, the Stanford-Binet, just in time for its adaptation to the screening of recruits into the United States Army during World War I. This redirection of effort to the needs of war dampened interest in sex differences. As Rosalind Rosenberg concludes, "by 1918 references to sex differences in intelligence were beginning to go out of style in psychology," and "by 1920 American psychologists had buried the doctrine of female uniqueness propounded by their mentors." Indeed they had buried it so deeply that the 1937 revision of the Stanford-Binet eliminated questions that favored one sex or the other, enforcing sex neutrality on the basic IQ test.[26]

Edward Thorndike at Columbia was one of the architects of this new consensus. Testing for general sex differences in intelligence, he wrote, could prove only "that the sexes are closely alike and that sex can account for only a very small fraction of human mental difference." By the time Havelock Ellis, gamely keeping abreast of the new research, was revising *Man and Woman* for the edition of 1929, he was able to report, citing Thorndike, that only small differences in intellect existed between the sexes. And he quoted the well-known British psychologist Charles Spearman as exclaiming, "The pack of investigators can be called off . . . they are following a false scent."[27]

The Variability Hypothesis Loses Its Charm

And yet the idea of sexual difference lingered on. Challenged on one front, it would, like Proteus, reappear in a new and more sophisticated guise. For intelligence, the variability hypothesis was that subtler guise. Granting that women might be of equal average intelligence with men, variability denied them, as we have seen, an equal share of departure from the average—there were far fewer female idiots, it was conceded, but by the same token, there were far fewer female geniuses. Columbia's psychology department under James McKeen Cattell was a stronghold of variability theorists. Cattell himself used the concept to explain why so few women appeared in his "Statistical Study of Eminent Men": intelligence took the form of a normal (bell-shaped) distribution, and "the distribution of women is represented by a narrower bell-shaped curve." Edward Thorndike, a Cattell student, likewise saw variability as the explanation (and the justification) for men's overshadowing women in "science, art, invention, and management." Social prejudice or discrimination did not enter into the situation: "If men differ in intelligence and energy by wider degrees than do women, eminence in and leadership of the world's affairs of whatever sort will inevitably belong oftener to men. They will oftener deserve it."[28]

It is hardly surprising that the first major American challenge to the theory of greater male variability, like the first challenge to the theory of sex differences in mental traits, was posed by a woman. Leta Stetter Hollingworth was a student of Edward Thorndike at Columbia, and her interest in the topic may well have originated in her contact with him. Failing to find in the literature on sex differences any data supportive of greater male variability in either physical or mental traits, Hollingworth (with a colleague, Helen Montague) examined the hospital records of 1,000 newborns of each sex for birth weight and height. The two researchers found either no evidence of differences in variability between the two sexes or a slightly greater variability among female infants. It is true that the significance of this finding for intelligence was lessened by the decline in psychologists' faith that physical and mental traits were correlated, but at the very least it suggested caution in the blithe (and empirically unfounded) assumption of greater male variability. Nor did Hollingworth rest her case there. Even were males proven to show more actual variation in intelligence, she wrote, that fact would not establish unalterable biological difference between the sexes: "It is undesirable to seek for the cause of sex differences in eminence in ultimate and obscure affective and intellectual differences until we have exhausted as a cause the known, obvious, and unescapable fact that women bear and rear the children, and that this has had as an inevitable sequel the occupation of housekeeping, a field where eminence is not possible."[29]

Lewis Terman dealt the variability hypothesis a more direct blow in 1917, when his survey of the results of IQ tests taken by thousands of American schoolchildren demonstrated no evidence of greater range in the boys' scores. Indeed, "the difference, if any exists, seems to be in the other direction." In the 1920s, however, after extensive studies of 1,000 gifted children, Terman reversed his position. More boys than girls appeared in his sample of students identified (by their teachers) as gifted, and this, Terman now concluded, accorded with "the hypothesis that exceptionally superior intelligence occurs with greater frequency among boys than girls." At almost the same time, on the other hand, Edward Thorndike was finding grounds for considerably more caution about variability than he had expressed in 1906.[30]

In general, according to Stephanie Shields, a reduction of interest in sex differences during and after World War I effected "a corresponding decline of interest in the social implications of the variability hypothesis." By the 1920s higher education for women and coeducation of the sexes were no longer controversial issues; they had become part of the birthright of the middle class. Educators were no longer prone to propose tailoring women's education to their intellectual mediocrity. Shields suggests that this lessening of the emotive social content freed variability to become "just one more dimension along which the sexes were compared." Then, too, increased statistical sophistication generated a variety of indices of variability, and these produced a variety of results. The ensuing confusion encouraged greater tentativeness among psychologists than had been evident at the turn of the century. Havelock Ellis, who had made variability the centerpiece of his analysis in *Man and Woman,* remained a true believer, but the theory, while not actually disproven, had become far too encumbered by complexity to serve as the favored explanation for male achievement.[31]

The Environmentalist Persuasion

A common intellectual thread united the female and male dissenters from the reigning doctrines of racial and sexual difference at the turn of the century. All repeatedly raised the claims of nurture over nature. Heirs of John Stuart Mill, they insisted that studies of human difference which ignored the effects of the environment were meaningless. Differences there might indeed be, but the explanation of those differences, if they existed, had to take account of social as well as biological fact. Human beings lived their lives in particular physical, intellectual, and social situations that shaped them profoundly, if not (yet) quantifiably. Feminist scholars had perforce to adopt this environmentalist perspective because nineteenth-century science was so ready to identify ability with achievement and to locate it in biology. The scientific argument was twofold: woman's lesser cultural achievements proved her mental deficiency, and her deficiency was rooted in her sex. From Maudsley and Galton through Thorndike and beyond, scientists proclaimed the biblical moral: to *him* who had (ability) would indeed be given (attainment). The elect enjoyed a kind of inevitability of eminence. No woman need apply.

Biological determinism of this kind could scarcely be palatable to any woman who sought to use her mind, let alone to the young women who sought graduate degrees in the social sciences during these years and who became dissenters from the scientific consensus on woman's nature. These women knew they were performing well in graduate school. More than most, they experienced in their own lives the obstacles raised in their path to achievement that made a mockery of the premise that talent would inevitably out. They were part of a remarkable assortment of American women who made their mark in the first decades of the twentieth century as academics, professionals, and social reformers, supported and sustained by a vigorous feminist movement.

When the aspirant academics arrived, as so many of them did, at the University of Chicago, they found support for the environmentalism to which the very living of their lives had led them in the work of younger faculty members like John Dewey, James R. Angell, and George Herbert Mead. The new psychology which these men were helping to shape drew from Darwinism the lesson that human beings, like all organisms, adapted themselves to their environment; the mind was a useful tool in this adaptation. Hence minds needed to be situated in particular environments: "Only when the mind is studied in its social context, they believed, can mental activity be fully understood." Thus intellectually reinforced, the young feminist scholars turned to environmentalism as a kind of survival mechanism, a way to maintain intellectual self-respect, and a far truer transcript of reality than the traditional view. They were in the forefront of the effort to create a new, more positive view of female potential.[32]

The intellectual atmosphere in the years after about 1915 was promising to the environmentalist persuasion. These were the years when anthropologists and sociologists moved vigorously to free themselves from tutelage to the natural sciences. They did this by severing the cord that had bound them to biology, declaring that culture and society were autonomous fields with their own proper methods of inquiry, not reducible to biological explanations. In practice, this meant denying that the hereditarian categories by means of which the natural sciences catalogued human beings—race, sex, and ethnicity preeminent among them—went very far in explaining human culture. Social scientists like Franz Boas insisted that nature did not dictate culture. Any discipline that wished to understand human behavior in society must examine the substance of cultural life—social institutions, language, religion, values—and not rely on biological analogies or hereditary models of evolution.[33]

As an explanatory concept nurture did not displace nature in the social sciences, but it did gain a respectable foothold. By 1910 Helen Thompson (now Woolley) thought she could discern a movement away from innatist explanations for sex differences in mind. Seven years earlier she had noted ruefully that environmentalist interpretations were often met with "derision." Now she reported that "one might characterize the drift of recent discussion as a shift of emphasis from a biological to a sociological interpretation of the mental characteristics of sex. The very small amount of difference between the sexes in those functions open to experimentation, the contradictory results obtained from different series of investigations, and the nature of the differences which prove to be most constant, have led to the belief that the psychological differences of sex are of sociological rather than of biological origin."[34]

Woolley's generalization, though probably premature, denoted the early stage of a social-scientific trend toward concern with the nonbiological determinants of behavior that culminated with Margaret Mead's celebrated and controversial *Sex and Temperament in Three Primitive Societies* (1935). By 1940 psychologists found the question of nature versus nurture unrewarding when couched in either/or terms. The preferred model viewed both factors as inextricably woven together in the fabric of human behavior. From the perspective of the turn of the century, this new understanding represented a legitimization of the claim, so frequently made by the pioneer academic feminists, that environment mattered.[35]

Can New Ideas Change Old Ideas?

This recitation of some of the most pertinent developments in science gives rise to a basic question: How much did these new developments actually contribute to altering nineteenth-century views about differences between women and men? The question is not one that can be definitively answered, but some reflections are in order. In the first place, it was to be expected that the implications of the new research for sex differences would be resisted, by scientists as well as by the laity. People dislike disturbances to their beliefs, particularly when these are strongly held, and above all when they concern issues of personal moment. If scientists were immune to this reluctance to embrace the new, the history of science would exhibit the eager and uniform replacement of faulty hypotheses by better ones and the steady triumph of truth over falsehood. Such is not the case. Science progresses, in the words of Loren Eiseley (paraphrasing the physicist Max Born), "through a series of intersecting and confusing alleys rather than down the broad and ever-widening highway that is the illusion fostered by our technological successes. Through these obscure alleys slip elusive shadows of thought that sometimes vanish only to reappear in a succeeding century." Shadows of thought vanish and reappear for many reasons, of course, including (as with Mendel) the obscurity of the original source or (as with evolution before Darwin) an insufficiency of evidence, but one reason is surely our human antipathy to altering the substance of our convictions. And if this is so in areas of no pressing significance for society, it will be all the more the case when the social and personal repercussions of the ideas in question are large.[36]

Ideological resistance can readily be seen in the dispute over gender-based ability. Contrary evidence was ignored or disputed or dismissed as the exception to the rule. Readers were reminded of the grave dangers to civilization that impended if the social relations of the sexes were disturbed. James McGrigor Allan warned that upgrading women's education and status "on the assumption of an imaginary sexual equality" ran counter to nature and threatened "a most baneful effect in unsettling society." Almost thirty years later Alpheus Hyatt spelled out the danger more precisely, using the language of recapitulation: the human race, he feared, was already "phylogerontic," that is, nearing the end point of its racial cycle. It faced a probable future of retrogression and eventual extinction. Thus imperiled, it must at all cost avoid hastening its fate by narrowing the social distance between the sexes, for "such changes would be convergences in structure and character, and women would be tending to become virified, and men to become effeminised, and both would have, therefore, entered upon the retrogressive period of their evolution."[37]

Admixtures of science and social prescription, suggesting as they do the presence of motives other than the strictly scientific, lend substance to the claim made by some scholars that new scientific data cannot significantly affect received habits of thought in sensitive areas like the nature and differences of the sexes. These scholars assert that the causal arrow in fact runs the other way, with social ideology governing the choice of scientific ideas that a scientist holds. Ruth Schwartz Cowan, for example, suggests that Francis Galton's political philosophy—emphatically inegalitarian and elitist—governed his denial of the Lamarckian supposition as to the inheritance of acquired characteristics. Hence, "it is not unreasonable to assume that initially he rejected Lamarckian ideas on philosophical grounds alone." Cowan labels Galton's first article of 1865, "Hereditary Talent and Character," not a scientific work but a contribution to a debate in political philosophy, "an exercise in political rhetoric." So also Douglas Lorimer attributes the race science of the London anthropologists to their political views, rather than the reverse: "The scientific racism of James Hunt and his like-minded colleagues in the Anthropological Council was a product of their underlying assumptions about the nature of man and society."[38]

Janet Sayers has applied this argument to the topic at hand with considerable effectiveness. Considering the rise and fall of the claim that women are less intelligent because they have smaller brains, she vigorously challenges Elizabeth Fee's view that new data like that of Franklin Mall made it scientifically untenable, and Stephanie Shields's view that it declined in part because of the development of mental tests. These conclusions could not be correct, Sayers argues, because, in the first case, scientists with an axe to grind were quite capable of ignoring, or reinterpreting, contrary evidence, and in the second, intelligence tests were designed on the principle of mental equality between the sexes, hence were the product, rather than the cause, of a new attitude toward women. Sayers prefers to ascribe the demise of the "great brain theory of intelligence" with its corollary of female insufficiency to social rather than scientific factors: "the cause of the decline of this thesis in the early years of the twentieth century, like that of its first emergence in the late 1860s, is to be found in changes that were then occurring in women's status."[39]

It would be hard to deny Sayers's charge of scientific selectivity. Some nineteenth-century scientists did have an easy way with the evidence; it was difficult for them to treat it impartially when they already knew what they would find, and they were quite likely to feel strongly about it. As Havelock Ellis wrote, with rueful detachment, "The history of opinion regarding cerebral sex differences forms a painful page in scientific annals. It is full of prejudices, assumptions, fallacies, over-hasty generalizations. The unscientific have had a predilection for the subject; and men of science seem to have lost the scientific spirit when they approached the study of its seat. Many a reputation has been lost in these soft and sinuous convolutions."[40]

Sayers is also clearly right to point to events in the wider world outside the community of science as precipitating factors in discrediting these theories. It mattered that middle-class women were finding employment and proving themselves capable workers in offices and shops. It mattered even more that colleges and universities were opening their doors to women and that women were responding, both at the undergraduate and graduate level, with enthusiasm and, in many cases, academic excellence. Helen Thompson Woolley certainly believed this at the time. With pardonable pride (she was, after all, one of the best students John Dewey and James R. Angell ever had), she noted that "even the time-honored belief that men are more capable of independent and creative work is beginning to give way in view of the successful competition of women in graduate work and in obtaining the doctorate."[41]

Yet Sayers's critique is not entirely convincing. There is less difference between her own interpretation and that of the writers she faults than she supposes. Neither Fee nor Shields ignores the connection between social factors and scientific theories. Shields writes, for example, "When issues faded in importance, it was not because they were resolved but because they ceased to serve as viable scientific 'myths' in the changing social and scientific milieu." And Fee, who can write of Franklin Mall as "deliver[ing] the *coup de grace* to craniology" in 1909, and of "[Karl] Pearson and his students . . . demolish[ing] the craniological enterprise" by 1906, also emphasizes at some length the changes in the lives of middle-class women that brought them into the marketplace and university and that began to alter old beliefs: "Experience, after all, seemed to demonstrate that many of their prior assumptions about the incapacities of women were simply incorrect. Female triumphs on the campuses compelled reassessment of women's supposed intellectual inferiority . . . Women's supposed inability to survive the hustle and bustle of the work place similarly did not stand up . . . Scientists lived in the world and could not help but be affected by their daily encounters with the new women." Indeed, Fee goes on to spell out even more explicitly a theory of scientific change that entirely accords with that of Sayers: "It may be that scientific theories on the subject [of women's abilities] are rather closely related to the actual current status of women, that they tend to be concerned with either justifying or condemning that position . . . It would follow that as the position of women changes—a change most often generated by transformations in the economy—scientists begin to reevaluate their previous conceptions in the light of new social evidence."[42]

Persuasive as this model of scientific change may be, the question needs to be asked whether it leaves sufficient room for alterations in the scientific evidence, for factual or interpretative disproof, correction, emendation. Do theories merely dance to the piping of contemporary trends in society? Surely they do not. Without disputing the power of social factors, a strong case can be made that developments within the sciences themselves made a difference, and an important one. There were things one simply could no longer say in 1915 that had been perfectly acceptable in 1880. No reputable scientist could any longer say, for example, that metabolism determined sex, and that anabolism characterized the female as katabolism epitomized the male. No scientist could suppose that the mental and physical chasm between men and women was widening. No one was any longer likely to look for intellectual capacity in the size and contours of the brain. And the fact that these things could no longer be said was the result of the cumulative labors of the scientists themselves at their desks and in their laboratories. This does not mean that any particular scientist's fundamental attitude necessarily changed, at least not immediately: a scientist who was skeptical about women's intelligence before the turn of the century might still be skeptical in 1915. But the grounds of the argument had shifted. Such a scientist could not continue to press his case in terms of women's lesser brains now that brain size had been determined to be irrelevant. Nor could he argue in terms of a difference in average intelligence, once IQ tests had shown such differences to be insignificant. These developments had a logic and momentum of their own, not entirely divorced from contemporary social trends, to be sure, but not entirely dependent on them either.

One can see the dynamic of the new research at work in the writings of Edward Thorndike. A hard-nosed empiricist and congenital skeptic, Thorndike is a useful example precisely because he never held any brief for women's mental equality with men. He nonetheless found himself driven to conclude, on the basis of his studies of schoolchildren, that sex accounted for very little of the differences in intelligence among them. In fact, he admitted, "the sexes are closely alike." Differences between individuals were enormously more significant than differences between the sexes: "we may say roughly that the difference in any purely intellectual capacities between the average for men and the average for women will be less than *one-twentieth* the difference between the highest and lowest four per cent of men." It is true that Thorndike then called on the variability hypothesis to explain the masculine "monopoly of genius," and relegated women to "the mediocre grades of ability and achievement." Yet Thorndike allowed that, middling as their skills were, women might become scientists and engineers, lawyers, doctors, and architects. It meant something—indeed, much—to grant to female intelligence a rough parity with male intelligence, however wanting it might be in eminence. Thorndike belongs among that group of Columbia experimental psychologists whose work, as described by Rosalind Rosenberg, set the stage for a new view of women's potential: "For all of their prejudices against women, they slowly put together the skeptical elements of a psychological system that could accommodate a very different view of feminine behavior from the one their own biases allowed."[43]

An interactive model that imagines ideas and social change in constant relationship, each affecting and being affected by the other, surely comes closest to describing the way new beliefs take shape. Rosalind Rosenberg provides a nice case study in her discussion of the Chicago sociologist William I. Thomas. Beginning as a disciple of Geddes and Thomson and their metabolic distinction between the sexes, Thomas underwent a remarkable transformation that left him doubting women's mental uniqueness and emphasizing the social determinants of character. The reasons for his volte-face are both experiential and intellectual. A number of the women in his classes did not conform to his expectations of "feminine frailty and intellectual mediocrity." But in addition Thomas was swayed by the influence of Chicago's cluster of functionalist psychologists—Dewey, Angell, and Mead, who persuaded him to rethink his physiological determinism. Both the personal and the intellectual stimuli were important.[44]

Ideas do have consequences; people do learn from new information, however reluctantly, as well as from new experience. It is hard, otherwise, to see why feminist scholars at the turn of the century cared about overturning scientific wisdom on the nature of women. They could simply have waited for social and economic conditions to render the old ideas obsolete. But they did not. They clearly saw their research as making a difference. And in the end, I believe, it did. Scholars may not move mountains, but they can sometimes, if only a little, move minds.

CHAPTER 7

Women and the Cosmic Nightmare

Such . . . indeed is the audacity of the human intellect, that the discovery of limits usually proves hopeless in only one case, namely, when they are perceived to apply to a different race, class, or sex, from that to which the investigator himself belongs . . . It is true that men have inquired with great research into the influence exerted upon the general organization of man by the special character and working of his sexual organization, but it is rare that this influence has been regarded as "limiting" in its nature.

—Mary Putnam Jacobi (1886)

The support of scientific opinion can be plausibly claimed for the defence of the inequalities of the social organism: these inequalities, it can be urged, are only part of what exist inevitably throughout the physical world. The creed of Liberty, Equality, Fraternity can be discarded as a metaphysical fiction of the unscientific eighteenth century. The aspirations of socialism can be put aside as the foolish denial of the everlasting economic competition which is sanctioned by nature as only one phase of the general struggle for existence.

—David G. Ritchie (1889)

In the hush of the British Museum reading room, Virginia Woolf examined a large volume by Professor von X entitled *The Mental, Moral, and Physical Inferiority of the Female Sex*. Professor von X was an angry man. On her notepaper she sketched his face—jowly, with small eyes and a red face. He appeared to "jab his pen on the paper as if he were killing some noxious insect as he wrote, but even when he had killed it that did not satisfy him; he must go on killing; and even so, some cause for anger and irritation remained." So too with the other learned men whose books on women Woolf perused: they were all angry. These books "had been written in the red light of emotion and not in the white light of truth."[1]

As a topic of study, women's bodies and women's minds, and the ways in which they resemble or differ from men's, have challenged the norms of scientific objectivity. Time and again in the late nineteenth century scientists took the rostrum to lecture women on their biological destiny. Clearly these discourses were not science. But what about the facts and theories on which they were based? We today, looking back on ideas that we do not share, find it easy to dismiss them out of hand as not truly scientific at all—as bad science or pseudoscience or ideology. Janet Sayers, for example, speaks of the "absurdity" of many of the claims of Geddes and Thomson in *The Evolution of Sex*. Yet their work was widely read and widely acclaimed at the time of its publication; its "absurdity" is clearly a modern judgment, and one that rests on hindsight. It is worth considering for the moment whether the scientific work that testified so unambiguously to a chasm between masculine and feminine nature might not have been good (if subsequently discredited) science in its day—good in the sense that it conformed to the canons of scientific method in the late nineteenth century. We have no right to expect either the data or the perspectives of the twentieth century in men of the nineteenth. We do have a right to ask them to live up to their own scientific credo.[2]

A good example of that credo is readily accessible in the writings of one of the foremost Victorian scientists, the physicist John Tyndall. A towering figure in the scientific community, Tyndall, unlike his eminent scientific contemporary Charles Darwin, made himself publicly prominent as a popularizer and propagandist for the scientific enterprise. In the course of his long career Tyndall spelled out at some length his understanding of the norms that governed scientific work. They included the following points:

1. Science is empirical. It rests on observable facts and seeks to verify theory by comparing "the deductions from it with the facts of observation."

2. But science is also theoretical, moving beyond the observed facts to seek out causal principles: "Our science would not be worthy of its name and fame if it halted at facts, however practically useful, and neglected the laws which accompany and rule the phenomena."

3. Science is always skeptical, accepting no authority other than the facts of nature.

4. Science is objective knowledge uncontaminated by personal interests, emotions, or biases.[3]

Tyndall's list is in no way remarkable; it is an assemblage of scientific truisms to which all practicing scientists in his time would have assented. Let us see how his principles accord with the scientific literature we have been examining in these pages.

By way of preliminary we need to recall the near-total absence of information in the field of sex differences, which made it inevitable that ideas now seen as preposterous were not preposterous at the time. Michael Ruse is at pains to point out in his treatment of Darwin's theory of pangenesis that Darwin "was not being stupid or reactionary by the scientific standards of his day," and that the theory was not, therefore, "some aberrant extravaganza of a brilliant mind." So too with the metabolic theory of sex determination proposed by Geddes and Thomson, and the conviction that the size and shape of the head revealed qualities of mind. In all these instances the hypotheses were legitimate, if ultimately misguided.[4]

It is also helpful to remember that statements of fact with which we should now disagree—that women are less courageous than men, for example, that they lack powers of abstract thought, that they are more wily or devious than men—may well have had some semblance of truth in the Victorian period, when courage and intellect were unlikely to be cultivated or even encouraged in girls, and when mature women normally found themselves dependent upon men for support. And, too, sometimes the scientists had their facts straight, however dubious we may be about their interpretations: women's brains are, by and large, smaller than men's—as are their bodies. Their metabolisms are different. Adult women do retain a greater morphological resemblance to children than do men; they really are neotenous.

Testing Tyndall's Credo

Returning to Tyndall's list, we begin with the concept of the empirical nature of science. The determination to render the study of humanity empirical was certainly the driving force behind the accumulation of anthropometric and craniological measurements in the early days of physical anthropology. By the end of the century a great deal had undoubtedly been learned about the range of variation in the human head and body, and certain facts had emerged—for example, the generally smaller mass and lighter weight of the female brain as compared with the male. Yet it must be said that scientific commitment to fact seems to have been pliable with regard to the nature of women—and this in two ways. In the first place, observable fact seems to have been quite loosely construed; the standard for admission as fact was not high. Susan Mosedale has remarked on George J. Romanes's disturbing propensity to attribute traits to women on the basis that their existence was "proverbial," "a matter of ordinary comment," and "a matter of universal recognition." Nor is Romanes at all exceptional. Even the calm and normally judicious Darwin is not above reproach. Flavia Alaya complains of Darwin's "*ben trovato* conclusions" and "not even minimal scientific documentation." One can respond in Darwin's defense, what is perfectly true, that adequate documentation was not to be had and that he did couch much of his discussion of men and women tentatively (it is "at least probable" that mental differences between men and women exist; women "seem to differ" mentally from men chiefly in their greater tenderness and unselfishness). But there does seem to be something of a double standard of proof involved in Darwin's scrupulous concern for reliability with regard to information on plant and animal breeding (he wrote to Thomas Henry Huxley that he was immersed in treatises and journals but "*The difficulty is to know what to trust. No one or two statements are worth a farthing; the facts are so complicated.*") and his casual and exclusive reliance when it came to African women on the popular travel journals of Mungo Park.[5]

In the second place, observable fact seems at times to have been malleable to preconceptions. Such was the case in the parable of the cerebral lobes as told by Havelock Ellis. Up until recent times, Ellis recounted in *Man and Woman,*

> it has over and over again been emphatically stated by brain anatomists that the frontal region is relatively larger in men, the parietal in women. This conclusion is now beginning to be regarded as the reverse of the truth, but we have to recognise that it was inevitable. It

was firmly believed that the frontal region is the seat of all the highest and most abstract intellectual processes, and if on examining a dozen or two brains an anatomist found himself landed in the conclusion that the frontal region is relatively larger in women, the probability is that he would feel he had reached a conclusion that was absurd. It may, indeed, be said that it is only since it has become known that the frontal region of the brain is of greater relative extent in the ape than it is in Man, and has no special connection with the higher intellectual processes, that it has become possible to recognise the fact that that region is relatively more extensive in women.

"Observable fact" in this story began as the larger size of the frontal lobe in men and ended as just the opposite. The scientists making the earlier calculations may of course have been incompetent, but that seems unlikely. More probably Ellis got the moral straight: empiricism became entangled with prior belief, and the results were shaped accordingly. Similar instances could be multiplied, from Francis Galton's bland refusal to consider Alice Lee's data on the lack of correlation between head size and intelligence because he "totally disagree[d]," to the recapitulationists' ignoring the plain evidence of neoteny and its meaning for racial and sexual stereotypes.[6]

The second item in Tyndall's set of norms is the belief in the theoretical and lawbound nature of science, its search for the causal laws lying behind empirical phenomena. It is fair to say that the scientists who considered sex differences did their best to live up to this aspect of the credo. Many of them, far from being satisfied with the physiology and psychology of sex, went to great lengths to subsume these facts under one or another of the available theoretical structures of nineteenth-century science. The ardor of their search for causal principles may not have been wholly disinterested: they were anxious to convert thorny questions of social policy into issues of science in part to enhance their own influence. But in this particular, at least, they do seem to have conformed to Tyndall's model of exemplary science.

Tyndall insisted, thirdly, that science was skeptical, heeding no authority but the facts of nature. It was open-minded and nondogmatic. In order to succeed as a scientist, Tyndall wrote, one must cultivate "patient industry, an honest receptivity, and a willingness to abandon all preconceived notions, however cherished, if they be found to contradict the truth." Victorian scientists of sex difference faltered badly in upholding this maxim, and, on the whole, they failed. "Honest receptivity and a willingness to abandon all preconceived notions" can hardly be said to have typified the response of Paul Broca, previously cited, to the proposal that craniologists consider brain size in relation to body size. "But," said Broca in a masterpiece of question-begging, "we must not forget that women are, on the average, a little less intelligent than men, a difference which we shall not exaggerate but which is, nonetheless, real. We are therefore permitted to suppose that the relatively small size of the female brain depends in part upon her physical inferiority and in part upon her intellectual inferiority." Such "permission to suppose" what is precisely at issue does not constitute "honest receptivity."[7]

Broca's attitude was common among his scientific colleagues. A very few exceptions do, however, exist. One is Havelock Ellis, who, after admitting that the extant evidence for a differential psychology was insubstantial, concluded *Man and Woman* with an admonition to open-mindedness. His results did not, he wrote, warrant dogmatism regarding the respective spheres of the sexes, and this was in itself a conclusion of considerable importance, one that "lays the axe at the root of many pseudoscientific superstitions." Another exception is Léonce Manouvrier, the one member of Broca's school of French anthropology who rejected belief in the inferiority of women. Both men excoriated the dogmatic lapses of their colleagues. Ellis described the history of writings on sex differences in the brain as "a painful page in scientific annals. It is full of prejudices, assumptions, fallacies, over-hasty generalisations." Scientists "seem to have lost the scientific spirit when they approached the study of its seat." Manouvrier lamented that women had been the target of scientific "commentaries and sarcasms more ferocious than the most misogynist imprecations of certain church fathers." Like those theologians who had asked if women had souls, modern scientists refused women a human intelligence. Manouvrier argued that these conclusions were the result of prejudice rather than scientific inquiry, because they were "not presented with the circumspection their authors would have considered essential in all other questions." Such calls to fair-mindedness are all the more remarkable for their scarcity; the writings of Ellis and Manouvrier found few echoes in the practices of the scientific community.[8]

A fourth hallmark of science in Tyndall's characterization was its status as objective knowledge untouched by personal interests, emotions, or biases. This article of faith has been the holy of holies for generations of scientists up until very recently, and in modified form probably still is. It supposes a universe in which human beings shed their social and emotional selves at the threshold of the laboratory and enter a world of pure science where theory-making is guided solely by previous research or the flash of individual inspiration, quite unrelated to the concerns of the outer world. In modern language, science and ideology are seen as polar opposites, with science representing spare and disinterested analysis leading to intellectual clarity, and ideology representing a committed and morally charged analysis that seeks to motivate action. Science is diagnostic and critical; ideology is justificatory and apologetic.[9]

It is obvious that very few of the scientists writing about the natures of the sexes honored this injunction to theoretical purity. Many of them, as we have seen, were perfectly open about their concern that women, acting in ignorance of the physical and mental limitations on their sex that science disclosed, were threatening the social equilibrium. There was nothing covert about this message. The editors of the *Popular Science Monthly,* for example, called their readers' attention to an article by Ely Van de Warker emphasizing the "penalty of sex" paid by women in reproduction as the reason they were unlikely to achieve success in professional work. This conclusion, the editors hoped, would be carefully pondered by "the promoters of their alleged reform [women's rights] . . . who are vehemently advocating 'revolution' in the social and industrial relations of women." So also the zoologist W. K. Brooks, affirming that "the positions which women already occupy in society and the duties which they perform are, in the main, what they should be if our view is correct," warned that "any attempt to improve the condition of women by ignoring or obliterating the intellectual differences between them and men must result in disaster to the race." Further examples would be superfluous. Indeed, the reader

who follows Michael Ghiselin's advice to read the scientific literature "from the point of view of ulterior motives, in which it
abounds," will find a rich harvest of tendentious prose.[10]

It is reasonable to conclude, then, that the Victorian literature on
sex differences was neither unbiased nor value-free. The scientists
who contemplated this topic failed to uphold the canon of objectivity enunciated by Tyndall. This means that, overall, they violated
three out of the four points that constituted for him the essence of
science. Their work was neither scrupulously empirical, nor skeptical, nor objective. Tyndall, as spokesman for Victorian science,
would certainly have had to condemn it as unscientific.

Science, Culture, and Ideology

Yet it needs to be said that many modern philosophers and sociologists and historians of science who have studied the way science is
actually done doubt that Tyndall's model of immaculately conceived science was ever a true description or even a practicable ideal.
Often taking a cue from Marxism, with its linkage of interests and
ideologies, these scholars have been chipping away at the classical
image of scientific practice. They point out the legitimating functions of scientific theories—their role, for example, in maintaining
middle-class dominance in the nineteenth century. Whether or not
one accepts a Marxist sociology of knowledge, the contextual
thrust of this scholarship is refreshing. Science is not disembodied
inquiry; it is the product of particular human beings living in
specific times and places, and these individuals, like all other human
beings, are affected by the circumstances of their lives. Hardly a
novel idea (recall Emerson's dictum, "No man can quite emanci-
pate himself from his age and country . . ."), the reconnection of
scientists with society suggests a reconception of the relationship of
science and ideology. According to the British historian of science
Roger Cooter, a consensus has arisen in his discipline as to the
meaning of the term *ideology:* it is simply a "worldview, or the
partial view of nature and human nature expressed by a group or
class which informs perception and conceptualization." So construed, science and ideology, far from being polar opposites, are
part and parcel of one another. Scientists cannot help but bring

cultural beliefs and interests into the construction of their theories. "We think and act on the basis of the resources our culture provides," observe Steven Shapin and Barry Barnes. "The use of cultural resources to construct scientific theories is an observation of what happens, not the casting of an aspersion."[11]

This view of science and scientists needs to be used with caution: scientists may not shed their social skins at the laboratory door, but the work that they do is something more than the transcription of their own particular cultural situation. Still there is value in the proposition that the beliefs—the preconceptions—of scientific practitioners do not necessarily destroy the validity of their results. In the case at hand, scientists of the Victorian era made their measurements and constructed their theories initially believing, for the most part, in the physical and mental inferiority of women. It would have been extraordinary had they not, for this belief was part of the intellectual atmosphere that enveloped them from infancy. Those who dismiss the sex-difference literature as falsified by the mere existence of prior beliefs among the anthropologists, biologists, and psychologists who created it demand an impossible ideological purity. At the same time good scientific practice, in the late nineteenth century as now, should not have permitted those preconceptions to distort the scientists' vision, to blinker them in such a way as to predetermine their conclusions. The moment that happened, preconceptions sabotaged inquiry. Manufactured facts, low standards of evidence, strained interpretations, hasty generalizations, question-begging, indifference to contradictory data, and bland dogmatism litter the intellectual landscape. However understandable in human terms, these are not the hallmarks of good science.

Science and Misogyny

The remarkable unanimity of scientific opinion about women's limitations was, not surprisingly, a source of outrage for feminists. Helen H. Gardener, one of the more outspoken of these, viewed it as an antifeminist conspiracy. In a speech delivered in 1886 she charged that with the decline of patriarchal religion, "Conservatism, Igorance and Egotism, in dismay and terror, took counsel together and called in medical science, still in its infancy, to aid in staying the march of progress which is inevitable to civilization and so necessary to anything like a real Republic. Equality of opportunity began to be denied to women, for the first time, upon natural and so-called scientific grounds." This piece of charged rhetoric is hyperbolic. Scientists never engaged in a conscious conspiracy against women, and they were by no means uniformly misogynistic. Charles Darwin, for example, though convinced of the intellectual superiority of men, believed that the improvement of women would benefit the human race and speculated about developing their minds through education. G. Stanley Hall, who clearly longed to turn back the clock, nevertheless found much to admire in the New Women of his day who were intellectually stimulating, "at home with the racket and on the golf links," "splendid friends," and indeed, "in every way magnificent, only they are not mothers . . ."[12]

There seems to have been a kind of geography of scientific misogyny, with the most overt and brutal antifeminism being voiced on the European Continent. Stephen Jay Gould has labeled Gustave Le Bon "chief misogynist of Broca's school" and Le Bon's work on women "the most vicious attack on women in modern scientific literature." (In fact, Le Bon would face stiff competition for the title from writers like Cesare Lombroso or P. J. Möbius.) M. Carey Thomas, later president of Bryn Mawr, discovered while a student at Leipzig the greater bluntness of Continental scholars. Writing to her mother in 1880, she exclaimed, "I wish I could convey to thee an idea of the way women are mentioned by the profs and in German books. I suppose American men regard them in that light—of course they do because they act thus, but at least they do not *say* so." In fact, the difference was more than verbal: opposition to women's rights, as evidenced, say, by resistance to suffrage, was much more pronounced in Italy, Germany, and France than in the United States.[13]

Paradoxically, Gardener was wrong, not because she claimed too much but because she claimed too little, not because she charged science with bigotry but because she did not push her charge far enough. No conspiracy of "Conservatism, Ignorance and Egotism" called on the aid of science to halt "the march of progress"

because no such conspiracy was needed: science itself was androcentric and patriarchal. It did not go to the aid of opponents of
social equality; it was a key source of that opposition. Nowhere in
the intellectual landscape of late-nineteenth-century life can one
find, despite individual differences of tact and tone, such a uniformly negative appraisal of woman's potential. How can this fact
be explained?[14]

The usual explanations are couched in terms of the scientists'
collective perception of the threat posed by educated women to
themselves and other male professionals, upon whose livelihood
these women would encroach; or to the entire male sex, whose
traditional prerogatives women would demand; or to the family,
whose stability they would undermine; or, finally, to society at
large, which would be gravely imperiled for all the above reasons.
Science, then, can be seen as a weapon used by men to rationalize
the perpetuation of traditional sex roles and men's continued domination of women. Arguments of this sort certainly provide a piece
of the puzzle. The determination of scientists to stop the infiltration
of women into new intellectual and occupational arenas was a
response to a threatened loss of power and authority. Such an
argument conforms precisely to the analysis of Milton Rokeach, in
The Open and Closed Mind, which identifies two needs served by all
belief systems—the need to know and the need to ward off threat:
"To the extent that the cognitive need to know is predominant and
the need to ward off threat absent, open systems should result
[systems that can accept new information and adapt or alter their
tenets as a result] . . . But as the need to ward off threat becomes
stronger, the cognitive need to know should become weaker, resulting in more closed belief systems." And closure is synonymous
with dogmatism, which the scientists of sex differences displayed in
abundance.[15]

But such arguments do not fully explain the unanimity and
strength of the scientific consensus. Other men had the same reasons for concern, yet some of them, at least, were able to discount
the threat and encourage women to fuller participation in society.
John Stuart Mill is the outstanding example of a male feminist in the
late nineteenth century, but there were a number of others—in
America men like Thomas Higginson, Wendell Phillips, Frederick

Douglass, Henry Blackwell, Andrew White, and Samuel Bowles; in England Jacob Bright, Richard Pankhurst, Henry Fawcett, William Woodall, and Richard Cobden. Yet one looks hard to find scientists or medical men on the roster. Lester Frank Ward, American paleobotanist turned sociologist who promoted the theory of "gynaecocracy," or the supremacy of the female, stands out as an exception, along with Franklin Mall, the Harvard physiologist Henry Bowditch, and a few doctors like Abraham Jacobi (married to the feminist Mary Putnam Jacobi). So too do Alfred Russel Wallace in England, and Léonce Manouvrier in France. But the great majority of male feminists among the educated classes were lawyers, ministers, journalists, and businessmen. By contrast, when Helen H. Gardener sought aid from American neurologists in combatting William Hammond's theory about sex differences in the brain, she found not one who believed in woman suffrage or sex equality.[16]

It cannot be that scientists were more endangered in their occupational security or masculine prerogatives than other educated male professionals. Women found more barriers to their entry into the sciences than into writing or law; they scarcely threatened the male hegemony of these disciplines. In other respects—political participation, for example, or domestic life—the lives of scientists were no more apt to be disrupted than those of other middle-class males. The intensity and unanimity of scientific opinion on the woman question remains, then, to be explained. I would suggest that an answer lies in contemporary scientific theory and practice.

Scientific Method and Group Differences

Feminists at the time sometimes lamented the masculine habit of viewing women as a group rather than as a collection of individuals. This habit was particularly galling to American women nurtured on a philosophy of individual right. It called forth one of the best efforts of Elizabeth Cady Stanton, a speech she delivered in 1892 entitled, significantly, "The Solitude of Self." Stanton called on her listeners to "think for a moment of the immeasurable solitude of self. We come into the world alone, unlike all who have gone before us, we leave it alone, under circumstances peculiar to ourselves. No mortal ever has been, no mortal ever will be like the soul just launched on the sea of life." She extolled "the infinite diversity in human character": "Nature never repeats herself, and the possibilities of one human soul will never be found in another. No one has ever found two blades of ribbon grass alike, and no one will ever find two human beings alike." And on this basis Stanton urged "the complete development of every individual," more specifically, the removal of "all artificial trammels" from a woman's chosen path. Stanton's associate Helen H. Gardener complained similarly (though less eloquently) about women's lack of individual rights: "As a person, she has no status with these consistent believers in 'equal rights to all mankind.' As a potential mother only, can she hope for consideration either by religious or medical theorist."[17]

Refusal to view women as individuals was the common intellectual stance of antifeminists, not something peculiar to the scientific community. Yet the normal practice of science itself strongly reinforced this stance. Scientists classify and categorize and generalize, and this often means that the scientist's vision is fixed on the larger collectivity rather than on the single individual. In the words of the novelist John Fowles, "Science is centrally, almost metaphysically, obsessed by general truths, by classifications . . . by functional laws whose worth is valued by their universality; by statistics, where a Bach or a da Vinci is no more than a quotum, a hole in a computer tape. The scientist . . . may study individuals, but only to help establish more widely applicable laws and facts."[18]

Fowles's description is not entirely fair—how else, one wonders, could generalizations be made?—nor even entirely accurate. Yet it has much in common with the definition of scientific method offered by Karl Pearson in 1892 in his influential *Grammar of Science:* "orderly classification of facts followed by the recognition of relationship and recurring sequence." Both Fowles's and Pearson's interpretations of how scientists work offer clues as to why scientists in Pearson's time were prone to ignore particular women in favor of a kind of composite Woman. Beginning as they did with the assumption that men and women should be classified separately, they were then committed to the further assumption that each group was relatively homogeneous: All women shared a basic feminine nature, all men a basic masculine one. The scientist therefore had a right and an obligation to focus not on individual particularity, but on the properties shared by the group. (An illuminating example of this attitude is Francis Galton's experiment with composite photography of particular groups—criminals, for example—with results he promoted as perfect visual instances of generalization.)[19]

But shuffling men and women into separate categories did more than simply flatten out individual idiosyncrasy. The logic of the practice also required emphasizing ways in which the two groups differed. Only by focusing on the fundamental differences between the sexes could their analytical separation be justified. Given their original assumption that what was most important about men and women was not their shared human nature but their separate sexual natures, scientists could hardly help but elaborate a kind of sociocultural apartheid based on sex.

The common practice of scientific analysis, then, powerfully encouraged a differential appraisal of men and women. But this appraisal also had roots in a pessimism widespread among scientists of the late nineteenth century about human potential in general. It is a commonplace that many intellectuals in Europe and America experienced feelings of anxiety and apprehension about the human condition, and Western civilization in particular, in the waning years of the nineteenth century. This mood has even acquired its own label, *fin de siècle*. Some of its manifestations, itemized by Edward A. Ross, a prominent sociologist of the time, included "naturalism in fiction, 'decadence' in poetry, realism in art, tragedy in music, scepticism in religion, cynicism in politics, and pessimism in philosophy." There were certainly many strands to this darkening mood, including economic depressions, labor strife, and a growing awareness of the social costs of industrialism, but for thoughtful people the revelations of science would have to count importantly among them.[20]

Evolution and Anxiety

Evolution, in particular, troubled the intellectual waters. It is true that many people, like the advocates of the Social Gospel, believed evolution to be a herald of hope, promising human and social betterment. It could be tamed to the uses of an optimistic philosophy of progress such as that fashioned by the ebullient Andrew Carnegie, in which "all is for the best since all grows better." Yet this cheerful gospel did not quell dismay at the revelations of strife and aggression in nature, which appeared to sanction the most violent aspects of contemporary society—fierce economic competition, industrial, racial, and national warfare, and the rule of the strong. Nor did it dispel the fears and uncertainties of those who, like the novelists Emile Zola, Frank Norris, Jack London, and Theodore Dreiser, brooded over the fragility of human nature. Kinship with the animals raised disturbing reflections, not least the possibility that civilization was no more than a thin veneer over the savage self. Evolutionary anthropology and psychology explored at length the sometimes frightening implications of continuity between mammals and men. In the work of Hughlings Jackson, human beings were seen to regress, through neurological impairment, to those lower levels of mental organization characteristic of the brutes. Carl Vogt similarly called the idiot "an intermediate stage between ape and man." These descriptions contained the unmistakable implication that full humanity was neither a birthright nor a secure possession. One could fail to achieve it, remaining, with the idiot, half-ape and half-man; or—what was perhaps worse—one could lose it once attained. Evolution disclosed the nightmare vision of a humanity so precariously situated on the path of organic perfection that one accident, one fatal hereditary flaw, could plunge the hapless individual into the bestial abyss. A universe so fluid was a universe not to be trusted.

The naturalization of mind had further repercussions. Situating mind in body shrank its godlike plenitude to the mean dimensions of the human frame. Mind became liable to all the evils that flesh was heir to. If "nerve force" and mental energy were, like muscular exertion, products of oxidation, then they were equally subject to the law of energy conservation and equally prone to exhaustion and collapse if overtaxed. Thought did not come free, nor did emotion; both cost the body a measurable expenditure of force. Great intellect precluded athletic and gustatory prowess, not to mention a warm heart. Clipping the wings of thought, the physiologically informed individual did not allow his mind to soar at will, not, at least, unless assured that romance was not imminent and the muscles and digestive system were in repose. Thought was potentially dangerous, and the mind constructed by the physiologists—the mind incarnate—was also a mind at risk.

So too, of course, was the body. For certainly if the linkage of mind and body highlighted the vulnerability of mind, it also pointed to the fragility of the body. Bodies were liable to leanness, weakness, premature balding, and, finally, "early decay," if subject to excessive intellectual drafts on their energy reserves. The apprehension about the depletion of bodily resources through intellectual activity was at the heart, it will be remembered, of the medical injunctions against higher education for women.

The new view of mind created philosophical shock waves as well. From the time when phrenologists proclaimed that "the brain is the organ of the mind," through the work of Alexander Bain and Herbert Spencer in arguing for a "biology of mind," to the maturation of physiological psychology in the latter part of the century, the mind-body problem festered. During this period Wilhelm Wundt established as the program for physiology "the reduction of vital phenomena to general physiological laws," and this procedure was being applied with notable success to the brain. Psychiatrists, psychologists, and neurologists applauded this development, yet with each increment to the deepening understanding of the brain the philosophical issue intensified. If the mind depended in some sense on the activity of the brain, was mind no more than brain? Was there really no such thing as mind at all, but only the complex interactions of neurons in the cerebral cortex? The mind of modern science could no longer be thought of as "a separate Immaterial existence, mysteriously connected . . . with a Bodily instrument." How then was it to be thought of?[21]

A number of scientists tried to duck the question by means of the doctrine of psycho-physical parallelism. But useful as this principle was methodologically, it did little to allay the metaphysical concerns of those who feared the reduction of mind to matter. This fear was far from idle. Traditionalists could hear the forces of materialism at the door in the persons of T. H. Huxley calling for "the . . . banishment from all regions of human thought of what we call spirit and spontaneity," and Henry Maudsley devaluing consciousness and denying free will. The impact on the educated public is suggested by the reaction of the popular writer and reformer Frances Power Cobbe. In her essay "Unconscious Cerebration," which gratefully acknowleged the guidance of William Carpenter, Cobbe asked whether thoughtful individuals could "face the real or supposed tendency of science to prove that 'Thought is a Function of Matter,' and yet logically retain faith in personal Immortality?" Using Carpenter's concept of "unconscious cerebration" to make the case for the separability of the conscious self from the physical brain, Cobbe returned a hopeful, if not entirely resounding, yes: "Let us then accept cheerfully the possibility, perhaps the probability, that science ere long will proclaim the dogma, 'Matter can think.' Having humbly bowed to the decree, we shall find ourselves none the worse. Admitting that our brains accomplish much without our conscious guidance, will help us to realize that our relation to them is of a variable—an intermittent—and (we may therefore venture to hope) of a *terminable* kind." So might the anxious continue to believe that " 'when the dust returns to the dust whence it was taken, the Spirit'—the Conscious Self of Man—'shall return to God who gave it.' "[22]

How many Victorians found solace in Cobbe's attempt at positive thinking it is not possible to know. But her essay, together with the sometimes strained reasoning of scientists like John Cleland and William Carpenter, is indicative of the apprehensive undercurrents stirred by the encroachment of empirical science on that bastion of human distinctiveness, the mind. The naturalization of mind, at worst, threatened to annihilate the human soul.

The Darkening Vision of the Future

Other sources of the darkening vision of late-nineteenth-century science and social thought include the failure of insane asylums to effect lasting cures of their patients, the intractability of poverty and vice, and the increasing emphasis on heredity rather than environment in shaping human character. These sources were interrelated. Physicians who, earlier in the century, had believed in the curability of a large proportion of the mentally ill, now found the statistics increasingly opposed to that hypothesis. Recovery rates in hospitals for the insane dropped markedly between 1870 and 1910. Social reformers met with little success in their efforts to improve the lives of the delinquent and the deficient. Mark Haller writes that physicians and social workers "found that the insane were largely incurable, the feebleminded proved to be untrainable, criminals returned to their lives of crime, alcoholics clung to their bottles, and the poor seemed often to prefer a life of indolence and want." Repeated difficulty in achieving the moral and mental reformation of the social outcast eventually encouraged reformers to move away from views of human nature that emphasized the role of environment toward one emphasizing heredity: "Since [social reformers] could not believe that normal people could act like this, they came to believe that these problem ones must be afflicted with a fatal flaw." Criminal anthropologists gave an academic gloss to this association of heredity and incurability with their theory of atavistic reversion: the "born criminal" could never be reformed.[23]

Belief in a fixed hereditary endowment was gathering strength at this same time among biologists. Two names will suffice to represent this trend. Beginning in the 1880s August Weismann mounted his powerful attack on the inheritance of acquired characters. The result was to create a distinction between the soma and the germ cells and to deny that somatic change in the parent could affect the offspring. Weismann did not argue that the environment had no importance in the development of individuals, nor did he claim that all traits were biologically inherited. But he did sever the link between environmental change in one generation and altered offspring in the next. This had the effect of minimizing the role of environment in evolution and spotlighting the role of heredity.[24]

In England Francis Galton was probably the single greatest influence in promoting hereditarianism. (Darwin, by contrast, remained much more latitudinarian about the mechanisms of inheritance, though after reading Galton's *Hereditary Genius* he confessed himself at least a partial convert to his cousin's views.) It pleased Galton to believe that his writings were instrumental in changing the popular conception of intelligence. In a preface to the second edition of *Hereditary Genius,* published in 1892, Galton wrote that "at the time when the book was written [1869], the human mind was popularly thought to act independently of natural laws, and to be capable of almost any achievement, if compelled to exert itself by a will that had power of initiation. Even those who had more philosophical habits of thought were far from looking upon the mental faculties of each individual as being limited with as much strictness as those of his body, still less was the idea of the hereditary transmission of ability clearly comprehended." Galton's pride in having shifted the climate of opinion toward "the hereditary transmission of ability" may well have been warranted. Certainly social thought moved in this direction, and he was one of the earliest and most insistent exponents of the new view. In the English-speaking world Galton's name became virtually synonymous with hereditarianism.[25]

Heredity and environment had not been seen as competing alternatives earlier in the nineteenth century, when it was supposed that both factors interacted. As Charles Rosenberg points out, hereditarianism was very much a part of the invigorating reformist climate of midcentury: "The mood which characterized the growing use of hereditarian ideas in the middle third of the century was one of confidence that man's most fundamental attributes could and should be manipulated." Health reformers like William Alcott and Sylvester Graham and the phrenologist Fowler brothers enthusiastically promoted knowledge of the laws of heredity as the means to creating new generations "having all that is great, and noble, and good in man, all that is pure, and virtuous, and beautiful, and angelic in woman." The heredity celebrated in these terms was not seen as a closed system, impervious to manipulation. Rather, hope rested in the belief that parents, ensuring their own physical and mental health by right living, could pass this health on to their offspring.[26]

Such confidence could be sustained only so long as the inheritance of acquired characteristics remained an intellectually viable belief. If Weismann were right, and no bodily change could be transmitted via the germ plasm to future generations, then hope for a direct route to social reformation vanished. Environmental reform or parental betterment would be of no avail; directed breeding alone could improve the race. This conclusion deeply distressed reform-minded social scientists like Lester Frank Ward, who lamented: "If nothing that the individual gains by the most heroic or the most assiduous effort can by any possibility be handed on to posterity, the incentive to effort is in great part removed . . . If, as Mr. Galton puts it, nurture is nothing and nature is everything, why not abandon nurture and leave the race wholly to nature?" "If Weismann [is] right," seconded Joseph LeConte, "then, alas for all our hopes of race improvement, whether physical, mental, or moral!" Rather than accept what he saw as an injunction to social laissez-faire, Ward preferred to fly the increasingly tattered banner of Lamarck well into the twentieth century.[27]

It would be wrong to see a simple causal relationship between the decline of Lamarckianism and the rise of neo-Darwinism, on the one hand, and the tough-mindedness and pessimism of fin de siècle thought, on the other. In the first place, Weismann's victory was not assured in the 1890s. America, indeed, had raised up a school of neo-Lamarckians that spoke for the majority of American biologists in challenging Weismann's theory. Further, Lamarckianism did not guarantee optimism. It could be construed to emphasize the fixing of negative traits acquired by ancestors in the hereditary makeup of subsequent generations. This was precisely the way degeneration occurred, when alcoholism or criminality, for example, entered the family lineage by way of an errant parent and accumulated in the germ cells of subsequent generations. The concept was a kind of secularized biblical moralism, the sins of the fathers being quite literally visited upon their children. It is true that most Lamarckians left open the possibility that degeneration could be reversed: if families lapsed into crime, insanity, pauperism, and immorality, so too they might be uplifted to health and virtue. But not all degeneration theorists were so hopeful. Henry Maudsley provides an example. Explaining that "in consequence of evil ancestral influences, individuals are born with such a flaw or warp of Nature that all the care in the world will not prevent them from being vicious or criminal, or becoming insane," Maudsley warned darkly that "no one can escape the tyranny of his organization; no one can elude the destiny that is innate in him." Maudsley could have been writing the script for Frank Norris's *McTeague,* in which the protagonist was the unwitting victim of a family taint that swept him inexorably to ruin. Norris's fictive universe, like that of his model Emile Zola, was one of Lamarckian determinism.[28]

Rather than assume that neo-Darwinism initiated a mood swing toward pessimistic determinism, it would probably be nearer the truth to suppose that it helped confirm it. There were many reasons for intellectuals and social reformers to feel grimmer about the human prospect late in the nineteenth century, and the loss of Lamarckian meliorism was not primary among them. Yet neo-Darwinism did narrow the options for meaningful reform, and the loss hurt. "In this century of pessimism," wrote an American reviewer of Weismann's work, "I know of no theory more pessimistic than the Weismann theory of heredity." Not only did it undercut much of the rationale for environmental reform, but it also threatened individual autonomy. In a perceptive analysis of European thought, Edward A. Ross charged Weismannism with attacking "the independence of the individual." To exalt the primacy of birth endowment was to subvert human freedom: "Heredity rules our lives like that supreme primeval necessity that stood above the Olympian Gods."[29]

All in all, the physical and biological ideas of the period from 1860 to about 1910 seem to have lent credence to a social philosophy of diminished expectations. Humanity had been rudely displaced from its former high status, a little lower in rank than the angels, and thrust into disquieting propinquity to the chimpanzee. Its godlike intellect was shorn of its metaphysical grandeur and firmly situated among the neurons of the cerebral cortex, its peerless powers shrunk to the measure of a frail and exhaustible frame. One result of the new focus on limitation and disability was an outspoken repudiation of political and social equality. As the noted Mendelian William Bateson proclaimed, "Of abstract rights, biology knows little: of equal rights, nothing." Liberty, equality, and fraternity came under scientific attack as discredited metaphysical fictions of the unscientific eighteenth century. Modern scientists had learned a different lesson: "nature in her arrangements is eminently hierarchical and not democratic." Specialization and division of labor inevitably created castes, and castes rested on "the predominance of the more over the less morally and intellectually gifted members of a community." Nature spoke in unambiguous terms: "the cuckoo cry of 'equality' is simply absurd." Dorothy Ross corroborates, in her biography of G. Stanley Hall, the easy association of scientific ideas with social inegalitarianism: "In an era of social Darwinism, Hall considered inequality the decree of nature."[30]

Francis Galton made a lifetime career out of the dissemination of this doctrine of natural inequality. Unrelentingly hostile to the ideas of the Enlightenment and hence to any reform measure based on egalitarianism, Galton exclaimed, "It is in the most unqualified manner that I object to pretensions of natural equality." Galton's disciple and biographer Karl Pearson referred to his mentor as "a thoroughgoing aristocrat, if such be involved in a denial of the equality of all men; he would have graded mankind by their natural aptitudes, and have done his best to check the reproduction of the lower grades."[31]

This vision of human hierarchy did not await the coming of Darwinism, but Darwinism certainly reinforced it, lending credibility to a number of frankly inegalitarian social policy proposals. Galton and Bateson were among those who centered their hopes for humanity on a thoroughgoing program of eugenics, which would encourage the reproduction of the talented and gifted while discouraging the reproduction of the less well-endowed. Another possibility lay in the testing and tracking of students in the schools. After the turn of the century newly devised intelligence tests could be used to assign pupils to different classes, or different levels of difficulty within the same class, on the basis of their test scores. G. Stanley Hall saw in such a program the solution to the conflict between natural inequality and social democracy. He would tailor education to individual variations, he wrote, and thus "bring discrimination down to the very basis of our educational pyramid." Human diversity for these biologists and psychologists, as well as for all those social scientists enraptured by the division of labor, remained the linchpin of social progress; distinctions of class and status were rather to be cherished than abolished. "It is the heterogeneity of modern man," wrote Bateson, "which has given him his control of the forces of nature. The maintenance of that heterogeneity, that differentiation of members, is a condition of progress. The aim of social reform must be not to abolish class, but to provide that each individual shall as far as possible get into the right class and stay there, and usually his children after him."[32]

The open espousal of a hierarchical order is, I would argue, part of the same intellectual universe that was absorbing the meaning of evolution for human nature and society. Science had disclosed that the cosmos was not as human beings might wish it, nor was their own place within it so singular as they had once been pleased to suppose. In the words of Henry Maudsley, the lesson of modern scientific inquiry was "more and more daily to show that man is but a part of nature, and not a small god for whom all has been created." A small god he had assuredly once been: "What a piece of work is a man," Shakespeare had exulted. "How noble in reason! how infinite in faculty! in form, in moving, how express and admirable! in action how like an angel! in apprehension how like a god! the beauty of the world! the paragon of animals!" But, godlike no longer, humanity stood revealed in all its creatureliness—so like the ape, so liable, as any machine is liable, to diminishment and depletion, so recently and precariously civilized.[33] In this new world of circumscribed horizons, where the table was spread not for all equally, but only for the brightest and the best, the language of invidious comparison sprang readily to the pen. Scientists became the prophets of an updated Calvinism, ordaining some—the white, the civilized, the European, the male—to evolutionary maturity, and others—the dark-skinned, the primitive, the female—to perpetual infancy. The cosmos itself disdained equality.

Under any circumstances it would have been extremely difficult for nineteenth-century scientists to arrive at some more favorable conclusions about women. The doctrine of female inferiority wore the habiliments of long familiarity: It was consonant with everything that scientists, like other men, had learned about women from childhood. It was preached from the pulpits of their churches. It fitted comfortably into scientific theories of impeccable standing. It explained, as it justified, the existing disparities in sex roles. Then, too, men's lives would in fact be immensely complicated by any abdication of women from the sanctuary of the home. Moreover, the stability of the established social order appeared at risk; hence women's derogation of duty was not just personal but societal.

But the circumstances just at this time were particularly precarious. During these years scientists were being asked to re-vision their universe: once orderly and stable, it was now to be perceived as evolving, mercurial, fickle. Nor was humanity preserved from the anarchic flux—it too changed and shifted, evolved and de-volved, was implicated in a hairy ancestry. How feeble and frail after all were human beings, how brief their tenure of the earth, how precarious their civilization. Sharing with other men the ap-prehension created by women's determined assault on the enclaves of masculine privilege, scientists had a particular need to reaffirm their ontological stature. In coming to terms with the evolutionary perspective, they sought to order their knowledge in a way that would affirm their own privileged status in the human hierarchy by contrasting it with that of those less fortunate. Self-definition de-manded an other, a not-self with characteristics different from one's own, against whom to measure oneself.

A dramatic incident in the life of William James is instructive here. Already in a state of "philosophical pessimism and general depression," the young James visited an insane asylum in France in 1872 and saw there "a black-haired youth with greenish skin, entirely idiotic, who used to sit all day on one of the benches, or rather against the wall, with his knees drawn up against his chin, and the coarse gray undershirt, which was his only garment, drawn over them enclosing his entire figure. He sat there like a sort of Egyptian mummy, moving nothing but his black eyes and looking absolutely non-human." The apparition terrified him: "*That shape am I,* I felt, potentially. Nothing that I possess can defend me against that fate, if the hour for it should strike for me as it struck for him." The unfortunate youth was an epileptic, and epilepsy was one of the diseases that Hughlings Jackson had identified as causing the mind to regress toward animality. Mindless, the boy was a genuine evolutionary aberration; epilepsy had destroyed his humanity.[34]

James's reaction to this vision was to internalize it: "*That shape am I.*" A would-be scientist who rebelled against the dogma and determinism of the science he studied, James was an extraordinarily sensitive and empathetic individual. His instinctive identification with the wretch in the asylum presaged his later career as a psychol-ogist who could write an entire essay on "the blindness with which we all are afflicted in regard to the feelings of creatures and people different from ourselves."[35]

In the eyes of the scientists whose dogma James rejected, however, that same epileptic youth could have a very different significance. They felt no temptation to empathy; quite the contrary. Like the idiot who grinned and chattered and displayed his genitals, like the savage who chopped off his toes to fit into his boots, this huddled shape of dubious humanity could stand between the scientist and the animal kingdom, a visible reminder that in the Great Chain of Being the scientist himself stood at least one link away from the ape. There was safety in distance.

In their more refined way, women subserved the same need. Far more numerous than idiots and more proximate than savages, women objectified a phase of evolution which men had transcended. They testified in their very otherness to masculine excellence. Women have always served, in Virginia Woolf's luminous metaphor, as looking-glasses "possessing the magic and delicious power of reflecting the figure of man at twice its natural size." No one knew better than post-Darwinian men of science how problematic man's natural size had become. Yet their affirmation of self required a simultaneous denigration of women, for, as Woolf continues, "if [women] were not inferior, they would cease to enlarge." Ceasing to enlarge—this was the crime women were committing when they demanded to vote, to attend college, to become economically independent. And they were doing these things just at the moment when psychic enhancement was more important than ever. The professorial anger which leaped off the page at Virginia Woolf in the library of the British Museum stemmed as much from fear as from arrogance. In a world turned topsy-turvy by evolution, it expressed apprehension, a sense of displacement.[36]

But do the ideas of a group of Victorian scientific gentlemen matter after all? Were they not simply utilizing the particular language of science to express ideas that were part of the wider culture? Yes and no. On the one hand, notions of female inferiority—physical, mental, and moral—dating as they did from antiquity, could hardly be considered novel. On the other hand, by virtue of the specificity of detail and inclusiveness of theory at its command, science was able to provide a newly plausible account of this inferiority. Measuring limbs, pondering viscera, reckoning up skulls, the new mandarins of gender difference were able to spell out in chapter and verse the manifold distinctions of sex. They spoke with

the confident voice of a profession that was at that moment successfully challenging the social authority of organized religion. Nature
was in the process of replacing nature's God as the final arbiter of
human affairs. Scientists, as the interpreters of nature, wielded an
authority that no other group commanded. When scientists spoke,
Victorians listened.[37]

Certainly the gentlemen themselves thought that what they were
saying mattered. Otherwise they would scarcely have been so
voluble and so tendentious. Certainly the women did too. We have
the testimony of M. Carey Thomas, growing up, she tells us,
"haunted . . . by the clanging chains of that gloomy little specter,
Dr. Edward H. Clarke's *Sex in Education*." Helen H. Gardener
knocked on the doors of neurologists seeking refutation of the
antifeminist neuroanatomy of Dr. William Hammond because of
her concern lest "educators, theorists, and politicians" accept the
findings of science and use them as a basis of action. Her fears were
warranted. At the University of Wisconsin in 1877 the Board of
Regents justified offering a special curriculum for women on the
basis of the limited-energy theory. "Every physiologist is well
aware," the Regents noted, that "at stated times nature makes a
great demand upon the energies of early womanhood."[38]

It seems reasonable, then, to accept all this testimony at face
value. Scientific ideas did more than reflect the status quo; they
helped maintain it. We shall never know how many "St. Theresas,
foundresses of nothing," floundered and failed, or never tried their
powers at all, discouraged by an uncongenial intellectual climate.[39]
It would not comfort them to know that their pain was inflicted by a
scientific establishment itself in the throes of a difficult adjustment
to a new and impersonal cosmos. Yet such, I believe, was the case.
The construction of womanhood by Victorian scientists grew out
of and was responsive to the very human needs of a particular
historical moment. It needs to be seen for the masculine power play
that it was, but it needs to be seen also as an intellectual monument,
etched in fear, of the painful transition to the modern world view.

Notes
Index

Notes

Introduction

Epigraphs: Virginia Woolf, *A Room of One's Own* (1929; London: Hogarth Press, 1974); Michael T. Ghiselin, *The Economy of Nature and the Evolution of Sex* (Berkeley: University of California Press, 1974), 61.

1. John Stuart Mill and Harriet Taylor Mill, *Essays on Sex Equality*, ed. and with an Introductory Essay by Alice S. Rossi (Chicago: University of Chicago Press, 1970), 125, 149, 148. On *The Subjection of Women* see also Josephine Kamm, *John Stuart Mill in Love* (London: Gordon and Cremonesi, 1977), and Eugene August, *John Stuart Mill: A Mind at Large* (New York: Charles Scribner's Sons, 1975).

2. Frances Power Cobbe, *Life of Frances Power Cobbe*, 2 vols. (Boston: Houghton Mifflin, 1893), 2:445. This vignette is mentioned in an unpublished essay by Jim Moore, "Woman's Place in Evolution: The Later-Victorian Ideology."

3. G. E. R. Lloyd, *Science, Folklore, and Ideology: Studies in the Life Sciences in Ancient Greece* (Cambridge: Cambridge University Press, 1983), 94–111; Carolyn Merchant, *The Death of Nature: Women, Ecology, and the Scientific Revolution* (San Francisco: Harper and Row, 1983), 158, 162.

4. The earliest physical anthropologists, it should be noted, were not enthusiasts for evolution, because as staunch racists they disliked the implications of a unitary descent for the human species. The president of the London Anthropological Society, James Hunt, asserted with pride, "If there be one society or one body of men who have more earnestly, more continually, persisted in attacking and endeavoring to refute the doctrines respecting man's origin by Mr. Darwin, or either of his disciples, that body is composed of men calling themselves Anthropologists." "President's Address to The Dundee Anthropological Conference," *Anthropological Review* 6 (1868), 77.

5. Reba N. Soffer, "The Revolution in English Social Thought, 1880–1914," *American Historical Review* 75 (1970), 1942n17, 1945.

6. Nina Morais, "A Reply to Miss Hardaker on the Woman Question," *Popular Science Monthly* 21 (1882); G. Stanley Hall, *Adolescence*, 2 vols. (New York: D. Appleton, 1904), 1:130–131.

7. Marvin Harris, *The Rise of Anthropological Theory* (New York: Thomas Y. Crowell, 1968), 78; see also Fred W. Voget, "Progress, Science, History, and Evolution in Eighteenth- and Nineteenth-Century Anthropology," *Journal of the History of the Behavioral Sciences* 3 (1967), 143.

8. Steven Shapin, " 'Homo Phrenologicus': Anthropological Perspectives on an Historical Problem," in *Natural Order: Historical Studies of Scientific Culture*, ed.

Barry Barnes and Steven Shapin (Beverly Hills, Calif.: Sage, 1979), 57; Frank E. Manuel, "From Equality to Organicism," *Journal of the History of Ideas* 17 (1956), 60.

9. George W. Stocking, Jr., Introductory Essay to James Cowles Prichard, *Researches into the Physical History of Man,* ed. George W. Stocking, Jr. (Chicago: University of Chicago Press, 1973), xxiv–xxxv.

10. General surveys of the nineteenth-century women's rights movement in America include the pioneering work of Eleanor Flexner, *Centuries of Struggle: The Woman's Rights Movement in the United States,* rev. ed. (Cambridge, Mass.: Harvard University Press, 1975); William O'Neill, *The Woman Movement: Feminism in the United States and England* (Chicago: Quadrangle, 1969); and Ellen Carol DuBois, *Feminism and Suffrage: The Emergence of an Independent Women's Movement in America* (Ithaca: Cornell University Press, 1978).

11. See Kamm, *John Stuart Mill in Love,* on Owenite and Benthamite feminism and its influence on Mill. Not all philosophical radicals were feminists, however; James Mill, for one, was not. On socialist feminism in England in the 1820s and 1830s see Barbara Taylor, *Eve and the New Jerusalem: Socialism and Feminism in the Nineteenth Century* (New York: Pantheon, 1983).

12. The movement for women's rights in England is treated in O'Neill, *Woman Movement;* Ray Strachey, *"The Cause"* (London: G. Bell and Sons, 1928); C. Bauer and L. Ritt, eds., *Source Readings in the Development of Victorian Feminism* (New York: Pergamon, 1979); Constance Rover, *Women's Suffrage and Party Politics in Britain, 1866–1914* (London: Routledge and Kegan Paul, 1967); and Richard J. Evans, *The Feminists: Women's Emancipation Movements in Europe, America, and Australasia, 1840–1920* (London: Croom, Helm; New York: Barnes and Noble, 1977).

13. Criticism of Blackwell's different-but-equal argument can be found in Evelleen Richards, "Darwin and the Descent of Woman," in *The Wider Domain of Evolutionary Thought,* ed. D. Oldroyd and J. Langham (Dordrecht: D. Riedel, 1983), 96; and Flavia Alaya, "Victorian Science and the 'Genius' of Woman," *Journal of the History of Ideas* 38 (1977), 261–262. Marjorie Spruill Wheeler, "Sex, Science, and the 'Woman Question': *The Woman's Journal* on Woman's Nature and Potential, 1870–1875," paper delivered at the Organization of American Historians, Detroit, 1980, gives a qualified rebuttal.

14. Richard Lewontin, "Biological Determinism as a Social Weapon," in The Ann Arbor Science for the People Editorial Collective, *Biology as a Social Weapon* (Minneapolis: Burgess, 1977), 8.

1. How to Tell the Girls from the Boys

Epigraphs: Luke Owen Pike, "On the Claims of Women to Political Power," *Journal of the Anthropological Society* 7 (1869), lviii; "Biology and 'Woman's Rights,' " *Popular Science Monthly* 14 (1878–1879), 204; W. I. Thomas, "The Mind of Woman," *American Magazine* 67 (1908–1909), 146.

1. J. G. Spurzheim, *Phrenology, or the Doctrine of Mental Phenomena,* 2 vols. (Boston: Marsh, Capen, and Lyon, 1833), 1:57.

2. George Combe, *Elements of Phrenology,* 18, quoted in A. Cameron Grant, "Combe on Phrenology and Free Will: A Note on XIXth-Century Secularism," *Journal of the History of Ideas* 26 (1965), 145; L. S. Jacyna, "The Physiology of Mind, the Unity of Nature, and the Moral Order in Victorian Thought," *British Journal for the History of Science* 14 (1981), 116; Angus McLaren's comment that phrenology functioned as an alternative to religion is quoted in R. J. Cooter, "Phrenology: The Provocation of Progress," *History of Science* 14 (1976), 220.

3. Robert M. Young, *Mind, Brain, and Adaptation in the Nineteenth Century* (Oxford: Clarendon Press, 1970), 16.

4. Spurzheim, *Phrenology,* 1:97; *Phrenological Journal,* quoted in David de Giustino, *Conquest of Mind: Phrenology and Victorian Social Thought* (London: Croom Helm, 1975), 72; Spurzheim, *Phrenology,* 1:182, 199, 185, 208, 181–182; George Combe, *Elements of Phrenology* (Boston: Marsh, Capen, and Lyon, 1835), 44.

5. Spurzheim, *Phrenology,* 1:150–152, 156; George Combe, *Lectures on Phrenology* (New York: Fowler and Wells, 1854), 30, 33.

6. Spurzheim, *Phrenology,* 2:78, 80; Hamilton quoted in David Bakan, "The Influence of Phrenology on American Philosophy," *Journal of the History of the Behavioral Sciences* 2 (1966), 214.

7. George Combe, *The Constitution of Man Considered in Relation to External Objects,* 2d ed. (Edinburgh: John Anderson Jun., 1835), 4, 11; O. S. and L. N. Fowler, *The Self-Instructor in Phrenology and Physiology* (New York: Fowler and Wells, n.d.), 11, 80; Fowler quoted in Bakan, "Influence of Phrenology," 204. Most commentators on phrenology have been impressed by its liberal reform orientation. R. J. Cooter, by contrast, emphasizes its uses in the control of the working class by the middle class: "Phrenology . . . provided a simple key to understanding the need to obey the Laws of Nature; radical social and political schemes were shown to be unnecessary—unnatural—for with phrenology the individual could improve himself. The old truism was reinstated; misery was really of one's own making." "Phrenology: The Provocation of Progress," 228. Phrenology was certainly not radical in its social implications, but Cooter's interpretation has to contend with the fact that enthusiasts for phrenology tended to be the very people involved in movements for social (not just individual) reform, such as abolitionism and women's rights.

8. Barbara Taylor, *Eve and the New Jerusalem: Socialism and Feminism in the Nineteenth Century* (New York: Pantheon, 1983), quote on 27–28.

9. Madeleine B. Stern, *Heads and Headlines: The Phrenological Fowlers* (Norman, Okla.: University of Oklahoma Press, 1971), 166.

10. Jessie A. Fowler, *Men and Women Compared; Or Their Mental and Physical Differences Considered* (London: L. N. Fowler, n.d.), 3, 9, 5.

11. On prize for critical essay, John Davies, *Phrenology: Fad and Science* (New Haven: Yale University Press, 1955), 66; Alexander Bain, *On the Study of Character, Including an Estimate of Phrenology* (London: Parker, Son, and Burn, 1861), 24–29.

12. Davies, *Phrenology,* 171; Bain, *On the Study of Character,* 16; Roger Smith, "The Background of Physiological Psychology in Natural Philosophy," *History of Science* 11 (1973), 86–87; Young, *Mind, Brain, and Adaptation,* 4, 21.

13. Lucille E. Hayme, "Physical Anthropology and Its Instruments: An Historical Study," *Southwestern Journal of Anthropology* 9 (1953), 413, 415–416.

14. George W. Stocking, Jr., *Race, Culture, and Evolution* (New York: Free Press, 1969), 45.

15. Marvin Harris, *The Rise of Anthropological Theory* (New York: Thomas Y. Crowell, 1968), 78; Fred W. Voget, "Progress, Science, History and Evolution in Eighteenth- and Nineteenth-Century Anthropology," *Journal of the History of the Behavioral Sciences* 3 (1967), 143, 145; George W. Stocking, Jr., "What's in a Name? The Origins of the Royal Anthropological Institute (1837–71)," *Man*, n.s., 6 (1971), 369–390. Terminology presents a problem in discussing nineteenth-century attitudes toward race. Stocking asserts that all scientists at that time were racists, although some were milder racists than others. James Cowles Prichard, *Researches into the Physical History of Man,* ed. and with an introductory essay by George W. Stocking, Jr. (Chicago: University of Chicago Press, 1973), lvii. Idus L. Murphree, on the contrary, absolves the evolutionary anthropologists, among them John Lubbock, Lewis Henry Morgan, and Edward Taylor, of the charge of racism: "Racism was not only generally absent from the evolutionary school, it was tacitly forbidden." Murphree, "The Evolutionary Anthropologists: The Progress of Mankind," *Proceedings of the American Philosophical Society* 105 (1961), 282. The contradiction can be resolved by making use of a helpful distinction between ethnocentrism, or the assumption of the superiority of one's own society on the basis of cultural ascendancy, and racism proper, or the assumption of a superiority based on biological inheritance. All nineteenth-century scientists believed in the preeminence of European civilization, but they differed as to its cause. In the terms defined above they were ethnocentrist to a man, but they were not all racist. Douglas Lorimer, in *Colour, Class and the Victorians* (New York: Holmes and Meier, 1978), 16, adopts this distinction, which he attributes to Pierre L. van den Berghe and Michael Banton.

16. Henry L. Shapiro, "The History and Development of Physical Anthropology," *American Anthropologist*, n.s., 61 (1959), 373; Donald Bender, "The Development of French Anthropology," *Journal of the History of the Behavioral Sciences* 1 (1965), 139–151. On Paul Broca, see the title essay in Carl Sagan, *Broca's Brain* (New York: Random House, 1969). William Stanton, *The Leopard's Spots: Scientific Attitudes toward Race in America, 1812–59* (Chicago: University of Chicago Press, 1960), is the standard source on American racial science before the Civil War. On Louis Agassiz's contribution see especially pp. 100–109. Hayme, "Physical Anthropology and Its Instruments," demonstrates the continuity of phrenology and physical anthropology in the person of Samuel Morton.

17. Typology in anthropology is discussed in Stocking, *Race, Culture, and Evolution,* 168–169, and especially in Herbert H. Odum, "Generalizations on Race in Nineteenth-Century Physical Anthropology," *Isis* 58 (1967), 5–18. Odum, in turn, is indebted to the work of Ernst Mayr on the anti-typological nature of Darwinism. See, for example, Mayr, "Darwin and the Evolutionary Theory in Biology," in The Anthropological Society of Washington, *Evolution and Anthropology: A Centennial Appraisal,* ed. Betty J. Meggers (Washington, D.C.: n.p., 1959), 1–10. Of the effect of typological thinking on early anthropology, Clifford

Geertz notes that "the differences among individuals and among groups of individuals are rendered secondary. Individuality comes to be seen as eccentricity, distinctiveness as accidental deviation from the only legitimate object of study for the true scientist: the underlying, unchanging, normative type." Geertz, *The Interpretation of Cultures* (New York: Basic Books, 1973), 51.

18. [James Hunt], "Race in Legislation and Political Economy," *Anthropological Review* 4 (1866), 116; Hunt, Fourth Presidential Address, *Journal of the Anthropological Society of London* 5 (1867), lx. On Hunt and the "fiercer spirits" of the London Anthropological Society, see Stocking, "What's in a Name?" and Ronald Rainger, "Race, Politics, and Science: The Anthropological Society of London in the 1860s," *Victorian Studies* 22 (1978), 51–70. According to Rainger unsigned articles in the *Anthropological Review* were probably written by James Hunt, its editor.

19. "Broca on Anthropology," *Anthropological Review* 6 (1868), 45–46; Carl Vogt, *Lectures on Man* (London: Longman, Green, Longman, and Roberts, 1864), 91. On British scientific attitudes toward race, see Nancy Stepan, *The Idea of Race in Science, Great Britain, 1800–1960* (Hamden, Conn.: Archon Books, 1982).

20. James McGrigor Allan, "On the Real Differences in the Minds of Men and Women," *Journal of the Anthropological Society of London* 7 (1869), ccxii; "Broca on Anthropology," 46.

21. Remarks of Mr. T. Bendyshe on James Hunt's paper, "On the Negro's Place in Nature," *Anthropological Review* 2 (1864), xxxvi–xxxvii; Hunt, "Race in Legislation," 115.

22. Havelock Ellis, *Man and Woman: A Study of Human Secondary Sexual Characteristics* (London: Walter Scott, 1894), 39, 41–43. Many scientists were less cautious than Ellis. Edward Drinker Cope, one of the foremost American paleontologists of his time, characterized the greater length of the Negro arm as "another approximation to the ape." Cope, *The Origin of the Fittest* (1887; New York: Arno Press, 1974), 147.

23. Ellis, *Man and Woman*, 53–54.

24. Vogt, *Lectures on Man*, 9, 81 (on men's and women's skulls as belonging to two different species Vogt was paraphrasing the German craniologist Welcker); Ellis, *Man and Woman*, 71–74.

25. G. Delauney, "Equality and Inequality in Sex," *Popular Science Monthly* 20 (1881–82), 184–185; Ellis, *Man and Woman*, 202, 210; William I. Thomas, "On a Difference in the Metabolism of the Sexes," *American Journal of Sociology* 3 (1897), 47–49. The comment about pianists is Delauney's (185).

26. McGrigor Allan, "On the Real Differences," cxcvii, cxcviii, cxcix.

27. Ellis, *Man and Woman*, 246, 256; Mary Putnam Jacobi, *The Question of Rest for Women during Menstruation* (New York: G. P. Putnam's Sons, 1886; rpt. Farmingdale, N.Y.: Dabor Social Science Publications, 1978), 2–3. Jacobi's was an authoritative voice, as she was one of the first to do empirical research into the effects of menstruation on women. Carroll Smith-Rosenberg discusses nineteenth-century medical attitudes toward menstruation in "Puberty to Menopause: The Cycle of Femininity in Nineteenth-Century America," *Feminist Studies* 1 (1973), 58–72.

28. Elizabeth Fee, "Nineteenth-Century Craniology: The Study of the Female Skull," *Bulletin of the History of Medicine* 53 (1979), 426; John S. Haller, Jr., *Outcasts from Evolution: Scientific Attitudes of Racial Inferiority, 1859–1900* (Urbana: University of Illinois Press, 1971), 15; Hayme, "Physical Anthropology and Its Instruments," 418. Carl Sagan visited the Musée de l'Homme in Paris, where Broca's own brain is preserved in a bottle, and imagined "the presence of nineteenth-century museum directors engaged, in their frock coats, in *goniometrie* and *craniologie*, busily collecting and measuring everything, in the pious hope that mere quantification would lead to understanding." *Broca's Brain*, 4.

29. Edward Anthony Spitzka, "A Study of the Brain of the Late Major J. W. Powell," *American Anthropologist*, n.s., 5 (1903), 586. On the development of physiological psychology see L. S. Jacyna, "The Physiology of Mind, the Unity of Nature, and the Moral Order in Victorian Thought," *British Journal for the History of Science* 14 (1981), 109–132; R. Smith, "The Background of Physiological Psychology in Natural Philosophy," *History of Science* 11 (1973), 75–123; and Kurt Danziger, "Mid-Nineteenth-Century British Psycho-Physiology: A Neglected Chapter in the History of Psychology," in *The Problematic Science: Psychology in Nineteenth-Century Thought*, ed. William R. Woodward and Mitchell G. Ash (New York: Praeger, 1982), 119–146.

30. Haller, *Outcasts*, 9–11; Vogt, *Lectures on Man*, 52; Hermann Schaaffhausen, "On the Primitive Form of the Human Skull," *Anthropological Review* 6 (1868), 424, 425; Ellis, *Man and Woman*, 4th ed. (London: Walter Scott, 1911), 91.

31. Stephen Jay Gould, *The Mismeasure of Man* (New York: W. W. Norton, 1981), 98–100; Topinard, *Anthropology* (London: Chapman and Hall, 1878), 236; Schaaffhausen, "On the Primitive Form," 414; Fee, "Nineteenth-Century Craniology," 423, 426. Topinard's *Anthropology*, with an approving introduction by his mentor, Broca, is a standard text. Havelock Ellis provides a good summary of the cephalic index in *Man and Woman*, 4th ed., 81–87.

32. Broca quoted in Stephen Jay Gould, "Women's Brains," *Natural History* 87 (1978), 44; Hammond, *A Treatise on Insanity in Its Medical Relations* (New York: D. Appleton, 1883), 13.

33. Topinard, *Anthropology*, 226–231.

34. Spitzka believed it "a legitimate claim of science that all persons, particularly those of superior intellectual capacity, permit themselves to become available for scientific study immediately after death." "A Death Mask of W. J. McGee," *American Anthropologist*, n.s., 15 (1913), 538.

35. Spitzka, "Powell's Brain," 610–611; Spitzka, "A Study of the Brains of Six Eminent Scientists and Scholars Belonging to the American Anthropological Society, Together with a Description of the Skull of Professor E. D. Cope," *Transactions of the American Philosophical Society* 21 (1908), 195.

36. Spitzka, "Powell's Brain," 602; Spitzka, "Study of the Brains of Six Scientists," 223–224.

37. Gould, *Mismeasure of Man*, 103; Vogt, *Lectures on Man*, 82; Hammond, *Insanity*, 102; Delauney, "Equality and Inequality in Sex," 185; Romanes, "Mental Differences between Men and Women," *Nineteenth Century* 21 (1887), 666.

38. Delauney, "Equality and Inequality in Sex," 186; Gould, *Mismeasure of Man*, 104–105; Vogt, *Lectures on Man*, 81.

39. Ashley Montagu, *The Natural Superiority of Women* (New York: Macmillan, 1954), 66; Fee, "Nineteenth-Century Craniology," 421; Helen H. Gardener, "Sex in Brain," in *Facts and Fictions of Life* (Boston: Arena, 1895), 112; Ellis, *Man and Woman*, 102. Cf. Joseph Simms, "Human Brain Weights," *Popular Science Monthly* 31 (1887), 358: "any reflecting person who has studied the brain-weights of eminent men as compared with ordinary intelligence must arrive at the same conclusion—that a great mind may belong to a person who carries a very small, a medium-sized, or a very large brain." Gould notes that Broca's own brain was an undistinguished 1,484 grams, and that Walt Whitman "managed to hear the varied carols of America singing with only 1,282 g." "Wide Hats and Narrow Minds," in *The Panda's Thumb: More Reflections on Natural History* (New York: W. W. Norton, 1980), 150.

40. Vogt, *Lectures on Man*, 86–87; Spitzka, "Powell's Brain," 591–592. How easily the evidence against ranking brains according to weight could be dismissed is seen in the continuing bias in favor of large brains up until the quite recent past. Writing in 1952, Ashley Montagu asserted, "I have never met anyone outside, and few in, scientific circles who did not believe that women had smaller brains and therefore less intelligence than men." *Natural Superiority of Women*, 66.

41. Ellis, *Man and Woman*, 95–99. See also Fee, "Nineteenth-Century Craniology," 421–428; Gould, *Mismeasure of Man*, 106, 104.

42. Spitzka, "Study of the Brains of Six Scientists," 224–225; Spitzka, "Powell's Brain," 604–606. Sartzee (more properly Saartjie), the Hottentot Venus, was a Bushwoman who earned her small niche in the annals of nineteenth-century anthropology primarily on the basis of two arresting physical characteristics: her steatopygous (extraordinarily large) buttocks and her *tablier*, or vaginal veil. On a less sensational note, scientists were also interested in the appearance of her brain, which they adjudged strikingly small and simple. Preserved in the Musée de l'Homme, it showed itself to be "palpably inferior to that of a normally developed white woman, and could only be compared with the brain of a white idiotic from arrest of cerebral development." Henry Maudsley, *Body and Mind* (New York: D. Appleton, 1874), 52. In the early 1980s Stephen Jay Gould visited the Musée de l'Homme and spotted Sartzee's genitalia pickled in a jar on the shelf above Broca's brain—a monument to the prurient racism of nineteenth-century anthropology. Stephen Jay Gould, "The Hottentot Venus," in *The Flamingo's Smile* (New York: W. W. Norton, 1985), 291–301.

43. Gould, *Mismeasure of Man*, 97.

44. Delauney, "Equality and Inequality in Sex," 186; Hammond, *Insanity*, 103, and "The Relations between the Mind and the Nervous System," *Popular Science Monthly* 26 (1884–85), 18.

45. Helen H. Gardener, letter entitled "Sex in Brain-Weight," *Popular Science Monthly* 31 (1887), 266. The subsequent controversy can be found on pp. 554–558, 698–700, and 846 of the same volume.

46. Gardener, "Sex in Brain," in *Facts and Fictions of Life*, 125, 101.

47. Charles Darwin, *The Descent of Man, and Selection in Relation to Sex*, 2d ed. (New York: P. F. Collier and Son, 1900), 586–587.

48. Darwin, *Descent*, 587. The converse would also be true. Cf. Karl Pearson, "Variation in Man and Woman," in *The Chances of Death and Other Studies in*

Evolution, 2 vols. (London: Edward Arnold, 1897), 1:323: "the existence of a higher average mental power in men, if it can be demonstrated, would not in the least touch the problem of the relative variability of the sexes."

49. Gardener, "Sex in Brain," in *Facts and Fictions of Life,* 109.

50. Romanes, "Mental Differences between Men and Women," 654. An interesting and helpful analysis of Romanes's views on women can be found in Susan Sleeth Mosedale, "Science Corrupted: Victorian Biologists Consider 'The Woman Question,' " *Journal of the History of Biology* 11 (1978), 16–24.

51. Romanes, "Mental Differences between Men and Women," 655–657.

52. Romanes, "Mental Differences between Men and Women," 657–658.

53. Romanes, "Mental Differences between Men and Women," 659–661.

54. Grant Allen, "Woman's Place in Nature," *Forum* 7 (1899), 258; Romanes, "Mental Differences between Men and Women," 663; Herbert Spencer, "Psychology of the Sexes," *Popular Science Monthly* 4 (1873–74), 31, 32; Thomas, "Difference in Metabolism," 60.

55. On the complex question of female sexuality in the late nineteenth century some helpful, though sometimes conflicting, interpretations are Carl Degler, "What Ought to Be and What Was: Women's Sexuality in the Nineteenth Century," *American Historical Review* 79 (1974), 1467–1490, and his *At Odds: Women and the Family in America from the Revolution to the Present* (New York: Oxford University Press, 1979); William G. Shade, " 'A Mental Passion': Female Sexuality in Victorian America," *International Journal of Women's Studies* 1 (1978), 13–29; Nancy Cott, "Passionlessness: An Interpretation of Victorian Sexual Ideology, 1790–1850," *Signs: A Journal of Women in Culture and Society* 4 (1978), 219–236; and G. J. Barker-Benfield, *The Horrors of the Half-Known Life: Male Attitudes toward Women and Sexuality in Nineteenth-Century America* (New York: Harper and Row, 1976). Campbell reports his findings on pp. 200–202 of *Differences in the Nervous Organisation of Man and Woman* (London: H. K. Lewis, 1891).

56. Campbell, *Differences in Nervous Organisation,* 210–212. Note the author's assumption that women not only could but would marry and bear children without the stimulus of sexual passion. Presumably he believed either that their desire for maternity would be sufficient motivation (a common view) or that, as weaker beings than men, they could not hold out against masculine ardor.

57. Ellis, *Man and Woman,* 193.

58. Francis Galton, *Inquiries into Human Faculty and Its Development* (1883; London: J. M. Dent and Sons, 1907), 20–21.

59. Romanes, "Mental Differences between Men and Women," 656–657.

60. Ellis, *Man and Woman,* 148–149.

61. Ellis, *Man and Woman,* 7th ed. (Boston: Houghton Mifflin, 1929), 265.

62. Galton's total disagreement with Alice Lee's finding that "skull capacity and brain power are not correlated" is given in Rosaleen Love, " 'Alice in Eugenics-Land': Feminism and Eugenics in the Scientific Careers of Alice Lee and Ethel Elderton," *Annals of Science* 36 (1979), 151; Galton, *Hereditary Genius* (1869; London: Macmillan, 1892), 35; Maudsley quoted in Vieda Skultans, *Madness and Morals: Ideas on Insanity in the Nineteenth Century* (London: Routledge and Kegan Paul, 1975), 21; G. Delauney, "Equality and Inequality in Sex," 192, paraphrasing T. L. W. Bischoff of Munich; Romanes, "Mental Differences between Men and Women," 655. "Shakespeare's sister," a creation of Virginia Woolf, was a "won-

derfully gifted" girl with a taste, like her brother's, for the theater, but, unlike him, with no schooling and no chance for training in her craft. Woolf tells us she would have ended her days a suicide, "buried at some cross-roads where the omnibuses now stop outside the Elephant and Castle." *A Room of One's Own* (1929; London: Hogarth Press, 1974), 70–73.

63. John Stuart Mill and Harriet Taylor Mill, *Essays on Sex Equality,* ed. and with an Introductory Essay by Alice S. Rossi (Chicago: University of Chicago Press, 1970), 186, 200–201. For a modern version of Mill's argument about negative facts, cf. David Hackett Fischer, *Historians' Fallacies: Toward a Logic of Historical Thought* (New York: Harper and Row, 1970), 62: "evidence must always be affirmative. Negative evidence is a contradiction in terms—it is no evidence at all. The nonexistence of an object is established not by nonexistent evidence but by affirmative evidence of the fact that it did not, or could not exist."

2. Up and Down the Phyletic Ladder

Epigraph: G. Stanley Hall, *Adolescence,* 2 vols. (New York: D. Appleton, 1904), 2:61, 192, 225–226.

1. William Coleman, *Biology in the Nineteenth Century: Problems of Form, Function, and Transformation* (New York: John Wiley and Sons, 1971), 47–49; E. S. Russell, *Form and Function* (London: John Murray, 1916), 256–257, 82.

2. Coleman, *Biology in the Nineteenth Century,* 52, quoting a standard manual of vertebrate embryology from the 1890s.

3. Quoted in Douglas A. Lorimer, *Colour, Class and the Victorians* (New York: Holmes and Meier, 1978), 148; "Thoughts and Facts Contributing to the History of Man," unsigned article, *Anthropological Review* 2 (1864), 179.

4. Arthur Lovejoy, *The Great Chain of Being* (Cambridge: Harvard University Press, 1936); Stephen Jay Gould, *Ontogeny and Phylogeny* (Cambridge: Harvard University Press, 1977), 23.

5. Quoted in Lorimer, *Colour, Class and the Victorians,* 146.

6. Carl Vogt, *Lectures on Man* (London: Longman, Green, Longman, and Roberts, 1864), 191–192; Harry Campbell, *Differences in the Nervous Organisation of Man and Woman* (London: H. K. Lewis, 1891), 155–160; Gould, *Ontogeny and Phylogeny,* 373, 438n9.

7. Paul Topinard, *Anthropology* (London: Chapman and Hall, 1878), 145; Topinard, quoted in William I. Thomas, "On a Difference in the Metabolism of the Sexes," *American Journal of Sociology* 3 (1897), 40; G. Delauney, "Equality and Inequality in Sex," *Popular Science Monthly* 20 (1881–82), 186; J. Ranke, German physiologist, cited in Thomas, "On a Difference," 41.

8. Campbell, *Differences in Nervous Organisation,* 162.

9. Edward Drinker Cope, *The Origin of the Fittest* (1887; New York: Arno Press, 1974), 159; G. Stanley Hall, *Adolescence,* 2:625.

10. J. McGrigor Allan, "On the Real Differences in the Minds of Men and Women," *Journal of Anthropology* 7 (1869), ccx; Vogt, *Lectures on Man,* 177, 180; Albrecht quoted in Thomas, "On a Difference," 42–43n3.

11. Ellis and Lombroso quoted in Gould, *Ontogeny and Phylogeny,* 124; Thomas, "On a Difference," 50.

12. Quoted in Havelock Ellis, *Man and Woman: A Study of Human Secondary Sexual Characteristics* (London: Walter Scott, 1894), 123–124.

13. Biographical material on Hall is from Dorothy Ross, *G. Stanley Hall: The Psychologist as Prophet* (Chicago: University of Chicago Press, 1972).

14. Hall, *Adolescence*, 2:62, 1:xviii.

15. Hall, *Adolescence*, 2:59, 50.

16. Hall, *Adolescence*, 2:719, 649. On Hall's racial attitudes see Ross, *G. Stanley Hall*, 213–216.

17. Hall, *Adolescence*, 2:61, 71, 1:x, xiii, xv.

18. Hall, "Some Aspects of the Early Sense of Self," in Alexander F. Chamberlain, *The Child: A Study in the Evolution of Man* (London and Felling-on-Tyne: Walter Scott, 1906), 228; Hall, *Adolescence*, 2:192, 194–195.

19. Hall, *Adolescence*, 1:xi–xii, x, xi.

20. Hall, *Adolescence*, 2:561–562.

21. Hall, *Adolescence*, 2:561, 646, 627, 646, 635.

22. Hall, *Adolescence*, 2:640, 623, 1:511.

23. Hall, *Adolescence*, 1:217–218, 2:623.

24. Ross, *G. Stanley Hall*, 97–98, 257, 266.

25. Thomas Laycock, "On the Naming and Classification of Mental Diseases and Defects," *Journal of Mental Science* 9 (1863), 166; "Periscope," *Journal of Nervous and Mental Diseases* 11 (1864), 538, quoted in S. P. Fullinwider, "William James's 'Spiritual Crisis,' " *Historian* 38 (1975), 46. The evolutionary conception of mind as developing from lower to higher centers is generally associated with the name of John Hughlings Jackson, eminent neurologist and student of Thomas Laycock, who was greatly influenced by the philosophy of Herbert Spencer. Hughlings Jackson also popularized the notion of the devolution or dissolution of the nervous system under the influence of disease. See, for example, J. Hughlings Jackson, *Remarks on Evolution and Dissolution of the Nervous System* (London: John Bale and Sons, 1888).

26. Cf. A. E. Carter, *The Idea of Decadence in French Literature* (Toronto: University of Toronto Press, 1958). Ironically, Zola's preoccupation with degeneration led to his being himself branded "a high-class degenerate" by Max Nordau in his popular appraisal of fin de siècle culture, *Degeneration* (New York: D. Appleton, 1895), 500. Frank Norris, *McTeague* (New York: International, 1900), 32; Jack London, *The Sea-Wolf* (1904; New York: Arcadia House, 1950), 75, 98.

27. Michael Ruse, *The Darwinian Revolution* (Chicago: University of Chicago Press, 1979), 24. I have followed Ruse's summary of pangenesis here.

28. Thomas Hunt Morgan, *Experimental Zoology* (New York: Macmillan, 1907), 58.

29. Charles Darwin, *The Descent of Man, and Selection in Relation to Sex* (1874; New York: P. F. Collier and Son, 1900), 56.

30. Chamberlain, *The Child*, 263; Hall, *Adolescence*, 2:194; Eugene S. Talbot, *Degeneracy: Its Causes, Signs, and Results* (London: Walter Scott, 1904), 33.

31. Chamberlain, *The Child*, 213–285. Quotations are found on pp. 255, 259, 280.

32. Charles Rosenberg, *No Other Gods: On Science and American Social Thought* (Baltimore: Johns Hopkins University Press, 1976), 43; Nathan G. Hale, Jr., *Freud and the Americans: The Beginnings of Psychoanalysis in the United States, 1876–1917*

(New York: Oxford Press, 1971), 75–78; Charles Rosenberg, *The Trial of the Assassin Guiteau: Psychiatry and Law in the Gilded Age* (Chicago: University of Chicago Press, 1968), 244–247.

33. Talbot, *Degeneracy*, 346–362. On reversibility or prevention of degeneration, cf. Rosenberg, *No Other Gods*, 34–47, and Hale, *Freud and the Americans*, 79. Rosenberg is at some pains to point out that hereditarian thought need not, and for much of the nineteenth century did not, entail pessimistic determinism.

34. Gould, *Ontogeny and Phylogeny*, 49–52; Topinard, *Anthropology*, 526.

35. Henry Maudsley, *Body and Mind* (New York: D. Appleton, 1874), 50, 48–49; Vogt, *Lectures on Man*, 202.

36. Nordau, *Degeneration*, 555–556, 283.

37. Arthur E. Fink, *Causes of Crime: Biological Theories in the United States, 1800–1915* (Philadelphia: University of Pennsylvania Press, 1938), 106.

38. Leonard Savitz lists these influences on Lombroso in the introduction to the reprint edition of Gina Lombroso-Ferrero, *Criminal Man According to the Classification of Cesare Lombroso* (1911; Montclair, N.J.: Patterson Smith, 1972). Havelock Ellis gives Darwin as the source of the "atavistic key" in *The Criminal* (London: Walter Scott, 1897), 38. Cesare Lombroso and Guglielmo Ferrero, *The Female Offender* (New York: D. Appleton, 1897), 1; Lombroso-Ferrero, *Criminal Man*, 5, xxiv–xxv.

39. James Weir, Jr., "Criminal Anthropology," quoted in Fink, *Causes of Crime*, 100. Later on, in response to criticism, Lombroso moved somewhat away from the category of atavism, adding the notion of developmental arrest and even suggesting that some anomalies, such as those caused by epilepsy, had no phyletic significance at all. Gould, *Ontogeny and Phylogeny*, 124; Ellis, *The Criminal*, 208–209; Gould, *Ontogeny and Phylogeny*, 124; George E. Dawson, "Psychic Rudiments and Morality," quoted in Fink, *Causes of Crime*, 101; Tarde quoted in Ellis, *The Criminal*, 208. Gould has pointed out that the criminal-child parallel is much more intelligible on the basis of a theory of arrested development rather than atavism. Because humans are neotenous (that is, human adults retain juvenile ancestral traits), "when the physical signs of an apish ancestry served as primary markers of the born criminal, children found no place in the argument . . ." (Gould, *Ontogeny and Phylogeny*, 125). Logically Gould is correct, but few anthropologists were aware of the significance of neoteny before 1900, and comparisons of children and apes flourished. See, for example, Chamberlain's section on "Monkey Atavisms" in his chapter, "The Child as Revealer of the Past," *The Child*, 227–231. In addition, as noted earlier, the categories of atavism and arrested development were frequently conflated, as, for example, in Havelock Ellis, *The Criminal*, 214: "In the criminal, we may often take it, there is an arrest of development. The criminal is an individual who, to some extent, remains a child his life long—a child of larger growth and with greater capacity for evil. This is part of the atavism of criminals."

40. Ellis, *The Criminal*, 212; Herbert Spencer, *Education: Intellectual, Moral, and Physical* (1860; Totowa, N.J.: Littlefield, Adams, 1969), 206; Henry Maudsley, *The Pathology of Mind* (London: Macmillan, 1895), 385; Lombroso and Ferrero, *Female Offender*, 151; "oil over marble" quote in Gould, *Ontogeny*, 122.

41. Lombroso and Ferrero, *Female Offender*, 151, 187–188; Marro quoted in Ellis, *The Criminal*, 217.

42. Dawson, "A Study of Youthful Degeneracy," quoted in Fink, *Causes of Crime,* 104.

43. Leonard Savitz, Introduction to Lombroso-Ferrero, *Criminal Man,* xvii; Hall, *Adolescence,* 1:334; Rosenberg, *Trial of Guiteau,* 248.

44. Russell, *Form and Function,* 126, 128; Gould, *Ontogeny and Phylogeny,* 129; Hall, *Adolescence,* 1:505, 2:565.

45. W. K. Brooks, *The Law of Heredity* (Baltimore: John Murphy, 1883), 110, 108–109.

46. Hall, *Adolescence,* 2:626; Allan, "On the Real Differences," cxcvii.

47. Maudsley, *Pathology of Mind,* 389.

48. The concept of complementarity will be discussed at some length in Chapter 5 in connection with social theory.

3. Hairy Men and Beautiful Women

Epigraph: Charles Darwin, *The Descent of Man, and Selection in Relation to Sex,* 2d ed. (Chicago: Rand, McNally, 1974), 554, 591–592.

1. Charles Darwin, *On the Origin of Species by Means of Natural Selection,* 6th ed. (Chicago: Encyclopaedia Britannica, 1975), 43; Darwin, *Descent,* 1.

2. Darwin, *Descent,* 205, 206, 207.

3. Darwin, *Descent,* 222, 510.

4. Darwin, *Descent,* 496, 517–518, 591, 592–594.

5. Darwin, *Descent,* 551. An anonymous article in the *British Quarterly of Science,* reprinted in the *Popular Science Monthly,* grudgingly admitted to lack of evidence regarding differences in intelligence in male and female mammals: "We are sorry to be compelled here to own that while we know that in most, if not all, mammalian species the brain of the male exceeds in size that of the female, we have no observation as to any corresponding difference in mental power." Such a difference the writer nonetheless took to be "highly probable," though less clear as one descended the developmental scale. "Biology and Woman's Rights," *Popular Science Monthly* 14 (1878–79), 204–205.

6. Darwin, *Descent,* 225, 227, 559.

7. Darwin, *Descent,* 560.

8. Ibid.

9. Darwin, *Descent,* 558.

10. Ibid. Harry Campbell, the British psychiatrist and disciple of Darwin, spelled out the Darwinian position more clearly. Both natural and sexual selection, wrote Campbell, played a role in differentiating the sexes. The sexually rivalrous male, subjected to "the law of battle," became "more courageous, powerful, and pugnacious than the female." She, on the contrary, experienced a deepening of "that round which her whole mental being centres, viz., the maternal instinct." In the different environments in which the two sexes were placed, natural selection continued to strengthen these dissimilar endowments; men and women followed "different modes of life." Competing with other breadwinners, men exercised both body and mind more than women did. Consorting constantly with children, women grew in emotional development. But "the emotional and intellectual

portions of our being [stand] to one another somewhat in inverse ratio." Harry Campbell, *Differences in the Nervous Organisation of Man and Woman* (London: H. K. Lewis, 1891), 40–41, 43, 46, 51, 82–84.

11. Darwin, *Descent,* 204.

12. Darwin, *Descent,* 236.

13. Charlotte Perkins Gilman, *Women and Economics* (1898; New York: Harper and Row, 1966), 18, 35, 37–39.

14. Gilman, *Women and Economics,* 86, 71. Cesare Lombroso described the male prerogative with his customary disregard for delicacy: "Man not only refused to *marry* a deformed female, but ate her, while, on the other hand, preserving for his enjoyment the handsome woman who gratified his peculiar instincts." Cesare Lombroso and Guglielmo Ferrero, *The Female Offender* (New York: D. Appleton, 1897), 109. In an article very congruent with Gilman's writings, Alfred Russel Wallace, like Gilman a socialist, looked to a future in which women, freed by economic and social independence from the necessity to marry, would become much more selective in their choice of husbands. They would reject the "idle," the "selfish," the "diseased," and the "weak in intellect," and humankind would make prodigious strides toward a better world. Wallace, in short, placed his hopes for a better world squarely on the shoulders of the "Woman of the Future." John Durant, "Scientific Naturalism and Social Reform in the Thought of Alfred Russel Wallace," *British Journal for the History of Science* 12 (1979), 49.

15. Gilman, *Women and Economics,* 340.

16. On this issue see George W. Stocking, Jr., *Race, Culture, and Evolution* (New York: Free Press, 1968), especially chapter 10; and Hamilton Cravens, *The Triumph of Evolution* (Philadelphia: University of Pennsylvania Press, 1978), chapters 3 and 4.

17. Evelleen Richards makes the point about Darwin's analogy of civilization to the process of domestication in her excellent article, "Darwin and the Descent of Woman," in *The Wider Domain of Evolutionary Thought,* ed. D. R. Oldroyd and Ian Langham (Dordrecht: D. Reidel, 1983), 78.

18. Durant, "Scientific Naturalism and Social Reform," 46, 53n12; Darwin, *Descent,* 95n5.

19. On the general disfavor into which Darwinism fell at the turn of the century, see Peter Bowler, *The Eclipse of Darwinism* (Baltimore: Johns Hopkins University Press, 1983); and on the specific issue of sexual selection, Nancy Stepan, *The Idea of Race in Science, Great Britain 1800–1960* (New York: Macmillan, 1982), 61–62.

20. The best accounts of the work of Geddes and Thomson are in Susan Sleeth Mosedale, "Science Corrupted: Victorian Biologists Consider 'The Woman Question,' " *Journal of the History of Biology* 11 (1978), 32–41; and Jill Conway, "Stereotypes of Femininity in a Theory of Sexual Evolution," in *Suffer and Be Still,* ed. Martha Vicinus (Bloomington: Indiana University Press, 1972), 140–154.

21. Patrick Geddes and J. Arthur Thomson, *The Evolution of Sex* (New York: Humboldt, 1889), 19.

22. Geddes and Thomson, *Evolution of Sex,* 250.

23. Harry Campbell, *Differences in Nervous Organisation,* 46–47; Geddes and

Thomson, *Evolution of Sex,* 247. Frederick Churchill makes the distinction between functional and essentialist theories in connection with the views of the
German zoologist Rudolph Leuckart, who "firmly rejected all theories of sexuality
that assumed that the sexes were fundamental polar opposites in essence and
influence . . . Sexuality and each of the sexes, he argued, must be viewed in terms of
their functional contribution to the species." Frederick Churchill, "Sex and the
Single Organism: Biological Theories of Sexuality in Mid-Nineteenth Century,"
Studies in the History of Biology 3 (1979), 158. Darwinian natural selection strongly
supports a functionalist interpretation of traits: traits have utility in a given environment, and if the environment changes, the traits can change in response.
Campbell notes that although "ages of subjection" had rendered women abjectly
dependent on men, the situation was changing as women were increasingly forced
to "take active personal share in the battle of life." They could be expected to shake
off the habit of dependency and behave with greater vigor and decisiveness.
Campbell believed that this change was already observable in America. *Differences
in Nervous Organisation,* 55–56.

24. Geddes and Thomson, *Evolution of Sex,* 247–249.

25. Darwin, *Descent,* 236–239.

26. W. K. Brooks, *The Law of Heredity* (Baltimore: John Murphy, 1883), 160;
Darwin, *Descent,* 219; Brooks, *Law of Heredity,* 82–83, 160.

27. Havelock Ellis, *Man and Woman: A Study of Human Secondary Sexual Characteristics* (London: Walter Scott, 1894), 359, 363–365, 102, 366.

28. Ellis, *Man and Woman,* 394; Cesare Lombroso, *The Man of Genius* (London:
Walter Scott, 1894), 137–138; Campbell, *Differences in Nervous Organisation,* 173.

29. Brooks, *Law of Heredity,* 257.

30. Brooks, *Law of Heredity,* 260–261; G. Stanley Hall, *Adolescence,* 2 vols.
(New York: D. Appleton, 1904), 2:567.

31. Ellis, *Man and Woman,* 7th ed. (Boston: Houghton Mifflin, 1929), 458; *Man
and Woman* (1894), 371.

32. Karl Pearson, "Variation in Man and Woman," in *The Chances of Death,* 2
vols. (London: Edward Arnold, 1897), 1:256–289. Discussion of Pearson's attack
is in Stephanie A. Shields, "Functionalism, Darwinism, and the Psychology of
Women," *American Psychologist* 39 (1975), 744; Shields, "The Variability Hy-
pothesis: The History of a Biological Model of Sex Differences in Intelligence,"
Signs: Journal of Women in Culture and Society 7 (1982), 776–778; and Rosalind
Rosenberg, "The Dissent from Darwin: The New View of Women among
American Social Scientists," Ph.D. diss., Stanford University, 1974, 72–75.

33. Rosenberg, "Dissent from Darwin," 59, quoting from Charlotte Perkins
Gilman, *The Man-Made World; Or, Our Androcentric Culture* (New York: Charlton,
1911), 156–160. Rosenberg's analysis of Herland is on pp. 60–62.

34. Anna Garlin Spencer, *Woman's Share in Social Culture* (1912; Philadelphia:
J. B. Lippincott, 1925), 171–172.

35. Flavia Alaya, "Victorian Science and the 'Genius' of Woman," *Journal of
the History of Ideas* 38 (1977), 261–280, and Evelleen Richards, "Darwin and the
Descent of Woman," are sharply critical of this approach. More positive are the
accounts of Marie Tedesco, "A Feminist Challenge to Darwinism: Antoinette L.

B. Blackwell on the Relations of the Sexes in Nature and Society," in *Feminist Visions: Toward a Transformation of the Liberal Arts Curriculum,* ed. Diana L. Fowlker and Charlotte S. McClure (University, Ala.: University of Alabama Press, 1984), 53–65; and Marjorie Spruill Wheeler, "Sex, Science, and the 'Woman Question': *The Woman's Journal* on Woman's Nature and Potential, 1870–1875," paper presented at a meeting of the Organization of American Historians, Detroit, 1980.

36. Karl Pearson, *The Life, Letters, and Labours of Frances Galton,* 3 vols. (Cambridge: Cambridge University Press, 1914–1930), 2:384–385.

37. Ellis, *Man and Woman,* 387. The "storm of protest" is mentioned in Janice Law Trecker's able survey of the impact of scientific ideas on women's education in the late nineteenth century, "Sex, Science, and Education," *American Quarterly* 26 (1974), 364.

38. Shields, "Functionalism, Darwinism, and the Psychology of Women," 744–745, 746–748; review of *Educational Psychology* in *Psychological Bulletin* 7 (1910), 343.

39. Edward Thorndike, "Sex in Education," *Bookman* 23 (1906), 212–213.

40. Richards, "Darwin and the Descent of Woman," 80–86.

41. "Darwin's Notebooks on Transmutation of Species, Part II, Second Notebook (February–July 1838)," *Bulletin of the British Museum (Natural History),* historical series, 2 (1960), 109; Henrietta Litchfield, ed., *Emma Darwin: A Century of Family Letters, 1792–1896,* 2 vols. (London: John Murray, 1915), 2:245.

42. Astonishingly, these quotations are from Antoinette Brown Blackwell, *The Sexes throughout Nature* (New York: G. P. Putnam's Sons, 1895), 221. Though herself a feminist, Blackwell fully accepted the polarization of masculine and feminine natures. Modern feminist critics are right to point out the difficulties inherent in her different-but-equal stance, as these words suggest. And yet it is interesting that in her own life Blackwell seems to have been quite successful in living out her feminist principles.

43. Geddes and Thomson, *Evolution of Sex,* 283–288.

4. The Machinery of the Body

Epigraphs: Herbert Spencer, "Psychology of the Sexes," *Popular Science Monthly* 4 (1873–1874), 31n1; George M. Beard, *Sexual Neurasthenia* (1884; New York: Arno Press, 1972), 60–61.

1. Miss M. A. Hardaker, "Science and the Woman Question," *Popular Science Monthly* (1881–1882), 583, 579, 581.

2. Hardaker, "Science and the Woman Question," 581, 583.

3. Nina Morais, "A Reply to Miss Hardaker on the Woman Question," *Popular Science Monthly* 21 (1882), 70–78, quotation on p. 78; Edward Youmans, ed., *The Correlation and Conservation of Force* (New York: D. Appleton and Co., 1869), xli.

4. For the history of the discovery of this principle see Yehuda Elkana, *The Discovery of the Conservation of Energy* (Cambridge, Mass.: Harvard University Press, 1974), and Thomas S. Kuhn, "Energy Conservation as an Example of

Simultaneous Discovery," in *Critical Problems in the History of Science,* ed. Marshall Clagett (Madison: University of Wisconsin Press, 1959), 321–356. A good discussion of the establishment of conservation principles and their cultural significance in an American context is Ronald E. Martin, *American Literature and the Universe of Force* (Durham, N.C.: Duke University Press, 1981).

5. Elkana, *Discovery,* 9, quoted in Martin, *American Literature,* 25.

6. Mayer quoted in *The Historical Development of Physiological Thought,* ed. Chandler McC. Brooks and Paul Cranefield (New York: Hafner, 1959), 254. See generally pp. 252–255, and Garland Allen, *Life Science in the Twentieth Century* (Cambridge: Cambridge University Press, 1975), xvi. John Theodore Merz defines metabolism as the "conception of a continuous exchange or circulation of matter and of energy in every living organism." It is the elementary typical form of the living process. *A History of European Thought in the Nineteenth Century,* 4 vols. (Edinburgh: William Blackwood and Sons, 1912–1914), 2:419.

7. Quoted in Bruce Haley, *The Healthy Body and Victorian Culture* (Cambridge, Mass.: Harvard University Press, 1978), 87–88. On Carpenter see L. S. Jacyna, "The Physiology of Mind, the Unity of Nature, and the Moral Order in Victorian Thought," *British Journal for the History of Science* 14 (1981), 109–132; and Roger Smith, "The Human Significance of Biology: Carpenter, Darwin, and the *vera causa,*" in *Nature and the Victorian Imagination,* ed. U. C. Knoepflmacher and G. B. Tennyson (Berkeley: University of California Press, 1977), 216–230.

8. Professor E. B. Rosa, "The Human Body as an Engine," *Popular Science Monthly* 57 (1900), 491, 495–499.

9. Rosa, "Body as Engine," 495.

10. The naturalization of mind is dealt with extensively in Jacyna, "Physiology of Mind," and in Roger Smith, "The Background of Physiological Psychology in Natural Philosophy," *History of Science* 11 (1973), 75–123. Of the so-called spiritualists William Carpenter wrote, "To them the Mind appears in the light of a separate Immaterial existence, mysteriously connected, indeed, with a Bodily instrument, but not dependent upon this in any other way for the conditions of its operation, then as deriving its knowledge of external things through its Organs of sense, and as making use of it to execute its determinations—so far as these are accomplished by Muscular effort." *Principles of Mental Physiology* (London: C. Kegan Paul, 1879), 7; Alexander Bain quoted in Haley, *Healthy Body,* 40; William Hammond's approving summary of Henry Maudsley's view quoted in Bonnie Ellen Blustein, "New York Neurologists and the Specialization of American Medicine," *Bulletin of the History of Medicine* 53 (1979), 173–174.

11. Carpenter, *Mental Physiology,* 14; Bain, "Correlation of Nervous and Mental Forces," Appendix to Balfour Stewart, *The Conservation of Energy* (New York: D. Appleton, 1881), 206–207, 218; Carpenter, *Mental Physiology,* 40.

12. John Cleland, *The Relation of Brain to Mind* (Glasgow: James Maclehose and Sons, 1882), 20–21; Robert Young, *Mind, Brain, and Adaptation in the Nineteenth Century* (Oxford: Oxford University Press, 1970), 208; Michael Clark, "The Rejection of Psychological Approaches to Mental Disorder in Late Nineteenth-Century British Psychiatry," in *Madhouses, Mad-Doctors, and Madmen: The Social History of Psychiatry in the Victorian Era,* ed. Andrew Scull (London: Athlone; Philadelphia: University of Pennsylvania Press, 1981), 283; H. Tristram En-

gelhardt, Jr., "John Hughlings Jackson and the Mind-Body Relation," *Bulletin of the History of Medicine* 49 (1975), 143–146; Nathan G. Hale, Jr., *Freud and the Americans: The Beginnings of Psychoanalysis in the United States, 1876–1917* (New York: Oxford, 1971), 54.

13. Thomas Henry Huxley, *On the Hypothesis That Animals Are Automata, and Its History* (Washington, D.C.: University Publications of America, 1978), 577; Clifford discussed in Jacyna, "Physiology of Mind," 127–128.

14. Cleland, *Relation of Brain to Mind*, 22; Carpenter, *Mental Physiology*, xviii.

15. See Barbara Sicherman, "The Paradox of Prudence: Mental Health in the Gilded Age," *Journal of American History* 62 (1976), 890–912.

16. Carpenter, *Mental Physiology*, 14; Hugh Campbell, *Nervous Exhaustion and the Diseases Induced by It* (London: Longmans, Green, Reader, and Dyer, 1873), 38; George M. Beard, *American Nervousness* (New York: G. P. Putnam's Sons, 1881), 98.

17. Rosa, "Body as Engine," 493.

18. Stewart, *Conservation of Energy*, 220, 222; Edward H. Clarke, *Sex in Education; or, A Fair Chance for the Girls* (Boston: James R. Osgood and Company, 1873), 40; Joseph LeConte, "Correlation of Vital with Physical Force," Appendix to Stewart, *Conservation of Energy*, 199.

19. Stewart, *Conservation of Energy*, 231; Cesare Lombroso, *The Man of Genius* (London: Walter Scott, 1891), 7; J. Leonard Corning, *Brain Exhaustion* (New York: D. Appleton, 1884), 30, 47; Stewart, *Conservation of Energy*, 234.

20. Stewart, *Conservation of Energy*, 228–229, 230. Cf. George M. Beard, *Sexual Neurasthenia*, 59.

21. Sicherman, "Paradox of Prudence," 898; Editor's Table, "The Progress of Mental Science," *Popular Science Monthly* 25 (1884), 267; Lombroso, *Man of Genius*, 30; Campbell, *Nervous Exhaustion*, 28.

22. The description of neurasthenics as delicate urban professionals is that of Beard in *American Nervousness*. As Barbara Sicherman points out, other physicians discovered neurasthenia in working-class patients as well. "The Uses of a Diagnosis: Doctors, Patients, and Neurasthenia," *Journal of the History of Medicine* 32 (1977), 44. Other discussions of neurologists' diagnoses of mental illness in the late nineteenth century include Charles E. Rosenberg, *The Trial of the Assassin Guiteau: Psychiatry and Law in the Gilded Age* (Chicago: University of Chicago Press, 1968), and Nathan G. Hale, Jr., *Freud and the Americans: The Beginnings of Psychoanalysis in the United States, 1876–1917* (New York: Oxford, 1971). Beard's description of the neurasthenic is in *Sexual Neurasthenia*, 61.

23. Corning, *Brain Exhaustion*, 47; Stewart, *Conservation of Energy*, 226; Max Nordau, *Degeneration* (New York: D. Appleton, 1895), 39–40. Some historians have tried to link a repressive sexual ethic supposed to characterize the nineteenth century with the needs of an industrializing capitalist society, at least partly on the basis of the period's use of economic metaphors for sexual acts. It is clear from the above examples, however, that while economic imagery was certainly popular, it was not restricted to discussions of sexuality.

24. Clarke, *Sex in Education*, 37; Henry Maudsley, "Sex in Mind and Education," *Popular Science Monthly* 5 (1874), 199; Clarke, *Sex in Education*, 38.

25. Clarke, *Sex in Education*, 40–41, 54–55.

26. Clarke, *Sex in Education*, 69–70, 71, 72.

27. Maudsley, "Sex in Mind," 211; Beard, *American Nervousness*, 9, 207; Harry Campbell, *Differences in the Nervous Organisation of Man and Woman* (London: H. K. Lewis, 1891), 88; Havelock Ellis, *Man and Woman: A Study of Human Secondary Sexual Characteristics* (London: Walter Scott, 1894), 279.

28. Herbert Spencer, "A Theory of Population Deduced from the General Law of Animal Fertility," *Westminster Review*, n.s., 1 (1852), 263.

29. Spencer, "Theory of Population," 265; Spencer, "Psychology of the Sexes," *Popular Science Monthly* 4 (1873–1874), 32.

30. Spencer, *Principles of Psychology*, 2 vols. (New York: D. Appleton, 1910), 1:368, 581.

31. Spencer, "Psychology of the Sexes," 36. Sigmund Freud similarly argued, though from different premises, that women lacked a mature sense of justice. So, much more recently, has the Harvard psychologist Lawrence Kohlberg.

32. Clarke, *Sex in Education*, 39; G. Stanley Hall, *Adolescence*, 2 vols. (New York: D. Appleton, 1904), 2:629, 636, 633.

33. Henry Maudsley, *Body and Mind* (New York: D. Appleton, 1874), 43. Personal details about Maudsley's life are from Elaine Showalter's excellent account in *The Female Malady: Women, Madness, and English Culture, 1830–1980* (New York: Pantheon, 1985), 112–120. Older biographical accounts are Aubrey Lewis, "Henry Maudsley: His Work and Influence," *Journal of Mental Science* 97 (1951), 251–277; and Peter Scott, "Henry Maudsley," in *Pioneers in Criminology*, ed. Hermann Mannheim (London: Stevens and Sons, 1960), 144–167. Kurt Danziger situates Maudsley in the mind-body debate in "Mid-Nineteenth-Century British Psycho-Physiology: A Neglected Chapter in the History of Psychology," in *The Problematic Science: Psychology in Nineteenth-Century Thought*, ed. William R. Woodward and Mitchell G. Ash (New York: Praeger, 1982), 135–140.

34. Danziger, "Mid-Nineteenth-Century British Psycho-Physiology," 139–140; Maudsley, *Body and Mind*, 35; Maudsley, "Sex in Mind," 203.

35. "Sex in Mind," 203–204.

36. Hall, *Adolescence*, 2:592, 593, 604, 602. On reasons for concern about declining fertility see, for the United States, Linda Gordon, *Woman's Body, Woman's Right: A Social History of Birth Control in America* (New York: Penguin, 1970), especially chapter 7, and Carl Degler, *At Odds: Women and the Family in America from the Revolution to the Present* (New York: Oxford, 1981), chapter 8; and for England, Joseph and Olive Banks, *Feminism and Family Planning in Victorian England* (Liverpool: Liverpool University Press, 1964).

37. Phyllis Grosskurth, *Havelock Ellis* (New York: Alfred A. Knopf, 1980), 90, 145, 171. On Pearson and his relationship to academic women see Rosaleen Lee, " 'Alice in Eugenics-Land': Feminism and Eugenics in the Scientific Careers of Alice Lee and Ethel Elderton," *Annals of Science* 36 (1979), 146–158.

38. Ellis, *The Task of Social Hygiene* (London: Constable, 1912), 95, 96; Ellis, *Man and Woman*, 7th ed. (Boston: Houghton Mifflin, 1929), 468. Cf. Flavia Alaya, "Victorian Science and the 'Genius' of Woman," *Journal of the History of Ideas* 38 (1975), 276: "In his divided mind, Ellis clearly feared the very thing he proposed. *Man and Woman* was from the point of view of the intellectual history of feminism, an early warning of the Freudian revolution, a strategic opening that would lead to

the eventual victory of biological determinism over moral freedom." I find this a bit overdrawn in the context of the times, in which the book looks quite open-minded on the capacities of women. Still, I think Alaya's point that Ellis executed a retreat from his original feminist commitment is correct. The limitations of Ellis's pro-woman stance are spelled out at length in Sheila Rowbotham and Jeffrey Weeks, *Socialism and the New Life: The Personal and Sexual Politics of Edward Carpenter and Havelock Ellis* (London: Pluto Press, 1977), 167–180.

39. Karl Pearson, *The Ethic of Freethought* (1887; London: Adam and Charles Black, 1901), 355; Pearson, *The Chances of Death and Other Studies in Evolution*, 2 vols. (London: E. Arnold, 1897), 1:232, 237.

40. Hall, *Adolescence*, 2:606. In the history of medicine some historians have challenged the portrait of the Victorian medical profession as paternalistic and condescending, even misogynistic, toward women, a portrait associated with Carroll Smith-Rosenberg and Charles Rosenberg, Ann Douglas, Ben Barker-Benfield, and others. The challengers argue that this picture is one-sided, that doctors frequently applied the same diagnoses and treatments, and were just as moralistic and authoritarian, to men. See, e.g., Barbara Sicherman, "Uses of a Diagnosis"; Regina Morantz, "The Perils of Feminist History," *Journal of Interdisciplinary History* 4 (1974), 649–660; and Gail Pat Parsons, "Equal Treatment for All: American Remedies for Male Sexual Problems: 1850–1900," *Journal of the History of Medicine* 32 (1977), 55–71.

41. Ely Van de Warker, "The Relations of Women to the Professions and Skilled Labor," *Popular Science Monthly* 6 (1874–1875), 466; Herbert Spencer, *Education: Intellectual, Moral and Physical* (London: Williams and Norgate, 1861), 179, quoted in Lorna Duffin, "Prisoners of Progress: Women and Evolution," in *The Nineteenth-Century Woman: Her Cultural and Physical World*, ed. Sara Delamont and Lorna Duffin (London: Croom Helm, 1978), 62; Robert Lawson Tait, *Diseases of the Ovaries* (1883), quoted in John Thorburn, *Female Education from a Physiological Point of View* (Manchester: J. E. Cornish, 1884), 11.

42. Ludwig von Bertalanffy, "Modern Concepts of Biological Adaptation," in Brooks and Cranefield, *Historical Development of Physiological Thought*, 267, 272–273.

43. Beard, *Sexual Neurasthenia*, 58; Beard, *American Nervousness*, 98; Stewart, *Conservation of Energy*, 224–225; Corning, *Brain Exhaustion*, 31; Beard, *American Nervousness*, 98–99, 317.

44. Stephen G. Brush, "Thermodynamics and History," *The Graduate Journal* 7 (1967), 494–495 and *passim*, 536; David Duncan, *Life and Letters of Herbert Spencer*, 2 vols. (New York: Appleton, 1908), 1:136. Discussions of Adams's use of thermodynamic concepts are in William Jordy, *Henry Adams: Scientific Historian* (New Haven: Yale University Press, 1952); Brush, "Thermodynamics and History," 535–539; and Martin, *American Literature*, chapter 4. Examples of twentieth-century scientific speculation on the relationship between physical theories and living organisms are L. Brillouin, "Life, Thermodynamics, and Cybernetics," *American Scientist* 37 (1949), 554–568, and Ludwig von Bertalanffy, *Problems of Life: An Evolution of Modern Biological Thought* (New York: John Wiley and Sons, 1952).

45. G. T. W. Patrick, "The Psychology of Woman," *Popular Science Monthly* 47 (1895), 225.

5. The Physiological Division of Labor

Epigraphs: Mrs. Mary K. Sedgwick, "Some Scientific Aspects of the Woman Suffrage Question," *Gunton's Magazine* 10 (1901), 336; J. Arthur Thomson and Patrick Geddes, *Problems of Sex* (New York: Moffat, Yard, 1912), 23.

1. E. E. Evans-Pritchard, *The Position of Women in Primitive Societies and Other Essays in Social Anthropology* (New York: Free Press, 1965), 39; Herbert Spencer, *Principles of Sociology,* 3 vols. (New York: D. Appleton, 1925), 1:725.

2. Silvan S. Schweber, "Darwin and the Political Economists: Divergence of Character," *Journal of the History of Biology* 13 (1980), 252, 255.

3. Herbert Spencer, *An Autobiography,* 2 vols. (New York: D. Appleton, 1904), 1:436–437, 446, 648.

4. Schweber, "Darwin and the Political Economists," 211–212.

5. Schweber, "Darwin and the Political Economists," 212; Herbert Spencer, *First Principles,* 5th ed. (New York: D. Appleton, 1880), v.

6. Schweber, "Darwin and the Political Economists," 264–271.

7. Schweber, "Darwin and the Political Economists," 286, 268.

8. Schweber, "Darwin and the Political Economists," 212, 269.

9. Cf. J. D. Y. Peel, *Herbert Spencer, The Evolution of a Sociologist* (London: Heinemann, 1971), 138: "But for all the apparent biologism of the theory of social progress . . . the major influences are, first and unacknowledged, Adam Smith, and then Malthus." Robert Young argues that the physiological division of labor supplied "a scientific guarantee of the rightness of the property and work relations of industrial society." "The Historiographical and Ideological Concepts of the Nineteenth-Century Debate on Man's Place in Nature," in *Changing Perspectives in the History of Science,* ed. Mikulas Teich and Robert Young (London: Heinemann, 1973), 375.

10. Henri Milne-Edwards, *Elemens de zoologie,* vol. 1 (1834), quoted in Schweber, "Darwin and the Political Economists," 251–252.

11. W. K. Brooks, *The Law of Heredity* (Baltimore: John Murphy, 1883), 313–314; E. S. Russell, *Form and Function* (London: John Murray, 1916), 19.

12. "Our Six-Footed Rivals," *Popular Science Monthly* 12 (1877–1878), 201.

13. Patrick Geddes and J. Arthur Thomson, *The Evolution of Sex,* rev. ed. (London: Walter Scott, 1901), 175, 178–179, 286, 289.

14. Geddes and Thomson, *Evolution of Sex,* 329–330.

15. J. W. Burrow, *Evolution and Society: A Study in Victorian Social Theory* (Cambridge: Cambridge University Press, 1966), 222–223.

16. Spencer, *Principles of Sociology,* 1:452; Spencer, *Principles of Biology,* 2 vols. (New York: D. Appleton, 1897), 1:161, 163, 2:370–371.

17. Herbert Spencer, "Progress: Its Law and Cause," in *Essays: Scientific, Political and Speculative* (London: Williams and Norgate, 1868), 17, 50, 2; Spencer, "The Social Organism," in *Essays,* 399–400. Cf. "Race in Legislation and Political Economy," *Anthropological Review* 4 (1866), 129: "Specialisation is the test of development. From the zoophyte to man the march is steadily in this direction." Higher human races therefore show greater individuality: "they are less foetal in their character, both morally and physically. It has long been observed that the

Negroid and Mongolic races are far less distinctly marked physiognomically than the Caucasian. They keep much closer to the common type; we may add, in mind as well as body."

18. Spencer, "Bain on the Emotions and the Will," in *Essays,* 313.

19. Spencer, *Principles of Sociology,* part 2, section 212, and part 1, section 6, quoted in J. D. Y. Peel, *Herbert Spencer: The Evolution of a Sociologist* (New York: Basic Books, 1971), 187. This curious disjunction can perhaps be linked to the well-known inconsistency of Spencer's analysis, which approved centralization in the biological organism but not in the social organism, the state.

20. On Spencer's methodological individualism see Peel, *Herbert Spencer,* 185–189; William B. Carpenter, "On the Correlation of the Physical and Vital Forces," in *The Correlation and Conservation of Force,* ed. Edward Youmans (New York: D. Appleton, 1869), 409–410.

21. Spencer, *Essays,* 12; Spencer, *Principles of Sociology,* 1:726, 729.

22. Spencer, *Principles of Sociology,* 2:289–290.

23. Alexis de Tocqueville, *Democracy in America* (New York: Doubleday, 1969), 601.

24. William Graham Sumner and Albert G. Keller, *The Science of Society,* 3 vols. (New Haven: Yale University Press, 1927), 1:130, 141, 140. Sumner actually died in 1910, bequeathing his notes to Keller, who adapted and supplemented them freely. The authorship of the resulting work was largely Keller's, but the ideas were very much shared.

25. Sumner and Keller, *Science of Society,* 3:1517; Herbert Spencer, *Principles of Ethics,* 2 vols. (London: Williams and Norgate, 1892–1893), 2:336.

26. E. E. Evans-Pritchard, *Social Anthropology and Other Essays* (New York: Free Press, 1964), 41.

27. G. Ferrero, "The Problem of Woman, from a Bio-Sociological Point of View," *Monist* 4 (1893–1894), 262–263, 266, 268–269.

28. Joseph LeConte, "The Woman Question," quoted in Lester D. Stephens, "Evolution and Woman's Rights in the 1890s: The Views of Joseph LeConte," *Historian* 38 (1976), 245; Edward Drinker Cope, "The Marriage Problem," *Open Court* 11 (1888), 1308.

29. G. Delauney, "Equality and Inequality in Sex," *Popular Science Monthly* 20 (1881–1882), 189–190.

30. Evans-Pritchard, *Position of Women in Primitive Societies,* 39.

31. Delauney, "Equality and Inequality in Sex," 192.

32. Sedgwick, "Some Scientific Aspects of the Woman Suffrage Question," 336, 337; Brooks, *Law of Heredity,* 266; Edward H. Clarke, *The Building of a Brain* (Boston: James R. Osgood, 1874), 53.

33. Brooks, *Law of Heredity,* 272–273.

34. Brooks, *Law of Heredity,* 259.

35. G. Stanley Hall, *Adolescence,* 2 vols. (New York: D. Appleton, 1904), 2:624–625.

36. Hall, *Adolescence,* 2:625.

37. Spencer, *Principles of Sociology,* 1:768–769; "Biology and 'Woman's Rights,'" *Popular Science Monthly* 14 (1878–1879), 213; LeConte quoted in

Stephens, "Evolution and Woman's Rights in the 1890s," 245; Geddes and Thomson, *Evolution of Sex,* 247; Hall, *Adolescence,* 2:636, 578; Thomson and Geddes, *Problems of Sex,* 33–34.

38. Delauney, "Equality and Inequality in Sex," 192; J. W. Jackson, "Iran and Turan," *Anthropological Review* 6 (1868), 128, 129.

39. William Graham Sumner, *What Social Classes Owe to Each Other* (1883; Caldwell, Idaho: Caxton Printers, 1978), 22–23; Carpenter reference is in note 16.

40. Charlotte Perkins Gilman, *The Home: Its Work and Influence* (1903; Urbana: University of Illinois Press, 1972), 84–85, 318, 90–91.

41. Gilman, *Women and Economics* (1898; New York: Harper and Row, 1966), 245, 242.

42. Gilman, *Women and Economics,* 316.

43. Gilman, *Women and Economics,* 340.

44. Spencer's well-known reliance on deduction rather than induction prompted Thomas Henry Huxley's quip that the definition of a tragedy for Spencer was a theory killed by an ugly fact.

6. The Victorian Paradigm Erodes

Epigraphs: Helen Thompson Woolley, "A Review of the Recent Literature on the Psychology of Sex," *Psychological Bulletin* 7 (1910), 340; Ralph Waldo Emerson, "Art," in *Essays* (1841), 290–291, quoted in Arthur Schlesinger, Jr., Review Essay, "Intellectual History: A Time for Despair," *Journal of American History* 66 (1980), 892.

1. Quoted in Hamilton Cravens, *The Triumph of Evolution: American Scientists and the Heredity-Environment Controversy, 1900–1941* (Philadelphia: University of Pennsylvania Press, 1978), 34.

2. Cravens, *Triumph of Evolution,* 159–165; Garland Allen, "Thomas Hunt Morgan and the Problem of Sex Determination, 1903–1910," *Proceedings of the American Philosophical Society* 110 (1966), 50.

3. Diana Long Hall, "Biology, Sex Hormones and Sexism in the 1920s," in *Women and Philosophy: Toward a Theory of Liberation,* ed. Carol G. Gould and Marx W. Wartofsky (New York: G. P. Putnam's Sons, 1976), 82–83, 86–87.

4. Stephen Jay Gould, *Ontogeny and Phylogeny* (Cambridge, Mass.: Harvard University Press, 1977), 6, 8, 302–305; Gould, *The Panda's Thumb: More Reflections in Natural History* (New York: W. W. Norton, 1980), 246.

5. Garland Allen, *Life Science in the Twentieth Century* (Cambridge: Cambridge University Press, 1975), 7; Jane Maienschein, "Cell Lineage, Ancestral Remembrance, and the Biogenetic Law," *Journal of the History of Biology* 11 (1978), 154–157; Thomas H. Montgomery, Jr., *The Analysis of Racial Descent in Animals* (New York: Henry Holt, 1906).

6. Edward J. Pfeifer, "United States," in *The Comparative Reception of Darwinism,* ed. Thomas G. Glick (Austin: University of Texas Press, 1974), 198–202; Peter Bowler, *The Eclipse of Darwinism* (Baltimore: Johns Hopkins University Press, 1983), 218–240.

7. Leta Stetter Hollingworth, "The Vocational Aptitudes of Women," in H. L. Hollingworth, *Vocational Psychology* (New York: D. Appleton, 1916), 241.

The theory of sex linkage of at least some mental traits has, however, recently been revived. See Robert G. Lehrke, "Sex Linkage: A Biological Basis for Greater Male Variability in Intelligence," in *Human Variation,* ed. R. T. Osborne, C. E. Noble, and N. Weyle (New York: Academic Press, 1978), 171–198; and Lehrke, "A Theory of X-Linkage of Major Intellectual Traits," *American Journal of Mental Deficiency* 76 (1972), 611–619.

8. Thomas Hunt Morgan, *Heredity and Sex* (New York: Columbia University Press, 1914), 50; Helen Thompson Woolley, "The Psychology of Sex," *Psychological Bulletin* 11 (1914), 354.

9. Hall, "Biology, Sex Hormones and Sexism," 86–88.

10. Kathryn Allamong Jacob, "Dr. Clelia Mosher: A Victorian Doctor Battles the 'Scientific' Sexual Myths," paper presented at the Organization of American Historians, April 3, 1980, 5, 7, 9.

11. Rosalind Rosenberg, *Beyond Separate Spheres: Intellectual Roots of Modern Feminism* (New Haven: Yale University Press, 1982), 95–99.

12. Nathan G. Hale, Jr., *Freud and the Americans: The Beginnings of Psychoanalysis in the United States, 1876–1917* (New York: Oxford Press, 1971), 141. See also Rosenberg, *Beyond Separate Spheres,* 93.

13. Quoted in Rosenberg, *Beyond Separate Spheres,* 133.

14. William James, "Herbert Spencer," *Atlantic Monthly* 94 (1904), 107.

15. William James, "The Energies of Men," in *Essays in Faith and Morals* (Cleveland: Meridian, 1962), 217, 218; James, "The Gospel of Relaxation," in the same volume, 244, 251. Barbara Sicherman points out this contrast in "The Paradox of Prudence: Mental Health in the Gilded Age," *Journal of American History* 62 (1975–1976), 912.

16. Joseph Simms, M.D., "Human Brain Weights," *Popular Science Monthly* 31 (1887), 358.

17. Alice Lee, "Data for the Problem of Evolution in Man. A First Study of the Correlation of the Human Skull," *Philosophical Transactions of the Royal Society of London* 196A (1902), quoted in Rosaleen Love, " 'Alice in Eugenics-Land': Feminism and Eugenics in the Scientific Careers of Alice Lee and Ethel Elderton," *Annals of Science* 36 (1979), 149–150.

18. Karl Pearson, "On the Correlation of Intellectual Ability with the Size and Shape of the Head. (Preliminary Notice.)," *Proceedings of the Royal Society of London* 69 (1902), 334, 342; and Pearson, "On the Relationship of Intelligence to the Size and Shape of the Head and to Other Physical and Mental Characters," *Biometrika* 5 (1906), 122, quoted in Elizabeth Fee, "Nineteenth-Century Craniology: The Study of the Female Skull," *Bulletin of the History of Medicine* 53 (1979), 432.

19. Franklin Mall, "On Several Anatomical Characters of the Human Brain, Said to Vary According to Race and Sex, With Especial Reference to the Weight of the Frontal Lobe," *American Journal of Anatomy* 9 (1909), 27, 32.

20. George W. Stocking, Jr., *The Shaping of American Anthropology, 1883–1911: A Franz Boas Reader* (New York: Basic Books, 1974), 216, 217.

21. Francis Galton, *Inquiries into Human Faculty and Its Development* (1883; London: J. M. Dent and Sons, 1907), 20–21; D. W. Forrest, *Francis Galton, The Life and Work of a Victorian Genius* (London: Paul Elek, 1974), 227. Pearson's letter is quoted in Love, " 'Alice in Eugenics-Land,' " 146.

22. Merle Curti, *Human Nature in American Thought* (Madison: University of Wisconsin Press, 1980), 202.

23. Michael M. Sokal, "James McKeen Cattell and the Failure of Anthropometric Testing, 1890–1901," in *The Problematic Science: Psychology in Nineteenth-Century Thought*, ed. William R. Woodward and Mitchell G. Ash (New York: Praeger, 1982), 330, 354, 339; Solomon Diamond, *Francis Galton and American Psychology: Theoretical-Historical Perspectives* (New York: Academic Press, 1980), 48. Jastrow received the first American Ph.D. awarded in psychology under G. Stanley Hall in 1886, so it is perhaps not strange that he took an interest in sex differences, believing "that his tests demonstrated the proper spheres of activity for each of the sexes." For his dispute with Wellesley psychologist Mary Whiton Calkins over the issue of sex differences in word association, see Rosenberg, *Beyond Separate Spheres,* 74.

24. Sokal, "James McKeen Cattell," 337–338; Rosenberg, *Beyond Separate Spheres,* 72–73.

25. Rosenberg, *Beyond Separate Spheres,* 70, 76, 80.

26. Cravens, *Triumph of Evolution,* 80–84; Rosenberg, *Beyond Separate Spheres,* 105, 107.

27. Edward Thorndike, *Educational Psychology* (1914), quoted in Stephanie Shields, "The Variability Hypothesis: The History of a Biological Model of Sex Differences in Intelligence," *Signs: Journal of Women in Culture and Society* 7 (1982), 781; Havelock Ellis, *Man and Woman: A Study of Human Secondary Sexual Characteristics,* 7th rev. ed. (Boston: Houghton Mifflin, 1929), 219–220.

28. Shields, "Variability Hypothesis," 779–787.

29. Shields, "Variability Hypothesis," 787; Leta Stetter Hollingworth, "Variability as Related to Sex Differences in Achievement," *American Journal of Sociology* 19 (1914), 529, quoted in Ludy Benjamin, Jr., "The Pioneering Work of Leta Hollingworth in the Psychology of Women," *Nebraska History* 56 (1975), 498. Rosenberg's figure of 20,000 newborn records (*Beyond Separate Spheres,* 101) is presumably a typographical error.

30. Lewis Terman, *The Standard Revision and Extension of the Binet-Simon Scale for Measuring Intelligence* (1917), quoted in Rosenberg, *Beyond Separate Spheres,* 106; Shields, "Variability Hypothesis," 792.

31. The "largely rewritten" 1929 edition of *Man and Woman* differs not at all from the first edition with regard to variability: "Genius is more common among men by virtue of the same general tendency by which idiocy is more common among men. The two facts are but two aspects of a larger zoological fact—the greater variational range of the male." Ellis was at pains to emphasize that the failure of women to demonstrate genius results not from lack of opportunity but from "an organic tendency, which no higher education can eradicate." Hence "spontaneous originality" will always be a male monopoly. Ellis, *Man and Woman,* 7th ed., 453–454, 454–455, 456. Stephanie Shields describes the declining significance of variability theory in "Variability Hypothesis," 789, 790.

32. Rosenberg, *Beyond Separate Spheres, passim;* quotation is on p. 61.

33. Cravens, *Triumph of Evolution,* 89–153.

34. Helen Thompson Woolley, "A Review of the Recent Literature on the Psychology of Sex," *Psychological Bulletin* 7 (1910), 341–342.

35. Cravens, *Triumph of Evolution,* 269–270.

36. Loren Eiseley, "The Intellectual Antecedents of the Descent of Man," in *Sexual Selection and the Descent of Man, 1871–1971,* ed. Bernard Campbell (Chicago: Aldine, 1972), 3.

37. James McGrigor Allan, "On the Real Differences in the Minds of Men and Women," *Journal of the Anthropological Society of London* 7 (1869), ccxiii, ccxv; Alpheus Hyatt, "The Influence of Women in the Evolution of the Human Race," *Natural Science* 11 (1897), 92–93, 91.

38. Ruth Schwartz Cowan, "Sir Francis Galton and the Study of Heredity in the Nineteenth Century," Ph.D. diss., Johns Hopkins University, 1969 (University Microfilms), 64–66; Douglas A. Lorimer, *Colour, Class, and the Victorians* (New York: Holmes & Meier, 1978), 154.

39. Janet Sayers, *Biological Politics: Feminist and Anti-Feminist Perspectives* (London: Tavistock, 1982), 84–97, quotation on p. 90.

40. Ellis, *Man and Woman* (London: Walter Scott, 1894), 94.

41. Woolley, "Recent Literature on the Psychology of Sex," 341.

42. Stephanie Shields, "Functionalism, Darwinism, and the Psychology of Women," *American Psychologist* 30 (1975), 740; Elizabeth Fee, "Science and the Woman Problem," in *Sex Differences: Social and Biological Perspectives,* ed. Michael S. Teitelbaum (Garden City, N.Y.: Anchor Books, 1976), 206; Fee, "Nineteenth-Century Craniology," 432; Fee, "Science and the Woman Problem," 204–205, 218.

43. Edward Thorndike, "Sex in Education," *Bookman* 23 (1906), 215, 214; Rosenberg, *Beyond Separate Spheres,* 91.

44. Rosenberg, *Beyond Separate Spheres,* 120–131.

7. Women and the Cosmic Nightmare

Epigraphs: Mary Putnam Jacobi, *The Question of Rest for Women during Menstruation* (New York: G. P. Putnam's Sons, 1886; rpt. Farmingdale, N.Y.: Dabor Social Science Publications, 1978), 1–2; David G. Ritchie, *Darwinism and Politics* (London: Swan Sonnenschein, 1889), 4.

1. Virginia Woolf, *A Room of One's Own* (1929; London: The Hogarth Press, 1974), 46–48.

2. Janet Sayers, *Biological Politics: Feminist and Anti-Feminist Perspectives* (London: Tavistock, 1982), 84–97, quotation on p. 90.

3. Thomas F. Gieryn, "Boundary-Work and the Demarcation of Science from Non-Science: Strains and Interests in Professional Ideologies of Scientists," *American Sociological Review* 48 (1983), 785–786. Gieryn includes more than four characteristics of good science, but the others are not relevant here.

4. Michael Ruse, *The Darwinian Revolution: Nature Red in Tooth and Claw* (Chicago: University of Chicago Press, 1979), 213, 214.

5. Susan Sleeth Mosedale, "Science Corrupted: Victorian Biologists Consider 'The Woman Question,' " *Journal of the History of Biology* 11 (1978), 17; Flavia Alaya, "Victorian Science and the 'Genius' of Woman," *Journal of the History of Ideas* 38 (1977), 265; Charles Darwin, *The Descent of Man, and Selection in Relation to Sex* (1871; New York: P. F. Collier and Son, 1900), 586, 587; Francis Darwin, ed., *The Life and Letters of Charles Darwin,* 3 vols. (London: J. Murray, 1888), 2:281–282. In complaining about the paucity of the evidence on which Darwin relied in

his psychological work, Alaya follows in the steps of earlier scholars who, like Albert G. Keller, the Yale sociologist, deplored Darwin's foray into "waters beyond his depth." Darwin's account of the origin of the moral sentiments was much too speculative for Keller's taste: "This part of the 'Descent' had better have been left unwritten, for, in default of the usual mountains of data from which he [Darwin] was wont to draw his weighty inductions, the great scientist was led to wander hopelessly among the unfamiliar and unfathomable quicksands of the metaphysical and intuitional." Albert G. Keller, *Societal Evolution* (New York: Macmillan, 1916), 11, quoted in Robert L. Carneiro, "Structure, Function, and Equilibrium in the Evolutionism of Herbert Spencer," *Journal of Anthropological Research* 29 (1973), 78n.

6. Havelock Ellis, *Man and Woman: A Study of Human Secondary Sexual Characteristics* (London: Walter Scott, 1894), 28.

7. Tyndall quoted in Gieryn, "Boundary-Work and the Demarcation of Science," 785; Broca quoted in Stephen Jay Gould, *The Mismeasure of Man* (New York: W. W. Norton, 1981), 104.

8. Ellis, *Man and Woman*, 386; L. Manouvrier, "Conclusions générales sur l'anthropologie des sexes et applications sociales," *Revue de l'école d'anthropologie de Paris* 13 (1903), 406.

9. Clifford Geertz, "Ideology as a Cultural System," in *The Interpretation of Cultures* (New York: Basic Books, 1978).

10. Editor's Table, "Science and Social Reform," *Popular Science Monthly* 6 (1874–1875), 504–505; W. K. Brooks, *The Law of Heredity* (Baltimore: John Murphy, 1883), 263; Michael Ghiselin, *The Economy of Nature and the Evolution of Sex* (Berkeley: University of California Press, 1974), 3.

11. Emerson is quoted in Arthur Schlesinger, Jr., Review Essay, "Intellectual History: A Time for Despair," *Journal of American History* 66 (1980), 290–291; Roger Cooter, "Deploying 'Pseudoscience' Then and Now," in *Science, Pseudo-Science, and Society*, ed. Marsha Hanen, Margaret J. Osler, and Robert G. Weyant (Waterloo, Ontario: Wilfrid Laurier University Press, 1980), 239; Steven Shapin and Barry Barnes, "Darwin and Social Darwinism: Purity and History," in *Natural Order: Historical Studies of Scientific Culture*, ed. Shapin and Barnes (Beverly Hills: Sage, 1979), 138. Cf. Peter L. Berger and Thomas Luckman, *The Social Construction of Reality* (Middlesex, England: Penguin, 1967), 145: "Institutions and symbolic universes are legitimated by living individuals, who have concrete social locations and concrete social interests. The history of legitimating theories is always part of the history of the society as a whole. No 'history of ideas' takes place in isolation from the blood and sweat of general history." This contextualizing of the work of scientists can be seen as consistent with a recent shift in historical practice, influenced by literary and linguistic theory, to denote "the contextually situated production and transmission of meaning." In his brief, helpful guide to this development, "Intellectual History after the Linguistic Turn: The Anatomy of Meaning and the Irreducibility of Experience," *American Historical Review* 92 (1987), 879–907, John E. Toew asserts that the writings of theorists like Michel Foucault, Jacques Derrida, and Hans-Georg Gadamer deny human knowers "access, even potentially, to an unmediated world of objective things and processes . . . Knowledge and meaning are not discoveries but constructions." Quotation on pp. 901–902.

12. Helen H. Gardener, *Facts and Fictions of Life* (Boston: Arena, 1895), 98; G. Stanley Hall, *Adolescence,* 2 vols. (New York: D. Appleton, 1904), 2:634–635.

13. Marjorie Houspian Dobkin, ed., *The Making of a Feminist: Early Journals and Letters of M. Carey Thomas* (Kent, Ohio: Kent State University Press, 1979), 232.

14. Gardener was also historically misinformed in her claim that science was being used against women for the first time. In fact, "the attempt to trace woman's social inferiority to her supposed biological inferiority is an old one, dating back at least to Aristotle." Londa Schiebinger, "The History and Philosophy of Women in Science: A Review Essay," in *Sex and Scientific Inquiry,* ed. Sandra Harding and Jean F. O'Barr (Chicago: University of Chicago Press, 1987), 25.

15. Milton Rokeach, *The Open and Closed Mind* (New York: Basic Books, 1960), 67–68. Clifford Geertz speaks of ideology as "a response to strain." It follows "loss of orientation," the time when the old rules have lost their hold. "Ideology as a Cultural System," 219.

16. Gardener, *Facts and Fictions of Life,* 101.

17. Ellen Carol Dubois, ed., *Elizabeth Cady Stanton / Susan B. Anthony: Correspondence, Writings, Speeches* (New York: Schocken, 1981), 248; Gardener, *Facts and Fictions of Life,* 99.

18. John Fowles, "Seeing Nature Whole," *Harper's* 259 (1979), 50, 67. This technique has been referred to as the "impoverishment theory of abstraction," since beginning with individual cases in all their particularity scientists "by a kind of comparison akin to factorial analysis . . . isolate the highest common factor of the lot, and from this . . . form an impoverished representation valid for a class of things." Patrick A. Heelan, S. J., *Quantum Mechanics and Objectivity* (The Hague: Martinus Nijhoff, 1965), 13.

19. Pearson quoted in Reba N. Soffer, "The Revolution in English Social Thought," *American Historical Review* 75 (1970), 1957; Karl Pearson, *The Life, Letters and Labours of Francis Galton,* 3 vols. (Cambridge: Cambridge University Press, 1914–1930), 2:231–232, 297.

20. Quoted in Robert Bannister, *Social Darwinism: Science and Myth in Anglo-American Social Thought* (Philadelphia: Temple University Press, 1970), 140; Nancy Stepan, *The Idea of Race in Science: Great Britain, 1800–1960* (New York: Macmillan, 1982), 117–118.

21. William Carpenter, *Principles of Mental Physiology* (London: C. Kegan Paul, 1879), 7.

22. Huxley is quoted in an article by Henry Calderwood in the *Contemporary Review* 16 (1871), cited in Lorraine J. Daston, "Theory of Will Versus the Science of Mind," in *The Problematic Science: Psychology in Nineteenth-Century Thought,* ed. William R. Woodward and Mitchell G. Ash (New York: Praeger, 1982), 104. Maudsley's denial of free will is discussed in Kurt Danziger, "Mid-Nineteenth Century British Psycho-Physiology: A Neglected Chapter in the History of Psychology," in the same volume, pp. 135–140. Frances Power Cobbe, *Darwinism in Morals and Other Essays* (London: Williams and Norgate, 1872), 306–307.

23. Nathan G. Hale, Jr., *Freud and the Americans: The Beginnings of Psychoanalysis in the United States, 1876–1917* (New York: Oxford Press, 1971), 75; Mark Haller, *Eugenics: Hereditarian Attitudes in American Thought* (New Brunswick, N.J.: Rutgers University Press, 1963), 25, 41.

24. Hamilton Cravens, *The Triumph of Evolution: American Scientists and the*

Heredity-Environment Controversy, 1900–1941 (Philadelphia: University of Pennsylvania Press, 1978), 37–38.

25. Francis Galton, *Hereditary Genius* (1869; London: Macmillan, 1892), vii.

26. Charles E. Rosenberg, *No Other Gods: On Science and American Social Thought* (Baltimore: Johns Hopkins University Press, 1976), 36, 41–42.

27. Lester Frank Ward, "Neo-Darwinism and Neo-Lamarckism," in *Glimpses of the Cosmos,* 6 vols. (New York: G. P. Putnam's Sons, 1913–1918), 4:291; LeConte quoted in Bannister, *Social Darwinism,* 139.

28. Rosenberg, *No Other Gods,* 47; Cravens, *Triumph of Evolution,* 36–37; Henry Maudsley, *Body and Mind* (New York: D. Appleton, 1874), 68. On the ambiguous significance of Lamarckianism see also Greta Jones, *Social Darwinism and English Thought: The Interaction between Biological and Social Theory* (Sussex: The Harvester Press; Atlantic Highlands, N.J.: Humanities Press, 1980), 82–83.

29. Bannister, *Social Darwinism,* 139, 140.

30. William Bateson, *Biological Fact and the Structure of Society* (Oxford: Clarendon Press, 1912), 29. Fittingly enough, Bateson made these remarks in the annual Herbert Spencer lecture. J. W. Jackson, "Iran and Turan," *Anthropological Review* 6 (1868), 125, 128, 129. Cf. Max Nordau, *Degeneration* (New York: D. Appleton, 1895), 472: "There is at the present time a widespread conviction that the enthusiasm for equality was a grievous error of the great Revolution. A doctrine opposed to all natural laws is justly resisted." Dorothy Ross, *G. Stanley Hall: The Psychologist as Prophet* (Chicago: University of Chicago Press, 1972), 311.

31. Galton, *Hereditary Genius,* 12; Pearson, *Life, Letters and Labours of Francis Galton,* 2:85.

32. Ross, *G. Stanley Hall,* 311; Bateson, *Biological Fact,* 31–32.

33. Henry Maudsley, "The Correlation of Mental and Physical Force; or, Man a Part of Nature," *Journal of Mental Science* 6 (1860), 52. Shakespeare's poetic tribute to humanity is in *Hamlet,* act 2, scene 2.

34. William James, *The Varieties of Religious Experience,* 160, 161, quoted in Howard M. Feinstein, *Becoming William James* (Ithaca: Cornell University Press, 1984), 242–243.

35. William James, "On a Certain Blindness in Human Beings," in *Essays on Faith and Morals* (Cleveland: World Publishing Company, 1967), 259.

36. Virginia Woolf, *A Room of One's Own,* 53, 54.

37. On British scientists' struggle for authority see Frank Turner, "The Victorian Conflict between Science and Religion: A Professional Dimension," *Isis* 69 (1978), 356–376; and Turner, "Public Science in Britain, 1880–1919," *Isis* 71 (1980), 589–608.

38. Carroll Smith-Rosenberg and Charles Rosenberg, "The Female Animal: Medical and Biological Views of Woman and Her Role in Nineteenth-Century America," *Journal of American History* 60 (1973), 341.

39. The reference to "St. Theresas" is from George Eliot's lament in *Middlemarch* over the obstacles hindering accomplishment in gifted women: "Here and there is born a St. Theresa, foundress of nothing, whose loving heartbeats and sobs after an unattained goodness tremble off and are dispersed among hindrances instead of centering in some long-recognizable deed." Quoted in Stephen Jay Gould, "Women's Brains," *Natural History* 87 (1978), 50.

Index